# Philip Doddridge
# of Northampton

*Malcolm Deacon*

HUM VIVIMVS VIVAMVS

PHILIP DODDRIDGE D.D.

born June 26. 1702

Philip Doddridge

MALCOLM DEACON

# Philip Doddridge
# of
# Northampton
## 1702-51

Northamptonshire
Libraries

1980

Published by
NORTHAMPTONSHIRE LIBRARIES
27 Guildhall Road, Northampton NN1 1EF

ISBN 0 905391 07 1

Designed by Bernard Crossland Associates
Type set in Monotype Bembo, 12/13 pt.
and printed on Abbey Mills Antique laid paper by
Stanley L. Hunt (Printers) Limited, Rushden,
Northamptonshire, England

To Stephanie, Tessa
and Julian

# Foreword

March 1980 marks the 250th anniversary of the ordination of Philip Doddridge to the ministry at Castle Hill (now Doddridge and Commercial Street United Reformed) Church, Northampton. Looking back in gratitude to the initiative of the church members of 1729 in calling Doddridge to the town, the present members of the church resolved to mark the occasion with a variety of special events and projects.

*Philip Doddridge of Northampton* is an outcome of that resolution, and we are grateful for the co-operation of Northamptonshire Libraries in making this much-needed biography of Doddridge possible. Thanks are expressed to Malcolm Deacon, a member of the 250th anniversary committee and an elder of the Duston United Reformed Church, for his research and effort in compiling this book. It tells of the life and influence of a man who served this church as minister, and who also entered fully into the life of the Town and County. By his writings, correspondence, and personal contact, Doddridge's influence spread far and wide, and is still active amongst us today.

Doddridge's life has present-day relevance in that one man, handicapped by a frail physique, was able to give so great a lead in the realm of spiritual, educational, medical and social life.

On behalf of the elders and members of Doddridge and Commercial Street United Reformed Church, Castle Hill, Northampton we commend this work in the hope that it will impart inspiration, and encourage further study of the life of the man by whose name our church is known.

ARTHUR E. WYATT: *Church Secretary*.
DENNIS G. WEBB: *Elder*.

# Contents

# List of Illustrations

# Notes on
# Sources and Acknowledgments

The main primary sources for the study of Philip Doddridge are his correspondence and diary. Thomas Stedman published a single volume of the letters in 1790, and Doddridge's great-grandson, John Doddridge Humphreys, published five volumes of the correspondence and diary in 1829-31. When the latter volumes appeared, many people were shocked by the publication of Doddridge's juvenile love letters, considering their exposure to the public gaze as detrimental to his character. Doddridge had his many critics in life as well as after death, but the dust has long settled on such controversies. Of more significance in the publication of the correspondence was the unsatisfactory manner of its editing; Humphreys in particular omitted many letters, conflated one with another, altered texts and confused dates. The *Calendar of the Correspondence of Philip Doddridge D.D.* by Dr Geoffrey Nuttall (jointly published by Northamptonshire Record Society and the Royal Commission on Historical Manuscripts) is a timely and welcome corrective which has greatly assisted the task of checking the accuracy of the texts and dates of the published correspondence.

Wherever possible original documents have been studied, especially the archives of Doddridge and Commercial Street United Reformed Church, Castle Hill, Northampton; letters preserved in the Northamptonshire Studies Collection at the Central Library Northampton; and the extensive archives at Dr Williams's Library, London. As Doddridge's letters are to be found in over thirty libraries in this country and abroad, reliance has had to be had in many cases on the published texts of the correspondence. References are made to Dr Nuttall's numbering of the letters (e.g. NUTTALL letter 146), and where they have been printed in other publications, references are likewise given (e.g. HUMPHREYS, vol. 3, p. 241). Wherever transcriptions vary and originals are not available, the wording of Nuttall's *Calendar* is always used; reliance has, however, been placed upon other publications where they include valuable or more detailed accounts of Doddridge's life. Whenever spelling has been modernised and punctuation added, this is indicated in the references; in all cases the contemporary use of 'ye' has been replaced by 'the', and abbreviated forms of words have been transcribed in full, with the exception of ' &' for 'and'.

Northamptonshire Libraries and the author gratefully acknowledge assistance given by the following: Dr Geoffrey Nuttall, who has given invaluable advice and practical help by reading the manuscript, and proof reading; Mr Victor Hatley for many helpful suggestions regarding the history of Northampton, for proof reading, and for the loan of books; Mr John Thornton; the Revd Fred Snape; the staff of the Central Library, Northampton; Mr John Creasey (Librarian of Dr Williams's Library); Mr Patrick King (Chief Archivist, Northamptonshire Record Office); Miss June Swann, MBE (Central Museum, Northampton); Miss Dorothy Sladden (secretary of the Northamptonshire Record Society); Dr Edmund King for help and advice; Mr John Blundell of Nottage Court, Glamorgan and Mrs Marjorie Perry of Madison, Tennessee for assistance with the Doddridge genealogy; and Mr Dennis Webb of the Doddridge and Commercial Street United Reformed Church, whose enthusiasm and encouragement have made this book possible. Grateful appreciation is also expressed to the elders and members of the Doddridge and Commercial Street United Reformed Church for unrestricted access to their archives, and to Mrs Sheila Benbow and Mrs Joyce Embrey for their readiness to type and re-type the manuscript during its various stages of composition.

Acknowledgement is made to Dr Williams's Trust for permission to reproduce the text of the *Constitutions Orders and Rules of the Academy at Northampton* (1743); and to Messrs Beedle & Cooper, Northampton, Mr R. Fielding, and Mr S. Pickering, for original photography.

### ILLUSTRATIONS

The following are thanked for permission to reproduce illustrations from their collections. Doddridge and Commercial Street United Reformed Church (Castle Hill) (frontispiece, 5, 7 11, 13, 15, 16, 17, 20, 23, 24, 25, 26, 28, 34, 40, 41, 42, 43, 49); Mr J. H. Thornton (46, 47); Mr Eric Cooper (30, 31); Northamptonshire Libraries have provided the following illustrations (1, 2, 3, 4, 6, 8, 9, 10, 12, 14, 18, 21, 22, 27, 29, 32, 33, 35, 36, 37, 38, 39, 44, 45, 48, 50); illustration 19 has been drawn by the author from an original photograph.

# Introduction

Philip Doddridge arrived in Northampton on Christmas Eve 1729 and finally left the town on 16 July 1751; between those dates he fulfilled an energetic ministry, ambitious in its scope and remarkable in its effectiveness.

The story of Doddridge's life needs to be told again so that others may come to appreciate the freshness, vitality and human warmth of the Town's most influential Nonconformist minister. Doddridge is presented within the context of the broad sweep of Free Church history; his unique impact upon his own and later generations is linked with his spiritual forefathers, who either chose to worship God outside the Church of England, or were forced by circumstances so to do. Yet Doddridge stands above denominational labels, as his tolerant spirit and ecumenical outlook did much to soften the religious divisions of his times. Northampton provides the main backcloth for his pursuits, although beyond the Town we glimpse his wider interests in this country and abroad. In all his activities Doddridge emerges as a man of flesh and blood; a loving husband and father, and a man of generous disposition; an advocate of justice and toleration, and an initiator of philanthropic schemes to benefit the community. His family motto 'dum vivimus, vivamus' (while we live, let us live), is an apt summary of his short yet eminent life.

# The Religious Background

While Thomas Bradbury, the minister of the Congregational Church in Fetter Lane, London, was preaching his morning sermon on 1 August 1714, a handkerchief fluttered from the gallery. It had been dropped deliberately by a messenger sent by Bishop Burnet as a pre-arranged signal to announce the death of Queen Anne. Upon concluding his sermon Bradbury offered prayers for the new monarch, the Hanoverian George I, and led his congregation in the singing of the 89th Psalm before preaching again from the text, 'Go, see now this cursed woman, and bury her; for she is a king's daughter'.

There was irony in the timing of the Stuart queen's death as all Nonconformists realised. The latest in a long list of attempts to destroy their influence, the Schism Act (see Appendix VII) was due to come into force that very day; now it was almost certain that it would be abandoned by the new king who had openly pledged his support to Nonconformity. It was the beginning of a new era in the struggle for religious liberty.

Fifteen years after this event a young Dissenting minister arrived in Northampton on the threshold of his life's work. Aged twenty-seven, Philip Doddridge faced the formidable task of being not only the minister of a large and flourishing church but also the principal of an academy. He was to become a major figure in the religious and educational life of the eighteenth century, and a vital catalyst in the formative years preceding the great evangelical awakening. In the twenty-two years of his ministry at Northampton, Doddridge's indefatigable industry laid a solid foundation upon which the expansion of Dissent was built. He was in constant friendly contact with men of affairs, religious leaders, and thinkers of all shades of opinion. In him were focused many of the important religious, political, and social issues of the day. His sound Christian moderation and powerful faith exerted an immense influence. It is with no exaggeration that Everitt writes:

Notes and references for this chapter begin on page 145

If any event can be regarded as beginning the Evangelical Movement it is probably the appointment of the Independent Philip
Doddridge to Castle Hill Chapel in Northampton in 1729, and
the transference of his Academy to the same town in that year.
These events antedated the conversion of John Wesley by nine
years, and the quiet but far-reaching influence of Doddridge, by
means of his teaching, his writings, and his hymns, prepared the
way for the reception of the new Movement amongst all sections
and classes of provincial society. By Queen Victoria's reign
virtually every Dissenting sect and the Church of England itself
had been largely transformed by it.[1]

Not only did the ministry of Philip Doddridge encourage and largely
direct the course of Dissenting evangelism in the eighteenth and nineteenth centuries, it provided a link with the earlier pioneering work of
the Independents[2] and the Moravian Brethren.[3] Doddridge had not been
long in Northampton when he was called upon publicly to champion
the cause of religious and educational freedom; the outcome of his fight
had national significance. In order to understand the importance of his
ministry, it is necessary first to trace the history of the Dissenters' struggle
towards religious toleration.

The course of the English Reformation in the sixteenth century is a
complex story characterised by ideologies that differed according to
changing regimes. Henry VIII's traumatic break with the Church of
Rome in 1534 was an act of state prompted by his own political, dynastic
and marital preoccupations. The real religious revolution came in the
reign (1547–53) of his son Edward VI. Under the influence of Edward
Seymour, Earl of Hertford (later Duke of Somerset) and Thomas
Cranmer, Archbishop of Canterbury, far-reaching changes were made.
Roman Catholic doctrines and practices were eliminated and replaced
by Protestant reforms. For a time England became a haven for Protestants
from more repressive European regimes, and their ideas became widely
disseminated.

Sharp reaction came in the reign of Mary Tudor (1553–8) who
endeavoured forcibly to reintroduce Roman Catholicism. Mary's
vigorous persecution of Protestant heretics achieved the opposite of her
intended purpose. John Foxe's *Book of Martyrs* (1563) ensured that the
two hundred and eighty-two people burned at the stake were never
forgotten; next to the Bible it became the most popular work of piety
of the age, and led to widespread sympathy for the Protestant cause.

This persecution was one major factor that ensured the ultimate triumph of the Reformation upon the accession of Elizabeth in 1558, but it was not the only one. Throughout the thirty years from 1529, powerful religious undercurrents had been flowing which even Henry VIII could not hold in check. The wide spectrum of viewpoints encompassed by the terms 'Nonconformist' or 'Dissenting',[4] strove for radical reform within the Church of England; their influence not only succeeded in changing its structure, but also deeply affected English society at large.

By the latter half of the sixteenth century, Dissent consisted of two distinct elements. On the one hand there were the Puritans—by far the more numerous—who sought to 'purify' the church from within. Many clergy refused to read parts of the liturgy, wear vestments or perform certain ceremonies that had been laid down by the authorities, considering them as Popish and contrary to the Christian gospel. Among them were those who felt that the Church of England should be reformed upon Presbyterian principles, its government and discipline controlled by a system of elders and synods, and not by the episcopate (i.e. the bishops). Presbyterianism met severe repression in the 1590s under Archbishop Whitgift, whose agents toured the Midland counties in search of those responsible for the Marprelate Tracts.[5] Yet in spite of the dashing of Presbyterian hopes, many Puritan clergy maintained control of those parishes where they were elected, not by a bishop, but by their parishioners. Such 'non-Separating Congregationalism' was later to be fused with the Separatist Independents in the crisis of 1662, thus forming the Dissenting Congregational body.

On the other hand there were those—more radical than the Puritans—who broke away completely, forming themselves into Separatist or 'gathered' communities modelled on the church of the early Christian centuries; to them the Church was the gathered community of confessing believers. Such a radical tradition owed its origins to the Lollard movement initiated by John Wycliffe in the fourteenth century. Wycliffe, 'the Morning Star of the Reformation', had stressed the need for freedom in worship, in church government, and in the understanding of the scriptures.

Robert Browne (c.1550–c.1633) gave dramatic expression to Separatism in the late sixteenth century; rejecting all forms of human authority over an individual's religion, he roundly condemned the Church of England for its exclusive and narrow aims. With Robert Harrison he established a Separatist church in Norwich, although eventually he became reconciled to the Church of England. The radical stream of Separatism was fed by Anabaptism in the first half of the sixteenth century; it was to overflow into the Quaker movement in the seventeenth century and be linked with the General Baptists[6] of the seventeenth and eighteenth centuries.

It took a great deal of courage and depth of conviction for anyone to depart from the doctrines and disciplines of the state church. The concept of 'the godly prince', who upheld the true religion in his realm, much appealed to Henry VIII who condemned to death Anabaptists and Roman Catholics alike. The governments of Edward VI and Mary Tudor also made use of this idea for their own differing purposes; in 1553 Bishop Hooper was burned to death for declaring that the state should not interfere in matters of religion. Although asserting that she did not intend to 'open windows into men's souls', Elizabeth I nevertheless equated religious conformity with that of political obedience. In the *Act of Supremacy* (1559) she was declared 'supreme governor' of the Church of England. In the *Act of Uniformity* of the same year harsh penalties were set out for those who departed from the liturgy of the church. A Court of High Commission was appointed to enforce obedience to the Crown's ecclesiastical policies. In spite of concerted efforts by the Puritans to effect reforms through the House of Commons, Elizabeth cleverly parried their thrusts and conceded very little.[7]

Matters did not greatly improve with the accession of the Stuarts in 1603. A petition presented to James I in 1604 by the Puritan clergy, in the hope of abolishing certain church ceremonies which they found offensive, was flatly and contemptuously rejected. Their pleas for greater religious freedom and relief from compulsory payment of tithes to maintain the clergy, fell on deaf ears. Yet in spite of persecution there were changes which heralded increasing religious liberty. After 1612 those who would not conform were no longer burned at Smithfield; instead of bodies, books were burned, and imprisonment was substituted for the death penalty. Of greater significance was the King's authorisation of a new translation of the Bible; little did James realise that by increasing public understanding of the scriptures, he was unwittingly putting into the hands of the reformers a powerful new weapon with which to attack the establishment.

Under Charles I (1625-49), Archbishop Laud[8] demanded external uniformity, and forced recalcitrant clergy before the ecclesiastical courts if they refused to conform to the Prayer Book and perform High Church[9] ceremonies. Punishments were severe; in 1637 the Revd Henry Burton was sentenced to stand in the pillory, have his ears cut off, fined £5,000,

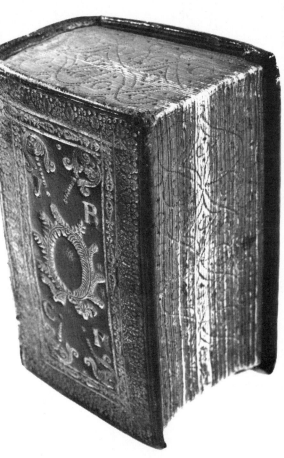

1. Doddridge's leather German Bible, printed in
Strasburg in 1626 and brought to England in
1646 by his maternal grandfather John Bauman.

2. Philip Doddridge learns his Bible stories at his mother's knee, assisted by the Delft tiles in the fireplace; an 1837 interpretation.

and spend the rest of his life in prison because he opposed Laud's policies.

In spite of such repressive measures Puritanism flourished, and resentment at High Church tendencies deepened. Many Puritans were impelled by force of circumstances into complete Separatism. As in the reign of Elizabeth, Separatists fled from England, especially to Holland, where their ideas took root and flourished; later when persecution in England eased, many returned.

The Puritan backlash found its expression in 1640 with the advent of the Long Parliament which destroyed the jurisdiction of the ecclesiastical courts and impeached Archbishop Laud. Within three years, episcopacy was abolished and 'The Solemn League and Covenant'[10] established. In 1645 *The Book of Common Prayer* was replaced by *The Directory for the Publique Worship of God*. In the following year Parliament ordered the reorganisation of the Church of England on Presbyterian principles. The boot of intolerance was now on the other foot, and one can feel the force of Milton's dictum, 'New Presbyter is but old Priest writ large'.[11]

Cromwell was a genuine lover of religious liberty, and although a dictator from necessity was exceptional in that he did not wish to impose religious uniformity upon the nation. He hated religious intolerance in any form. Although his sympathies lay with the Independents, he was prepared to accept Episcopalians and the Prayer Book as part of a general toleration; the only compulsion in things of the mind should be those of light and reason, he declared. Roman Catholics found themselves less severely treated, and Jews were allowed to settle in England for the first time since 1290.

The emergence of the Society of Friends (Quakers), together with a number of more radical groups, attests the degree of liberty gained by Separatism during the Commonwealth and Protectorate. In 1654 the government commenced a scheme under which the suitability of any incumbent aspiring to a living in the Church of England was scrutinised by a commission of thirty-eight 'Triers'. Composed of laymen and ministers, the commission was predominantly Independent and Presbyterian with some Baptist members. It was an attempt 'to graft the principle of the gathered church on to a national ecclesiastical system'.[12] Like the compulsory establishment of Presbyterianism in 1646, this first and last official attempt to incorporate Independents and Baptists within the state church was a failure.

There is no reason to disbelieve the declaration made by Charles II at Breda in the Netherlands in April 1660 that promised 'a liberty to tender consciences . . . that no man shall be disquieted, or called in question, for differences of opinion in matters of religion which do not disturb the peace of the kingdom'.[13] Charles' private sympathies with Roman Catholicism did not prevent him from desiring toleration for others; for a brief while Dissenters' hopes for peace were roused. Charles' major stumbling-block, however, was the power of Parliament which from its restoration in 1660 became fiercely reactionary against Dissent. An insurrection of Fifth Monarchists[14] in London, in spite of vehement protestations of loyalty from other Dissenters, led to scenes of malicious persecution. Within weeks of a royal proclamation on 10 January 1661, Baptists were dragged from their beds by armed soldiers, over four thousand Quakers were imprisoned, and at least one Baptist pastor was hanged, drawn, and quartered as a traitor.

Parliament rapidly formulated the Clarendon Code[15] with its four penal laws, the *Corporation Act* (1661), the *Act of Uniformity* (1662), the *Conventicle Act* (1664), and the *Five Mile Act* (1665) which were designed to break the political and educational influence of all Dissenters once and for all. Under the *Corporation Act* no conscientious Dissenter could hold municipal office unless allegiance to the King was sworn, and the sacrament of holy communion was taken according to the rites of the Church of England. Many Dissenters immediately lost their seats on borough councils, and some were deliberately elected to municipal office so that they could be heavily fined for not complying with the regulations. Some Baptists and Quakers who refused to swear oaths of allegiance to the crown were fined, imprisoned, or even transported. John Bunyan was arrested in November 1660 while preaching in the open air; this was the first of his imprisonments for Nonconformity which amounted to twelve years of his life. Bunyan's *The Pilgrim's Progress* and *Grace Abounding to the Chief of Sinners* and William Penn's *No Cross, No Crown*[16] are superb products of the faith and resolution with which Dissent faced persecution.[17]

Parliament's fears of rebellion had some foundation. In 1663 the King's attempt at easing the penal laws was frustrated by news of a small rising of radical Dissenters in the north of England.[18] After the execution of the ringleaders in January 1664 Parliament formulated the *Conventicle Act*, which forbade five or more people to meet for worship unless conducted in accordance with the Anglican liturgy. (For legislation affecting Dissenters, see Appendix VIII.) The *Five Mile Act* of the following year was particularly vindictive. London had been shaken by the return of plague, and some of the clergy had deserted their parishes. Many Dissenters had stepped in to care for the sick and bereaved, and to bury the dead. Sheltering at Oxford from the plague, Parliament prohibited Dissenting ministers from preaching or from coming within five miles of any place where they had ministered, and from any city, corporate town or any borough represented in Parliament.[19] The fine for disobedience was £40.

In 1670 the *Conventicle Act* was strengthened by increasing the penalties and encouraging informers, who could claim up to a third of the goods seized from convicted Dissenters' estates. Many Dissenters lost their homes, furniture, and even their bed-linen, and Dissenting workmen the very tools and materials of their trades. In 1673 the *Test Act* was passed which denied all naval, military or civil employment on behalf of the Government to any Dissenter.

Macaulay says, 'Every moderate man was shocked by the insolence, cruelty, and perfidy with which the Nonconformists were treated'.[20] Congregations were scattered and many individuals were fined, pilloried, imprisoned, or banished. Baptists and Independents met by stealth, stationing watchers on roof tops or at street corners to warn of informers. The Quakers suffered particularly: 'Their meetings were broken up by the military, and their attendants stunned by bludgeons or hacked by swords. The female members were stripped and flogged with shameless indecency.'[21] Thousands were thrown into prison where many hundreds died of disease, or were transported to the West Indies where they were sold as slaves.

Without doubt Parliament's overwhelming blunder was the *Act of Uniformity* which was passed on 19 May 1662. Aimed at rooting out Puritanism in the established church, the act represented an ultimatum; *The Book of Common Prayer* was made compulsory and every incumbent was ordered to declare his 'unfeigned Assent and Consent to all and everything contained and prescribed within it'. Little time was given for the Puritan ministers to consider the issues involved, as declaration had to be made on 24 August. 'Black Bartholomew's Day' came and some two thousand clergy[22] left their livings rather than compromise their consciences. Unable to collect their yearly tithes that were almost due, many of the ejected were plunged into immediate poverty. Richard Baxter wrote: 'Hundreds of able ministers, with their wives and children, had neither house nor bread.'[23] Driven from the towns, fined, pilloried, imprisoned and harassed, many were faced with utter destitution and misery.

This cruel persecution failed in its object, as few bent before the storm. 'Ministers continued to preach and congregations assembled to hear them. In the country they met for their illegal worship in the large kitchens and barns of solitary farm houses, or in the neighbourhood of woods into which they fled when surprised by soldiers or informers; in the towns they met in private houses by night, and sometimes the prayers and sermons lasted till dawn.'[24]

Many ingenious stratagems were devised to escape detection. Places and times of worship were frequently changed. In some houses trap doors were built so that preachers could escape or hide if disturbed. Where Nonconformists lived next door to each other passages were dug or walls removed. In some instances worshippers met provided with bread and cheese so that, if necessary, their meeting for devotion might be converted into a convivial gathering.[25] It is hardly surprising that scores of Free Churches date from the period of the Great Ejectment; from this crisis emerged organised Nonconformity which, fusing together the Puritan and Separatist streams of Dissent, became a powerful force completely outside the established church. The temporary Indulgence granted in 1672 gave Nonconformists a brief breathing space; of the 1,610[26] preaching licences that were allowed, the first to be granted was to John Bunyan. Although the Indulgence was cancelled in the following year, and the licences recalled in 1675, Nonconformity gained vital confidence.

Yet dangers still lay ahead. For much of his reign James II worked sedulously for the forcible reconversion of England to Roman Catholicism. News of the horrors of persecution in France brought by fleeing Huguenot refugees, united Protestants of all shades of opinion into action against the common danger. Anglicans became alarmed at the threat posed by the re-establishment of Roman Catholicism, and their opposition to Dissent began to wane. Both James and the established church attempted to gain Nonconformist support by making tempting offers of greater toleration. Putting aside their enmity against the Church of England, the Nonconformists remained loyal to the Protestant cause and sided against the King.

The flight of James with his wife and baby son to France and the landing of William of Orange in 1688, are dramatic events in the development of English democracy. William's accession to the English throne finally threw the balance of power in favour of Parliament rather than the monarchy, and this ultimately led to increased liberty for all.

In spite of the failure to reunite ('comprehend') two major sections of Nonconformity—the Independents and the Presbyterians—within the established church in 1689, Protestant Nonconformity as a whole secured important concessions. The *'Toleration Act'*, as it was popularly called, granted all Nonconformists a limited right to dissent in forms and ceremonies of worship; however, dissent from the doctrines of the established church, especially the doctrine of the Trinity, was forbidden. In return for taking an oath against Papal rule and supremacy, Nonconformists were exempted from the Elizabethan laws which compelled all people to attend their parish churches, although worship on the Lord's Day was still compulsory.

Nonconformists were not, however, freed from paying tithes and church rates. Dissenting places of worship had to be certified before the Bishop of the Diocese, his Archdeacon, or a Justice of the Peace. Dissenting teachers and preachers had to subscribe to the majority of the Thirty-Nine Articles, failing which they could be punished under the Clarendon Code.[27] Dissenting ministers were still unable to be jurors, churchwardens or overseers, and immediate imprisonment without bail could be exacted on any Dissenter refusing to take the oaths.

In spite of these restrictions, Nonconformists secured a considerable measure of religious freedom and were, in the main, content with the improvements. The established church lost much of its power to persecute, although it still held exclusive political and educational privileges; for instance, no Roman Catholic could enter Parliament and no Nonconformist the universities.

A period of reaction set in during the reign of Queen Anne that brought increased difficulties for Dissent. Initially grateful for the toleration they had been granted, Nonconformists expressed their loyalty to the monarchy. Even Dr Isaac Watts[28] wrote a eulogistic ode to the Queen, but afterwards retracted it as it became increasingly clear 'that Anne, had she dared, would have withdrawn every liberty from Dissenters, and [would] have given her heartiest support to any government which would propose to legislate according to the old Stuart pattern'.[29] Anne endeavoured to secure the position of the Church of England; in her 'Bounty'[30] to augment poorer livings, by the establishment of fifty new churches in London, and in numerous preferments and other ways, she pursued a course that was pro-High Church and anti-Dissent.

In both the *Occasional Conformity Act* of 1711 and the *Schism Act* of 1714 the same objectives of destroying Nonconformity were manifest. Daniel Defoe and others protested volubly at the former act, which levied fines of £40 on anyone holding civil or military office, or found frequenting a place of worship other than the established church. Of more sinister design was the *Schism Act* which required any person who wished to keep any public or private school, or to teach in any capacity, first to have taken the sacrament according to the rites of the Church of England during the preceding year. Upon such qualification the Bishop of the Diocese could issue a licence without which the penalty for teaching was to be imprisonment without bail. The act struck at the roots of Nonconformist strength—their academies, which were already beginning to provide a high standard of education. Underlying the act was another motive, namely the undermining of Nonconformist political influence in order to facilitate the continuation of the Stuart monarchy in the person of the Pretender.[31]

Ever since the *Act of Uniformity*, Nonconformist educational activity had been growing steadily in efficiency and popularity. In 1662 the exodus of ministers, university dons and schoolmasters from their posts flooded the country with able teachers. Out of necessity many began to open schools and academies, often in their own homes. Constantly under fear of prosecution, many of these schools frequently changed their location in order to avoid detection. Others, however, became firmly established and, under able leadership, developed into some of the finest educational establishments in the country, attracting pupils from a broad social and religious spectrum.[32]

Indeed, the curricula of many of the Dissenting academies surpassed those of Oxford and Cambridge, which greatly declined in the seventeenth and eighteenth centuries. With no tests of religious belief exacted on students, all-comers were accepted into the academies; thus numerous Anglicans and the sons of the aristocracy and well-to-do also found themselves within Dissenting establishments.[33] Candidates for the Dissenting ministry were educated with students who were intended for secular occupations, and who professed no particular Nonconformist allegiance; both groups benefited from each other and from the common core of theological lectures which they all attended. Some students entered the academies as young as fourteen, simply to complete their formal education; others, particularly theological students, came to pursue a rigorous higher education. Being essentially personal, and not institutional organisations, the academies fluctuated in relation to the changing fortunes of their individual tutors; as an academy's principal was normally a Dissenting minister, the location of the academy would change if the minister accepted the charge of another congregation. Students also moved from academy to academy in order to study under a tutor noted for excellence in a particular subject; for example Thomas Secker, who became Archbishop of Canterbury, studied in this way. There were different emphases in theology in some academies, and this produced migrations of students and staff; nevertheless, such movements 'helped to build up a corporate feeling among Dissenters, and to create a common standard of education throughout the country'.[34]

The hostility of sections of the established church to the academies was intense. In a sermon delivered in 1685 Prebendary South urged his congregation to 'employ the utmost of your power and interest both with the King and Parliament, to suppress, utterly to suppress, and extinguish, those private, blind conventicling schools or academies of grammar and philosophy, set up and taught secretly by fanatics, here and there all the kingdom over.'[35] Similarly, in 1709 Henry Sacheverell termed the academies 'fountains of lewdness', and hot beds of 'Atheism, Deism, Tritheism, Socinianism, with all the hellish principles of Fanaticism, Regicide and Anarchy'.[36]

Yet in spite of opposition, Dissenting academies continued to increase in numbers; before 1690 there were twenty-three and this number had increased to thirty-four within a few years. The products of the academies varied but some were men of considerable ability;[37] for instance, both Daniel Defoe and Samuel Wesley attended the progressive academy at Newington Green run by Charles Morton.[38]

The repression of 1662 resulted in a fortuitous redirection of educational effort. Freed from the narrow vision of the ecclesiastically controlled curriculum of the universities and grammar schools, which had changed little from medieval times, the Dissenting academies were able to broaden their concept of education. For a century and more writers had been urging a widening of the traditional classical curriculum to include modern languages and scientific subjects. As early as 1591 Sir Humphrey Gilbert had proposed an academy based upon continental prototypes, in which there would be a modern curriculum including scientific experiments, gunnery, civics, economics, and training in arms as well as Latin and Greek; above all, suggested Gilbert, instruction should be given in English and not in the traditional Latin. In 1644 John Milton's tract *Of Education* included the following definition of education: 'I call therefore a compleat and generous education that which fits a man to perform justly, skilfully and magnanimously all the offices, both private and public, of peace and war.' It was a strong call to make education relevant to the needs of the contemporary world where mathematics and science were influencing commerce, navigation and warfare; diplomats, statesmen and politicians needed modern languages as well as knowledge in geography and history. The opposing tendencies of the age were neatly juxtaposed by the fact that 1662 saw not only the repressive legislation of the *Act of Uniformity*, but also the reinvigoration of the Royal Society,[39] albeit initially frowned upon by the universities.

Men like Samuel Hartlib and Hezekiah Woodward, both staunch Puritans, believed passionately in the ideas of the Moravian reformer Comenius,[40] who emphasised that education should contain all aspects of knowledge. He advocated scientific experimentation, and in 1641 came to England at the invitation of Hartlib's Puritan coterie in order to establish a college in London. Nothing came of the venture owing to the outbreak of the Civil War, but Comenius' ideas took root and were later put into widespread use in the Dissenting academies. Daniel Defoe was proud of his education at Newington Green where he was taught five languages, philosophy, logic, history, geography, politics, mathematics, and science. At the academy at Sheriffhales in Shropshire (founded in 1663) John Woodhouse conducted courses in mathematics, logic, anatomy, physics, ethics, rhetoric, Greek, Hebrew, law and theology. A wide range of books was read in class, and recapitulated in such a way as to ensure that every author was read three times. Other practical work accompanied the lectures including land surveying, composing almanacks, dissecting animals, and constructing sundials.

Sheriffhales had profound influence upon John Jennings' academy, founded in 1715 at Kibworth in Leicestershire. Jennings likewise offered his students a wide curriculum, adding French and lectures in drama, as well as extending the proportion of time spent on scientific subjects. Eventually the mantle of John Jennings was to fall upon the shoulders of Philip Doddridge, who brought the academy with him to Northampton in 1729, commencing twenty-one years of intensive activity and widespread influence.

# The Young Doddridge

Philip Doddridge was a descendant of a long and prolific line which originated in Devonshire in Saxon times. In the parish of Sandford, near Crediton, there exist records of an ancient manor called Doddridge, or Dodderidge, which was given by the Conqueror to one of his knights, who subsequently took his name from the estate. The earliest written record of the family dates from 1218 when, in the second year of Henry III's reign, a Gilbert de Dodarig witnessed a 'recovery' of legal costs by Robert de Bremerige.

The spelling of the surname is an example of the somewhat haphazard regard for spelling that is found in documents dating from the Middle Ages; it also reflects the prolific nature of the family itself whose branches spread widely in both Devonshire and Somerset. It appears that the original spelling of the surname was Dudderidge but numerous variations appear: Douderygge (14th century), Dothderygge (1434), and Dotheridge (late 15th century). The form Doddridge became popular in the reign of Henry VIII, especially amongst the Devonshire branches of the family, although references to Dodaridge, Dodoredge, Dudderidge and Dodderidge and other variations (even for the same individual) appear in wills, letters and other documents.[1]

Philip Doddridge's ancestry becomes clearer with one John Dodderidge who lived at South Molton, Devon, in the fifteenth century. His son Richard established himself in Barnstaple where he became a prosperous merchant, magistrate, mayor and alderman. Richard had three sons, one of whom was the eminent King's Bench Judge Sir John Dodderidge (1555–1628). Sir John was a man of considerable learning, an author of numerous erudite works which had much contemporary influence, and a founder member of the Society of Antiquaries. He died without issue in September 1628, and is interred within an ornate black and white marble sarcophagus in Exeter Cathedral.

Notes and references for this chapter begin on page 152

He left all his estates to his brother, Pentecost Dodderidge, who became
a wealthy and influential merchant and M.P. for Barnstaple, where he is
described in the *Heralds' Visitation* for 1620 as 'a chiefe Burgess'. In 1637
he became the town's mayor and in 1642 we find him lending the town
council £50 in order to strengthen the town's fortifications against a
Royalist attack. His son, a second John Dodderidge, followed in his
uncle's (Sir John's) footsteps and became an author on legal subjects and
was chosen Recorder for Bristol; in 1646 he represented Barnstaple in
Parliament, and in the following year became a Justice of the Peace for the
County of Devon. He was instrumental in founding a library in Barnstaple in 1665, the Register Book of which records him as 'that worthy
and pious Benefactor, John Doddridg, Esquire; by whose Bounty it was
furnished with many worthy Books'.[2]

In 1628 Pentecost Dodderidge's coat of arms was 'confirmed and
allowed' to him by the College of Heralds. In the Harleian manuscripts
on Devonshire pedigrees (c.1630) Pentecost's brother Philip, the great-
grandfather of Dr Philip Doddridge, is mentioned under his shield of
arms: 'Argent, two Pales wavy, Azure; between nine Cross Croslets,
Gules.'[3] Philip's only son, a third John Doddridge, became the Rector of
Shepperton in Middlesex where he received a living of £130 per annum,
besides income from tithes and nineteen acres of glebe land. His ministry
covered a difficult period in which the conflicting loyalties and passions
of the Civil War disturbed his pastoral work. His conscience was sorely
tested by the *Act of Uniformity* in August 1662, and although he wavered
for six months he finally resigned his living. This was undoubtedly a
considerable personal sacrifice as his income had been substantial. He
retired to Twickenham with his wife and ten children, where he was
noted in 1672 as a pastor of a small Dissenting congregation who probably
met for worship in a private house. Dr Calamy, who had benefited from
the second John Dodderidge's generosity, spoke of him as 'an ingenious
man and a scholar; an acceptable preacher, and a very peaceable divine'.[4]
Affection and sorrow were expressed by his congregation upon his
sudden death in 1689 and there is little doubt that the example of John,
Philip Doddridge's paternal grandfather, was one of the formative
influences during the latter's youth.

Of John Doddridge's ten children only two sons, Philip and Daniel,
were alive at the time of his death. Philip 'was bred to the law' and
became a solicitor. For many years he was employed as steward to
William, 5th Earl Russell and 1st Duke of Bedford. He was, writes
Stanford, 'a genial gentleman, well versed in "the humanities", and

posted up in the knowledge of his times'.[5] He was the well-loved uncle of young Philip Doddridge, who frequently spent his holidays on the Duke and Duchess's estates in company with him. Young 'Philly' became a favourite with the Russell children some of whom remained his life-long friends. The Duchess, too, took a kindly interest in his affairs and was later to offer him strong inducements to become a clergyman in the established church.

John Doddridge's second son Daniel 'was evidently not the genius of the family',[6] although he too successfully made his way in the world by becoming a prosperous merchant trading, according to Job Orton, as 'an oilman' somewhere in London. Daniel married a young orphan girl named Monica Bauman whose father John Bauman had died in 1668 leaving her as his only issue. Bauman had fled from his native Prague forty-two years before, leaving behind considerable estates. As a Hussite Protestant[7] his religious position in Bohemia became untenable following the ejection of Frederick, the Protestant Elector Palatine, by the forces of Roman Catholicism. Persecution forced Bauman to disguise himself as a peasant and 'in the emergency of the moment could not carry with him into banishment more than a hundred broad pieces of gold, which for the purpose of concealment were carefully plaited into the leathern girdle, at that time a necessary part of his rude costume'.[8]

Bauman must have been terrified of being caught, and this may have been the cause of his forgetting to buckle on his belt after staying at some obscure inn. Finding out his loss when he arrived at another inn, he resolved to go back there and then to search for the belt. Eventually his patience was rewarded when a servant woman found it thrown amongst a pile of rubbish under a staircase.

If John Bauman could have forgotten his gold, he had a greater treasure which he held tenaciously as his most precious possession; everywhere he travelled his Luther's Bible went with him. It was to become a precious heirloom to Philip Doddridge who in 1724 wrote this inscription on the fly leaf:

> P. Doddridge 1724.
> These Bibles, my Honoured Grandfather, Mr John Bauman, brought with him from Germany, his Native Countrey, when he fled on Foot from the Persecution there on Account of the Protestant Religion. . . .[9]

Bauman spent some years in Saxe Gotha and eventually in 1646 arrived in London armed with excellent academic references from his

university and from several Protestant divines. He established a grammar
school at Kingston-upon-Thames, married, and upon his death left his
teenage daughter Monica as the future mother of Philip Doddridge.

Philip Doddridge was born at an unknown location in London on
26 June 1702. His mother had been in difficult labour for thirty-six hours.
Philip appeared stillborn, but the midwife noticing a slight movement of
his chest, slapped the baby into life. Named after his uncle, Philip never
enjoyed robust health and remained frail and consumptive-looking all
his life. He and his elder sister, Elizabeth,[10] were the only survivors of
twenty children, the other eighteen having died before Philip was born.

The family background profoundly impressed the growing boy,
especially the stories of his grandfather Bauman's escape from persecution,
exemplified by the black Luther Bible which was preserved in the house.
Similarly grandfather John Doddridge's ejectment was another potent
influence:

> . . . he [i.e. John Doddridge] had a family of ten children un-
> provided for; but he quitted his living, which was worth to him
> about two hundred pounds per annum, rather than he would
> violate his conscience in the manner he must have done, by
> submitting to the subscriptions and declarations required, and the
> usages imposed by the Act of Uniformity, contrived by some
> wicked politicians to serve their own interest, and most effectually
> humble those who had been most active in that general struggle
> for public liberty, in which the family of the Stuarts had fallen.[11]

Philip's mother naturally lavished her care upon the two survivors of
her large family. She was a woman of great piety and assiduously taught
her children the stories from scripture. In later life Doddridge recalled
that his mother had taught him the history of the Old and New Testaments before he could read, by means of some blue Dutch tiles in the
chimney place of their sitting room.[12] No doubt he listened wide-eyed
at his mother's knee as she recounted the incidents depicted in blue and
white glaze: 'The apple tree with a serpent in it; Noah looking out from
the window of an ark smaller than himself; Eli falling back from the top
of a five barred gate; a very great Jonah coming out of a very little
whale; Peter sailing over the Sea of Galilee in a Dutch three-decker; a
Prodigal Son in a periwig; and so on.'[13] Such impressions formed at an
early age a mind sensitive and receptive to religious truths.

Philip's parents employed a tutor, Mr Stott, to give him his first lessons in 'grammaticals' and classical literature until he was old enough to be boarded at a private school. In 1712 at the age of ten Philip found himself at a grammar school in Kingston-upon-Thames studying under the Revd Daniel Mayo, the son of a former vicar of Kingston who had been ejected in 1662. Mayo was a man of considerable education, a writer of religious treatises, and minister of the Nonconformist congregation which assembled in the Gravel Pit meeting in Kingston. In later years Philip Doddridge was to acknowledge his indebtedness to Mayo's influence, especially his method of teaching by catechisms and his interest in and friendship with his pupils.

Philip was only eight years old when his mother suddenly died on 12 April 1711. It was a heavy blow which was followed four years later, on 17 July 1715, by the death of his father. To make matters worse his much loved uncle Philip also died in the same year as his father. Although orphaned at such a tender age, young 'Philly' could write in his diary a deeply held statement of faith and a remarkably mature resolution to do as his parents would wish:

> God is an immortal Father, my soul rejoiceth in Him; He hath hitherto helped me and provided for me; may it be my study to approve myself a more affectionate, grateful, and dutiful child.[14]

In later life he alluded to his own experiences in a sermon entitled 'The Orphan's Hope':[15]

> I am under some peculiar obligations to desire and attempt the relief of orphans, as I know the heart of an orphan; having been deprived of both of my parents at an age in which it might reasonably be supposed a child should be most sensible of such a loss.[16]

The guardianship of the orphaned boy was assumed by a gentleman named Downes who removed him from Kingston to a school in St Albans. The principal of Philip's new school was Dr Nathaniel Wood, a Nonconformist minister of a small local congregation. Dr Wood was an impressive disciplinarian and 'a thorough and careful scholar'. Under his tutelage 'Philly' began 'to acquire the habit, which so distinguished him in after life, of working methodically, exactly, and instantly, at whatever he aimed to do; and of finding, as he said "that the best recreation is in the change from one work to another" '.[17]

He became acquainted with the Revd Samuel Clark, a local Presbyterian minister and author of *A Collection of the Promises of Scripture*

(1720). Deeply influenced with Dr Clark's holy life and warm heart, Philip confessed his Christian faith and on 1 January 1718 joined Clark's church. In his diary he recorded his feelings:

> I rose early this morning, read that part of Mr Henry's book on the Lord's supper, which treats of due approach to it. I endeavoured to excite in myself those dispositions and affections which he mentions as proper for that ordinance. As I endeavoured to prepare my heart, according to the preparation of the sanctuary, though with many defects, God was pleased to meet me, and give me sweet communion with Himself, of which I desire always to retain a grateful sense.[18]

Later in the day, after further study and prayer, Doddridge reviewed the events of the day: 'I then looked over the memorandums of this day, comparing the manner in which I spent it, and blessed be God, I had reason to do it with some pleasure, though in some instances I found cause for humiliation.'[19]

Clark virtually became Philip's father-substitute when it was learned that Downes, the guardian in name only, had become bankrupt; precarious financial speculations in the City had failed, bringing in their wake ruin on several wardships for which Downes was responsible. In the financial crash most of the Doddridge inheritance was lost. Yet in a characteristic gesture Philip sold what family plate he had left in order to extricate his guardian from the debtors' prison. Downes promptly set about further speculative ventures, including a scheme to supply water to London from St Albans.

The effect on Philip's life was traumatic. Reduced to desperate circumstances, he immediately left Dr Wood's school to seek the comfort of his only close relative, his sister; Elizabeth had recently married the Revd John Nettleton, a Dissenting minister, and they lived close by the windmill on Hampstead Heath. It was to their house that the sixteen-year-old boy retired to collect his thoughts and redirect his life.[20]

Philip's spirits soon rallied under the care of John and Elizabeth Nettleton, and he told them that he had set his heart on becoming a minister of religion. On hearing of this and of his misfortunes, the Duchess of Bedford sent him an offer which would have made him financially secure for the rest of his life. If he would become a conforming member of the Church of England, she would pay for his education at university and would ensure preferment in the Church. It was a tempting proposition but Philip's nonconformist background and deeply-held beliefs were too powerful an obstacle; with politeness he declined the Duchess's offer.

Perplexed as to his next step, Philip requested an interview with the eminent Nonconformist divine Dr Edmund Calamy[21] who, possibly thinking that the weak-looking youth before him could never stand the tough ministerial life, gave him some depressing advice. 'I waited upon Dr Edmund Calamy to beg his advice and assistance, that I might be brought up a minister, which has always been my great desire,' wrote Doddridge, 'He gave me no encouragement in it, but advised me to turn my thoughts to something else. It was with great concern, that I received such advice; but I desire to follow Providence and not force it. The Lord give me grace to glorify Him in whatever station He sets me: then, here am I, let Him do with me what seemeth good in His sight.'[22]

Three weeks later a chance was presented to him to study for the law; a family friend named Horseman knew of Doddridge's abilities and introduced him to a lawyer named Eyre. Impressed by the young man, Eyre intimated that he would accept Philip for legal training, and made him a generous offer. The dilemma tore at Doddridge's heart; resolving to seek guidance in prayer he set aside a day in order to make his decision. His agony of mind was interrupted by the arrival of a letter from St Albans. Recognising Samuel Clark's[23] familiar handwriting, Philip could hardly believe his eyes when he read of Clark's offer to provide him with a home and the wherewithal to support his studies until a place could be found at an academy.

Seeing this as the decisive hand of God in his life, Doddridge wrote: 'This I looked upon almost as an answer from heaven, and, while I live, shall always adore so seasonable an interposition of Divine Providence. I have sought God's direction in this matter, and I hope I have had it. My only view in my choice hath been that of more extensive service, and I beg God would make me an instrument of doing much good in the world.'[24]

Doddridge's stay with Clark lasted only a few months, as the latter soon secured a place for his young friend at the Dissenting academy at Kibworth[25] in Leicestershire.

The Kibworth academy was founded in 1715 and conducted by the Revd John Jennings, son of an ejected minister and himself an Independent minister of high academic status and cultured outlook. His *Two Discourses, Preaching Christ* and *Particular and Experimental Preaching*, published four years after Doddridge joined the academy, received high acclaim in theological circles. Mrs Jennings' father was Sir Francis Wingate of

Harlington Grange, Bedford, who had committed John Bunyan to
Bedford jail. Doddridge felt great affection and respect for both Mr and
Mrs Jennings who showed great interest in his academic progress. He
particularly appreciated Mrs Jennings' 'uncommon sprightliness and wit,
solidity of judgement; and delicacy of taste'.[26]

Doddridge commenced his studies in October 1719, supported financially by Clark. On 3 January 1722 he wrote to his patron:

> Rev. Sir
> The principal reason of my writing now is to transmit you the
> following account which I received of Mr Jennings last week:
> 'Bill to Christmas, [1721]; half year's board and tuition, eight
> pounds ten shillings; King's Inquiry, four shillings and three
> pence; Appendix to Logic, two shillings and six pence; a New
> Testament interleaved, three shillings and eight pence, in all nine
> pounds and five pence; received of Mr Taylor's fund, two pounds
> ten shillings; remains due six pounds ten shillings and five pence,
> payable to John Clark, bookseller'.[27]

Doddridge continued to attack his studies eagerly; the interleaved New
Testament was used by him to make notes and observations on his
reading:

> In my last, sir, I sent you an account of the course of our public
> studies for this last half year, and you will perceive that they are
> of such a nature as to require a considerable exercise of thought,
> and that the references are generally long, and consequently that,
> though we have no evening lecture, still we have less time for our
> private studies than we ever had in any of our former half years;
> however, I generally find about an hour and a half in a day for the
> study of the Scriptures. The New Testament I read in the original
> without any commentator, but more of my time is spent in the
> Old, . . . I do not entirely neglect the classics, though I have but
> little time for them. . . .[28]

He had found time, however, to study some of the works of Horace,
Cicero, Isocrates, Homer, Lucian and Xenophon in addition to modern
English writings; Bishop Burnet's *Sacred Theory of the Earth* (1681) he
had avidly consumed as he did the writings of Locke. Doddridge did not
absorb uncritically all that he read; Lord Shaftesbury's works he considered 'a strange mixture of good sense and extravagance'.

There is no doubt that Doddridge was following Clark's advice:

3. Doddridge as a young minister.

4. Strength of character and good humour radiate from what Doddridge considered his best likeness.

The Church of Christ in Northampton sendeth greeting —

Rev'd S'

The dispensation of Gods providence towards us, in suffering the removeal of our late Pastor from us, is very Awfull, and we hope hath lay with weight upon all our hearts, and has put us upon prayer & supplication to God the great Shepherd, that he would appear for us & direct us in this Difficult & weighty matter; and send one amongst us, that he will Eminently own, and make a great blessing unto us.

S' we have had some taste of your ministerial abilities in your occasional labours amongst us, which gave a general satisfaction to the Congregation; but this matter being so important, we humbly apply our selves to you, that you would come to us and preach amongst us a month as a Candidate in order for whole Satisfaction; you being the first after Mr Miles that has been Invited on such an account. we shall leave our Brethren that bring this to use what further arguments they think fitt with you, to accept of this Invitation, And shall recomend you to the wisdom and Conduct of the divine Spirit and Continue our Prayers & supplications to the great God for our Direction and do Subscribe our names under written by the order & Consent of the whole Church —

Sep't 28. 1729 —    Geo: Mason    Malory Wooston
                     Wm: Bliss
                     Edward Pinkley        Rich Noton
                     Richard         Jm
                     Henry Bunyan    Wm Manning
                     Benj: Shott     James Hackleton
                     Josiah Brine

5. The letter sent from Castle Hill Church to Doddridge asking him 'to preach amongst us a month as a Candidate', 28 September 1729.

that he should be 'furnished, not with a bare superficial taste of literature, but with so rich a stock of solid knowledge as may abundantly qualify you for whatever service God may call you to in his church. Therefore now is your time for thorough improvement . . .'.[29]

When only fourteen years of age Doddridge had resolved to put every minute of his time to good use. At Kibworth he set himself high standards of self-discipline and wrote down eighteen rules for the direction of his conduct as a student:

> Let my first thoughts be devout and thankful.
> Let me rise early, immediately return God more solemn thanks for the mercies of the night, devote myself to Him, and beg His assistance in the intended business of the day.[30]

Doddridge decided to pray regularly, to read the scriptures and not to 'trifle with a book with which I may have no present concern'. No unnecessary expenses were to be incurred. He resolved to eat moderately, to avoid procrastination, to guard against pride and to consecrate his sleep and all his recreations to God. He desired to be useful to other people and intended to cultivate 'a tender, compassionate, friendly behaviour'. He would regularly survey his conduct in the light of such rules, remembering 'that the Souls of Men are immortal, and that Christ died to redeem them'.[31]

There is little wonder that Doddridge became a model student rising at five every morning, summer and winter, and praying even as he dressed himself. It was a habit that he retained for the rest of his life. In addition to the intensive course pursued at the academy, he managed to read sixty extra major works, making copious annotations as he did so.

Some biographers of Doddridge have sought to excuse many of his youthful letters as indiscretions or merely boyish fantasies. Doddridge was by nature of a friendly and gregarious disposition; one must look with sympathy at a young man closeted in his study, often for over ten hours a day and pursuing intensive and exacting studies, as in need of some emotional outlet and relaxation.

At times Doddridge was simply lonely and wrote long and intimate letters to his sister, to Samuel Clark, and other personal friends. To Mrs Farrington he wrote in April 1722:

> You are really the best mamma I have in the world; and if you will give me leave to say it, I have a vast deal of filial affection for you, and so I hope you will write, if it be possible, by the next post.[32]

Several changes of address did not ease his loneliness. Early in 1722 he moved with the academy to Hinckley which he compared unfavourably with Kibworth. From his new study window Doddridge could see and hear the noisy operations of building a new meeting house; he missed the rural delights of Kibworth. In July 1723 when he moved again from Hinckley to take up his pastoral duties at Kibworth, he lodged with the Freeman family at Stretton; his loneliness at times seemed acute although somewhat relieved by the interests of the countryside around; he wrote to Clark on 6 July 1723:

> . . . [I] live with a substantial farmer, who is one of the heads of our congregation. The housekeeping is plain and very good; but what I most delight in is a pleasant garden, orchard, and close. I am treated with a great deal of kindness and respect; but they are so taken up with their business that I am sometimes alone twenty-one hours in the twenty-four; nay, I frequently breakfast, dine and sup by myself. This is a very disagreeable circumstance, especially to me who have always been used to good company.[33]

Doddridge relished his vacations in which he could renew his acquaintances. On returning to Stretton from a visit to his sister and the Clark family in August 1723 he referred to himself as 'a fish out of water' and continued: 'I have had so much good company at London and St Albans, and especially at Hampstead, that I hardly know how to bear up under the loss of it, and the solitude to which I am condemned is a thousand times more disagreeable than it was a few weeks ago. Had I but one agreeable, constant companion, I could be easy, but it is my misfortune to be quite alone, and can you wonder that it has almost made me stupid.'[34]

Doddridge occasionally met young people of his own age and social circle; the conversation would revolve around the latest books and current affairs. In the fashion of the day, good manners and graceful deportment were deemed vital to social intercourse. At times his letters show excessive playfulness; classical allusions were made so that Doddridge became 'Hortensius', his friend Obadiah Hughes 'Atticus' and Jennings' daughter Jenny 'Theodosia'. On one occasion Doddridge signed himself Sultan Bajazet after describing a hilarious evening when he and his fellow students performed Nicholas Rowe's play *Tamerlane* in nightgowns, borrowed petticoats and pudding tins for helmets.[35]

His letters are often amusing and show a natural exuberance; 'I must put on a more melancholy air,' he promised, and in the exaggerated epistolary style of the period he would often apologise for his 'impertinences' before signing himself an 'affectionate and dutiful servant'. There was inevitably an element of fantasy for a time. He admitted to Hannah Clark that 'I find it absolutely necessary to have some subject of amorous contemplation'.[36] On other occasions he referred to his heart as 'an uninhabited box' and to himself as Adam in Paradise but 'bereft of his Eve'. He constantly sought advice from his friends, thus compensating for the lack of any close family life, where advice could be easily sought and readily given.[37] He anxiously asked Clark: 'Particularly I desire you would let me know, upon your own experience, whether a married life be most expedient for a minister, and what are its peculiar advantages.'[38]

In a letter to Hannah Clark it is clear that he had decided to proceed with caution:

> I have indeed no thoughts of marrying very soon, and whenever I come to take that master-work in hand, I hope I shall remember the important article of a provision for a family; for I have a mortal aversion to the cares of the world, and am fully convinced that it is impossible for the most agreeable woman it contains to preserve her beauty or good humour, if she has nothing to subsist upon but compliments and kisses.[39]

In December 1722 Doddridge wrote to his 'much respected Aunt', Rebecca Roberts, confiding that he was 'most violently in love' with seventeen year-old Kitty Freeman, his Kibworth host's daughter whom he called Clarinda:

> I have a heart exactly prepared to receive the fondest and tenderest impressions. . . . I forget everything but Clarinda. I dream of her in the night; and rave of her in the day. If my tutor asks me a question about predestination, I answer him, that Clarinda is the prettiest creature in the world! Or if I sit down to make a sermon against transubstantiation, I cannot forbear cautioning my hearers against the excesses of love.[40]

Doddridge's infatuation for Kitty lasted for several years and passed through the various stages of such amours. He was perplexed by a conflict between his own natural feelings and the claims of prudence; financially he was unable to support a wife and his future was uncertain yet, he expostulated, 'how can I answer it to my own conscience, if I should neglect the opportunity?'[41] He duly proposed marriage to Kitty who gave him an equivocal reply and continued to keep him in suspense. Matters became difficult at his lodgings as Kitty's parents, reluctantly

6. The old Meeting House, Market Harborough. Doddridge moved to Harborough in 1725 to share the pastoral responsibilities of Kibworth and Harborough with David Some, senior.

agreeing to the prospect of him as a son-in-law, desired him to move out of the house until the situation could be resolved.

On 30 September 1725, Doddridge moved to Market Harborough but kept up his relationship with Kitty, hoping that fondness would grow with absence. Kitty, however, found fault with him, accused him of flirting with one Rachel Wingate and demanded that he break off all his female friendships. Exasperated by the quarrelling, Doddridge presented Kitty with an ultimatum, and the affair came to an unhappy end. Writing in July 1727 he could still entertain a faint hope that he might be 're-engaged with Kitty' but within a few weeks he gloomily reported to his sister that 'for aught I know, [Kitty] may be married before, or within a fortnight'.[42]

John Jennings had noted the great potential in Philip Doddridge and was anxious to see him established as a fully qualified minister. Usually a student was not allowed to preach outside the academy. However, in a letter to his sister on 30 July 1722, Doddridge excitedly announced 'a piece of news':

> I preached my first sermon on Sunday morning, to a very large auditory, from 1 Cor. xvi 22. If Mr Jennings had not been very

urgent, I had not begun till Christmas; but he told me, he believed it would be most for my improvement to begin now, and there was great need of some assistance, and so I submitted.[43]

Evidently Doddridge's conduct of the service at the Hinckley meeting house, especially the striking words of his sermon, made a favourable impression on the congregation. Doddridge was nervous of his youthfulness, but was greatly cheered by his hearers' response.

On 28 January 1723, Doddridge wrote to Clark including details of his debts to Jennings for tuition, board and other necessities; one item was for a new gown costing one pound fourteen shillings and two pence (£1.71). The old one 'had lasted me two years', wrote Doddridge, 'and had been turned and mended several times, and was at first but an ordinary calimanco of eighteen-pence a yard, so that it was very necessary to have another'.[44]

In the same letter he mentioned the result of the examination conducted at Leicester by three local ministers to ascertain his fitness for the ministry:

> Last Thursday my class fellow, Mr [David] Some [junior] and I were examined by his father [David Some of Market Harborough], Mr Bridgen [John Brogden of Narborough] and Mr [John] Norris [of Welford], three neighbouring ministers, remarkable for their affability, candour and catholicism, as well as their learning and good sense. They were pleased to declare themselves thoroughly satisfied; and we are to receive a certificate of approbation and recommendation from all the ministers of the county next general meeting; that is, about the middle of May.[45]

Following his acceptance for the Christian ministry Doddridge soon found himself called upon to preach in the neighbourhood; by the end of the following month he had preached at Kibworth, Nuneaton and Bedworth, travelling mostly on horseback. He sensibly accepted the advice of his brother-in-law, the Revd John Nettleton, regarding 'the management of my voice in preaching. I am sure I have need enough of it, for it is very certain that I always speak a great deal too fast, and all my friends are so kind as to tell me of it'.[46]

It was not long before he accepted the unanimous call of the congregation at Kibworth to the pastorate which became vacant upon the premature death of John Jennings at the age of thirty. In June 1723 Doddridge commenced his preaching duties in a building where the Ten

Commandments were lettered on the wall behind the pulpit. His congregation, numbering about forty in the morning and one hundred and fifty in the evening, were mainly 'shepherds, farmers, graziers, and their subalterns'; a homely unaffected people.[47] His salary was to be £35 per annum, although he reckoned that with ample country provisions he could live on £10.

One of his friends commiserated with him on being 'buried alive' in such an obscure village; he replied that such a life suited him admirably, especially the beautiful countryside with its distinct sounds: 'the chirping of sparrows, the cooing of pigeons, the lowing of kine, the bleating of sheep, and, to complete the concert, the grunting of swine and neighing of horses'.[48]

Doddridge drew up a set of personal rules in respect of his ministerial duties, promising to 'spend some extraordinary time in devotion every Lord's day . . . and [I] will then preach over to my soul that doctrine which I preach to others'. He resolved to spend half an hour every second evening in the week in praying for his congregation, to review weekly and monthly his accomplishments 'and whether I advance or lose ground in religion', to pray regularly on matters of importance and public welfare, and in all his 'duties of the oratory, I will endeavour to maintain a serious and affectionate temper'.[49]

It was an ideal time for him to continue his studies away from the charms of ensnaring city life; although there was a streak of loneliness in his constitution his situation gave him 'so many favourable advantages for the most serious and important purposes of devotion and philosophy, and, I hope I may add, of usefulness too'.[50]

He therefore pursued his studies with indefatigable zeal, reading deeply and widely. Some of his favourite theological writers were Tillotson, Howe and Baxter,[51] and he found immense delight in the elegance of French literature. Of his beloved tutor Doddridge wrote:

> I go on very agreeably with my studies. I have almost finished Mr Jennings's system of divinity; and the better I am acquainted with it, the more I admire it. He does not entirely accord with the system of any particular body of men; but is sometimes a Calvinist, sometimes a Remonstrant, sometimes a Baxterian, and sometimes a Socinian, as truth and evidence determine him. He always inculcates it upon our attention, that the scriptures are the only standard of orthodoxy, and encourages the utmost freedom of inquiry. He furnishes us with all kinds of authors upon every

subject, without advising us to skip over the heretical passages for fear of infection. It is evidently his main care to inspire us with sentiments of CATHOLICISM, and to arm us against that zeal, which is not according to knowledge.[52]

This is a key passage in the understanding of Doddridge's outlook on life; he admired people for their candour and catholicity and not for any doctrinal bigotry. It was a period in which fierce controversies were waged among Dissenters, and attempts to ensure orthodoxy by compulsory agreements ('subscriptions') to doctrinal statements were made; the famous Salters' Hall[53] controversy in 1719 over the Trinity excited passionate interest throughout the country.

Doddridge could see the dangers of such disputes and firmly refused to subscribe to any formulation of words. At this time he was being pressed from many quarters to accept larger and more remunerative pastorates. One London congregation entreated him to accept their call. In a letter to Clark dated 4 February 1724, he gave his reasons for his decision to decline the offer:

> Considering the temper of the people, I thought it very probable that I should have been required to Subscribe, which I was resolved never to do; for as I had been accustomed, under my dear tutor, to that latitude of expression which the Scriptures indulge and recommend, I could not resolve upon tying myself up in trammels, and obliging myself to talk in the phrases of the assembly's catechism.[54]

Nothing could have been more foreign to a man who held scripture to be the highest arbiter in all matters; nothing more irksome to a mind open and alert in the search for truth. Doddridge could admit that from 1723 to 1730 he had seriously reflected on the claims of various theological notions currently being disputed. In 1723 he had stated that he was 'moderately inclined' to 'the congregational form',[55] but it is clear from his correspondence that he steadfastly held that he was foremost a servant of God and refused to be encompassed by man-made formulas of faith.

In April 1723 a congregation of over twelve hundred at Coventry wanted him as their assistant minister. In the following August a similarly large congregation of Independents and Baptists requested him to settle at Pershore in Worcestershire. In November, Girdlers' Hall, London, a centre of powerful scholarly preaching, urged him to succeed Mr Foxon. In February of the following year many of the civic and religious leaders of Coventry, including the mayor and several aldermen, tempted Doddridge with the offer of over six times his current stipend. Four years later in 1728 two separate congregations in Nottingham (Castle Gate and the High Pavement) competed for his services; he was not impressed by the rigid religious views of some of the people and declined both offers. Other calls had come from Lincoln's Inn Dissenting congregation and Bradfield, but Doddridge refused to be distracted from his responsibilities. His love for his people, and his fear that the cause would suffer if he left, were his main motives.

Violent sickness and sudden death were a common feature in the eighteenth century. We see Doddridge writing with great concern hoping that his sister Elizabeth and her children would recover from their maladies; on one occasion he enclosed 'His Majesty, King William' (i.e. a half guinea), to help their family finances. Throughout the correspondence there are frequent references to illness especially to the scourge of smallpox. On 6 July 1723 he wrote to Elizabeth:

> The agreeable Mrs Roberts died the first of June, of a violent fever, and good Mr Jennings is fallen ill of the small-pox. It is the very worst sort, and I am afraid he will be dead before this comes to your hand. May God avert so dreadful a loss to the dissenting interest in general, and especially to this part of England.[56]

His fears were well-grounded; John Jennings was dead within a few days. It was a savage blow that jeopardised the academy. Yet Jennings, long before he died, had quietly encouraged Doddridge to review his whole course of lectures and make annotations and improvements where necessary. 'Our young divine did not then suspect what was the motive of Mr Jennings in giving him this advice. But he was afterwards informed, that his tutor had declared it to be his opinion, that, if it should please God to remove him early in life, Mr Doddridge was the most likely of any of his pupils to pursue the schemes which he had formed; and which, indeed, were very far from being complete. . . .'[57]

When Doddridge moved to Market Harborough in October 1725 he united his pastoral work at Kibworth with that of the Revd David Some (senior). The latter was conscious of the void created by the closing of the academy; an attempt to reopen it under Thomas Benyon[58] was 'rendered abortive, by the premature death of that promising young man'.[59] Doddridge had written a letter to Thomas Saunders of Kettering giving a detailed account of Jennings' system of education. The letter was taken to London by Some for the scrutiny of the celebrated Isaac Watts. In due course Watts' comments were received:

... The diversity of genius, the variety of studies, the several intellectual, moral, and pious accomplishments, the constant daily and hourly labours necessary to fill such a post can hardly be expected from any one person living!

Yet if there be one person capable of such a post, perhaps it is the man who has so admirably described this scheme of education; and as he seems to have surveyed and engrossed the whole comprehensive view and design, together with its constant difficulties and accidental embarrassments, and yet supposed it to be practicable, I am sure I can never think of any person more likely to execute it than himself; although, if an elder person joined with him, for the reputation of the matter, at least, it would be well. ..."[60]

On 10 April 1729, the local Dissenting ministers met at Lutterworth for a day of humiliation and prayer for religious revival. The sermon was preached by David Some on Revelation iii. 2: 'Be watchful, and strengthen the things that remain, that are ready to die; for I have not found thy works perfect before God.' With Dr Watts' encouragement Some proposed that Doddridge, young as he was, should be asked to reopen the academy at Market Harborough. The assembled ministers were unanimous in their support, and they 'engaged to render every encouragement and assistance in their power'.[61]

David Some had carefully prepared the ground, pre-empting any contrary arguments Doddridge might put up, by finding potential students and being prepared to take on the bulk of the work of the combined Harborough/Kibworth pastorate. He was a man of persuasion and pressed Doddridge to accept. True to his nature Doddridge consulted his friends, especially Clark whose first reaction was to advise him to take on the pastorate of a city church; but Clark soon realised the importance of the post and Doddridge's unique qualities for such an office, and encouraged him to accept.

'At Midsummer,' writes Stanford, 'in obedience to the wish thus recorded, he set up his academy at Harborough. Mrs Jennings, with her kind motherliness, her notable faculty of management, and her remarkable gift of utterance, came to take charge of the key-basket. The waggon brought the furniture and her family. Students arrived, more were coming, and everything seemed full of promise, when in a few months, to the surprise of everybody, he had to leave Harborough for Northampton.'[62]

# Northampton and Marriage

Northamptonshire has a long tradition of Dissent. As far back as the late fourteenth century the town became a centre of Lollard activity when supporters of John Wycliffe gained access to important civic and ecclesiastical positions in the town. In 1392 the Mayor of Northampton, John Fox, was accused of using his powers to allow Lollards to preach in All Saints Church; it was alleged that on one occasion Fox forcibly prevented the Vicar from saying Mass until a Lollard preacher had completed his sermon. The Lollards denied the doctrine of transubstantiation, and in the reign of Mary Tudor attempts were made to root out such viewpoints; in August 1557 the Chancellor of the Bishop of Peterborough pronounced sentence of death upon a shoemaker, John Kurde of Syresham, who was duly burned to death in the stonepit adjacent to the North Gate of Northampton[1] by the officers of the Sheriff, Sir Thomas Tresham.

For two eventful years (1570–2) Northampton became the centre of a revolutionary Puritan experiment. Introduced to the town by a group of local puritan gentry, Percival Wiburn (who had been exiled for his beliefs during Mary Tudor's reign) quickly established himself as a leading figure in the radical transformation of the town's religious and civic life. By the 'order' of Northampton on 5 June 1571 the authorities of both bishop and mayor were 'joined together . . . [so that] ill life is corrected, God's glory set forth and the people brought in good obedience'.[2] In practical terms it meant compulsory attendance for all townspeople at weekly sermons, catechisings and services on Sundays, and quarterly solemn communions. Discipline was exacted by ministers and churchwardens in co-operation with the mayor and bailiffs. A fortnight before every quarterly communion each household was visited by the ministers and churchwardens to ascertain their spiritual state.

Wiburn also established 'exercises of prophesying'[3]—weekly meetings on Saturdays for the clergy of town and country in order systematically

Notes and references for this chapter begin on page 155

to study and discuss the scriptures. By their popularity and success in educating the more ignorant clergy in theology and preaching method, the prophesyings did more than anything else to establish Puritanism in Elizabethan England.[4]

Such a regime met fierce opposition, especially from Roman Catholics and others who had no love for Wiburn's restrictions. Encouraged by the Pope's excommunication of Elizabeth I, an anonymous rhymester attacked the Puritan reformer in Northampton:

> Maister Wyborne, alias tiburne tyke,
> Here dwelleth in this towne,
> Which sought by all the meanes he could,
> The Easter [sepulchre] to pluck downe.
>
> But I of hym do well pronounce,
> And tyme the truth shall try,
> That he shall trust unto his heeles
> Or els in Smithfield fry.[5]

Although Wiburn did not 'in Smithfield fry' he did take 'unto his heeles' after pressure from his enemies ensured his dismissal from Northampton. Retiring to Whiston, Wiburn continued his Puritan activities there.

Elizabeth viewed with suspicion the growth of Puritanism. When the Archbishop of Canterbury, Edmund Grindal, refused the Queen's order to reduce the number of licensed preachers to three or four per county, and to suppress the prophesyings, he was suspended from office and confined to his palace. In his place Edmund Freke of Norwich began the task of silencing Puritan preachers. In 1577 the Privy Council ordered a general suppression of all prophesyings throughout the country; the Northampton prophesyings, which centred upon All Saints Church, were duly prohibited, and ceased.

The Presbyterians within the Church of England were fundamentally concerned with the nature of the church and the exercise of authority within it. During the last decades of the sixteenth century Presbyterian principles began to be adopted in Northampton, Daventry and Kettering where committees or 'classes' were set up to control church life and appoint ministers. In Northampton, Edmund Snape, curate of St Peter's, was imprisoned in 1590 for denying episcopal ordination and advocating Presbyterian doctrines.

If the Presbyterians wished to reform the church on more democratic lines, the Separatists challenged the church with the revolutionary concept of the 'gathered' church. Northamptonshire has its link with the earliest of the Separatists, Robert Browne, who was born at Tolethorpe Hall, Little Casterton in Rutland. Browne was vociferous in his opposition to the authority of the bishops. He was imprisoned frequently for his extreme Separatist views, but in 1591 seemed reconciled to the Church of England when he was instituted as rector of Thorpe Achurch in Northampton-shire. A local tradition held that he led a double life, conducting services for the Puritans in a nearby cottage after he had finished his duties at the parish church. In 1617 he was suspended from his duties for not conform-ing to the Prayer Book, and was finally excommunicated in 1631. His violent temper got the better of him in 1633 when he assaulted the village constable. Browne was imprisoned in Northampton where he died; his memorial can be seen in St Giles' churchyard.

After 1583, when Whitgift was made Archbishop of Canterbury, Northamptonshire became the centre of Puritan pamphleteering. John Penry of Northampton was probably the writer of several of the Martin Marprelate Tracts, at least one of which was secretly printed and collated at Fawsley, the home of Sir Richard Knightley,[6] another leading Puritan. Northampton retained its strongly-held principles of freedom from clerical domination into the seventeenth century; in 1638 the churchwardens of All Saints were excommunicated for disobeying the instructions of the Archbishop of Canterbury. From 1641 to the Restoration Puritanism held the ascendancy, and in Northamptonshire forty High Church clergymen were replaced in the resultant purges. Quakerism emerged as an aggressive force, and in the County as elsewhere attempts were made to stem its growth by harsh means.

Not long after the battle of Naseby in 1645 several dissenting con-gregations (Presbyterian, Independent and Baptist) emerged in the County. In Northampton a Presbyterian church was in existence well before 1674. In Rothwell an Independent church had been formed in 1655. After 1689 the Rothwell Church came under the direction of the Revd Richard Davis,[7] a powerful and persuasive evangelist; as a result of his work, numerous 'meetings' were established within a radius of eighty miles of Rothwell, and members of the church were drawn from over sixteen towns and villages. Such growth alarmed the Presbyterians who, conscious of Davis' poaching of some of their flocks, labelled it *a Most Horrid and Dismal Plague begun at . . . Rowell.*[8]

In Northampton Davis found a small group of Dissenters who met regularly for worship and established a 'Congregational Church'. This church met in the house of the Dowager Lady Fermor situated in the

'South Quarter', a residential part of the town in Bridge Street and close to the Nene. Lady Fermor, although a member of the established church, was a generous and sympathetic patron of Dissenters. The church was formally established in 1697 and continued to meet in Lady Fermor's house until a site was purchased in College Lane, and a meeting house erected in 1711. Subsequent history was to see the development of cordial relations between the College Lane Church (which later became College Street Baptist Church) and the church at Castle Hill; Philip Doddridge's ministry in particular was to cement their essential religious unity and destroy the rivalries of their early history.

The oldest records of Castle Hill Church (dated 1694) mention the departure of the minister, Mr Blower, whose successful ministry had been exercised for some years. The origins of the church are obscure, although it is doubtful whether it was in existence before the Great Ejectment of 1662. Nor can evidence be found to support the theory that the Castle Hill Church was directly formed by the ejectment of the Revd Jeremiah Lewis[9] from St Giles' Church; there are no clear records of any substantial numbers of Nonconformist parishioners leaving with him, and Lewis died soon after in December 1662. What is likely is that the Ejectment encouraged Nonconformists to assemble in private houses and barns. Northampton's relatively tolerant spirit freed them from the savage persecution exacted in other parts of the country; although preachers were gaoled, they were outsiders, and in general Nonconformist prisoners were treated reasonably well by the townsfolk. Dr Conant, himself a former Presbyterian and Vicar of All Saints from 1671, had close relations with those in 'private congregations' and his powerful moderating influence in the town 'cannot be over-estimated in judging of the conditions and even moral forces which led to formation of the early Nonconformist Church'.[10]

In 1672 King Charles' Indulgence[11] eased the situation for Nonconformists. Richard Hooke, ejected from his living at Creaton in 1662, preached for a time in his own house before removing to another property in the Drapery, Northampton where, under the Indulgence, he obtained a licence as a Presbyterian minister. John Harding,[12] ejected from his livings in Oxfordshire and Wiltshire, came to the town where he continued as a licenced Presbyterian minister. Religious services were also allowed in the houses of John Clarke, Valentine Chadock, Samuel Wolford (or Welford), Alexander Blake and the barn and house of Robert Massey (Marsey or Marley). Samuel Wolford, whose house was licensed for Presbyterian teaching, was an early member of Castle Hill Church.[13]

Under Parliamentary pressure the Indulgence was cancelled within a year and in 1675 all licences were recalled as part of renewed persecution; even Northampton felt the change. The overall effect, however, was to strengthen Nonconformist congregations as many people who had hitherto 'occasionally conformed' by minimally attending their parish churches, were goaded into declaring their full Nonconformity. Numerous Nonconformist churches date their existence from 1662 and 1672 respectively.[14]

On 20 September 1675, in St Mary's Street, close to Castle Hill, a serious domestic fire broke out. Assisted by a strong westerly wind the fire rapidly took hold of the thatched roofs of other nearby cottages. The town was packed with goods, the tradesmen having returned from Stourbridge fair laden with their annual supplies. Hayricks, timber, oil stores and maltings were quickly engulfed in a sea of flame which in several hours destroyed about three quarters of the town and rendered seven hundred families homeless. All Saints Church was gutted, the bells crashing down from the tower. There was some looting of goods packed into the Market Square for safety, and eleven people died.[15]

The clerk at the Church of the Holy Sepulchre recorded details of the fire which 'burnt all the Horse markit, most part of Gold Street, all the Chequer, part of Bridge Street, part of the Sheep markitt, all Newland, almost all Abington Street, and all St Gile's street, except heare and there an odd house'.[16] 'Nothing standing above the cellars that was combustible, which was not either burnt or burning down to Ashes. No Timber left, from great Beams even to Cheeks of Doors and Lintels.'[17] Some of the houses licenced for preaching purposes, Richard Hooke's in the Drapery and Robert Massey's in the Chequer (Market Square) were destroyed. Alexander Blake's house in St Martin's (Broad Street) probably escaped unscathed, and Massey's barn survived.

As to the fate of the properties of Valentine Chadock, John Clarke, and John Harding little is known. The locations where Nonconformists met until the meeting house on Castle Hill was built in 1695, are equally obscure. There are, however, a few stray pieces of evidence which centre on the activities of John Clarke. Described as a draper and a prominent citizen (Chamberlain in 1687 and Mayor in 1691–2) Clarke was a staunch Presbyterian. The diary of Thomas Isham of Lamport mentions Clarke as 'preaching and building a house',[18] and it is known that sometime before the fire Clarke had purchased from Francis Pickmer, attorney, and others the *Swan* inn situated in the Drapery. It may be that the *Swan* was the building mentioned by Isham, as the Fire Court of 1677–8[19] ruled that Clarke's duty was to rebuild his property. That Nonconformists had regular meeting places there is little doubt. In the Church Book at Castle Hill is a curious entry in the handwriting of Thomas Shepard: 'Dec. 11. I married Mr Buswell's Son and Daughter of Kettering in our Meeting House.'[20] It was written in 1694, a year before the Castle Hill meeting house was erected.

It is also believed that Robert Massey's barn provided another centre for Nonconformist activity, the group meeting there eventually moving to Lady Fermor's house in Bridge Street before becoming College Lane (Baptist) Church. John Harding was also influential, gathering round him a strong nucleus of worshippers, many of whom joined the Castle Hill meeting in 1695.

The arrival of the Revd Samuel Blower to Northampton was to result in the welding together of many of the disparate Nonconformist elements within the town. It is not known when Blower actually came to Northampton, although it is certain that he was active early in 1690. He was a man of considerable learning and had been ejected in 1662 from his Fellowship of Magdalen College, Oxford, and forbidden to preach at Woodstock where he held the living.[21] Some accounts state that he was in Northampton either in 1674 or early 1675 but these are unsubstantiated. Edmund Calamy describes him thus:

> He was a man of meek temper, peaceable principles, and a godly life. He had, like St Austin, very exalted thoughts of Divine Grace and Redeeming Love. He discovered a very tender regard to young persons, and would often address himself very affectionately towards them, not only in his sermons but in his visits, and rejoiced much in their hopefulness. He affected not a pompous way of preaching. . . . He was very desirable as a friend, being free and communicative, candid in the last degree, of a very sympathising spirit with those in affliction, and particularly mindful of them in his prayers. . . . Wherever he had an interest, he was for improving it for God to his utmost; and took all opportunities to do so.[22]

Such remarkable qualities of character helped to form a distinct tone in the life of the church, so much so that when Philip Doddridge came to Castle Hill he felt that he had entered a spiritual home.

Although he was of 'meek temper', Blower in 1692 attacked Richard Davis for his activities within the town, especially his administering the Lord's Supper to the gathering in Lady Fermor's house. For several years

Dissenting ministers had been outraged by Davis' activities, and it is a reasonable assumption that Davis' work in Northampton had caused a considerable withdrawal of members from the church, mostly those with Baptist leanings.[23] A study of the earliest names in the Castle Hill and College Lane Church Books reveals that at least sixteen persons who were members of Castle Hill in 1694 or shortly afterwards later became members of College Lane. Thus there was a split in the Nonconformist church over principles of baptism, as well as tensions between Presbyterian and Congregational concepts of ecclesiastical church government. Nevertheless Blower's ministry had lasting influence, and upon his departure for Abingdon in 1694 he left a strong membership of one hundred and sixty-four.

The Church, after meeting for prayer, sent a 'Unanimous Call' to the Revd Thomas Shepard to succeed Samuel Blower. Like his father Shepard had been an Anglican clergyman but had had differences of opinion with his Bishop in his former living at Haversham. From Haversham he left for Oundle where his father lived, and thence came to Northampton at the age of twenty-nine. Shepard seems to have insisted on the Church Covenant being read and signed by all members:

> We this Church of Christ whose names are underwritten, having given up ourselves to the Lord and one to Another according to the Will of God, do promise and Covenant in the presence of God, to walk together in all the Laws and Ordinances of Christ according to the Rules of his Gospell thro' Jesus Christ so strengthening us.[24]

Shepard was an accomplished poet and was already well known as the co-author with John Mason of *Penitential Cries*, a series of thirty-two recently published hymns. In later life and in co-operation with Mason he wrote *Spiritual Songs* which eclipsed his earlier work; their writing prepared the way for Watts and Doddridge.

Shepard had made his ministry conditional on pastor and people walking 'comfortably together in all the ways and Ordinances of the Lord'. Evidently his political views upset some, and perhaps there were religious differences too. On 11 September 1696, the church meeting agreed that 'their present pastor was not under any obligation to a continuance with them by virtue of any conditional consent or promise made upon setting down'.[25] Thomas Shepard's 'engagement to the church' therefore ceased and he left Northampton.[26]

The most important event in Shepard's ministry was the building of

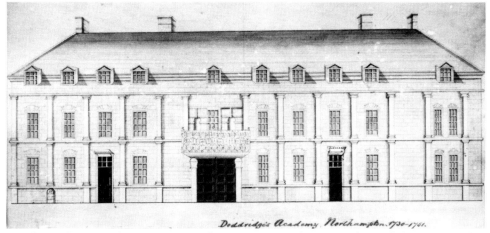

7. The academy in Sheep Street, Northampton. Formerly a town house belonging to the Earl of Halifax, the building provided sufficient accommodation for the increasing number of students. Doddridge lived here from 1740 until his death in 1751, when the academy moved to Daventry.

8. The academy in 1979. Approximately a third of the original building at the northern end has been removed to make way for a road.

Col. James Gardiner
Slain at Preston Pans Sep. 21 1745 Æt 58.

9. Colonel James Gardiner, whose death at the battle of Prestonpans in 1745 galvanised Doddridge into action in defence of the country.

10. Title page from Doddridge's biography of James Gardiner.

SOME

REMARKABLE PASSAGES

IN THE

# LIFE

Of the HONOURABLE

## Col. James Gardiner,

Who was SLAIN at the BATTLE
of PRESTON-PANS,

SEPTEMBER 21, 1745.

WITH

An Appendix relating to the antient Family
of the MUNRO's of *Fowlis*.

*By* P. DODDRIDGE, D.D.

———*Juſtior alter*
*Nec Pietate fuit, nec Bello major & Armis.* Virg.

*L O N D O N:*

Printed for JAMES BUCKLAND, at the *Buck* in
*Pater-noſter Row*; and JAMES WAUGH, at
the *Turk's-Head* in *Grace-church-Street.*

M,DCC.XLVII.

11. Revd Job Orton, student then tutor at the Northampton academy, elder at Castle Hill Church, minister at Shrewsbury, Doddridge's biographer, and publisher of his hymns.

12. Title page of Doddridge's *Hymns founded on Various Texts in the Holy Scriptures*, published by Job Orton in 1755.

# HYMNS

FOUNDED ON

## VARIOUS TEXTS

IN THE

### *HOLY SCRIPTURES.*

By the late Reverend
*PHILIP DODDRIDGE*, D.D.

Publiſhed from the AUTHOR's Manuſcript
By JOB ORTON.

*I eſteem* Nepos *for his Faith and Diligence, his Comments on Scripture, and many Hymns, with which the Brethren are delighted.*
Euſeb. Eccl. Hiſt. L. 7. C. 24.

*SALOP,*
Printed by J. EDDOWES and J. COTTON:
And Sold by J. WAUGH and W. FENNER,
at the *Turk's Head* in *Lombard Street*;
and J. BUCKLAND, at the *Buck* in
*Pater-noſter Row,* LONDON.
M.DCC.LV.

64 And on this Sad Occasion the following Order was unanimously agreed to by the Church

It is the unanimous Judgement of this Church that the frequent Acts of Bankrupcy which have happened in Dissenting Congregations, as well as elsewhere, have brought so great a Dishonour on Religion & occasioned so much Mischief & Reproach, that we think our selves obliged in Duty to enter our publick Protest & Caution on this Head. And we do hereby declare that if any person in stated Communion with us shall become a Bankrupt, or as it is commonly expressed fail in his world, he must expect to be cut off from our Body, unless he do within two Months give to the Church by y Elders either in word or writing, such an Account of his Affairs as shall convince us that his Fall was owing not to his own Sin or Folly but to the afflicting Hand of god upon him. In which Case, far from adding affliction to y afflicted, we hope that as god shall enable us we shall be ready to vindicate comfort & assist him as his Friends & Brethren in Christ. Signed in the Name & Presence of the Church this first Day of May . 1741

P Doddridge  Pastor

J Orton
S Haworth
John Brown    Elders
John Evans

The Names of William Harris, Henry Swoine, James Langley, Francis Parker, Thomas Manning, & George Webb were mentioned

13. A letter from Doddridge and his four elders on the problem of bankruptcies of church members (1 May 1741). Bankruptcy was considered a particularly heinous sin for any Christian. The handwriting is Doddridge's.

the meeting house on 'Castle Hills', a rubble and dung-strewn piece of wasteland adjacent to the site of the old Norman castle, and close to the former Church of St Mary's. In a Deed Poll under the hand and seal of Thomas Warner of Daventry, who was selling the property on behalf of his orphaned niece, Joyce Talbott aged fourteen, we learn that the property consisted of remains of two tenements which had recently been destroyed by fire. The purchasers of the property were Thomas Dust, Richard Pendrick, William Burcott, John Buswell, Robert Chambers, John Sanders, George Mason, Thomas Rabbitt, and 'their heirs and assigns'. £26 was paid for the property and work soon commenced in 1695; so rapidly did the building proceed that the meeting house was completed before the winter set in that year.

The structure was a square barn of a place built from the russet-coloured stones that lay nearby in profuse heaps, the ruins of the ancient town walls and castle. The windows were heavily shuttered,[27] and over one of them was a sundial with the motto 'Post est occasio calva 1695'.[28] Inside was the same puritanical simplicity, which remained basically unchanged until the church was enlarged in the mid-nineteenth century. One account describes it thus:

> Space for about seven hundred persons. Roof propped up by two great white wooden pillars, one a little bandy—the 'Jachin' and 'Boaz' of the temple. White galleries, clumsy white pulpit, a great sounding board over it. Right and left of it, glazed with small, gray-green panes, two tall windows of the lattice kind. Straight before the pulpit, a long massive communion-table; and over this table, on a chain that dangled from the rafters, a mighty brass branched candlestick. All the pews near the walls were deep and square. There were no lobbies. You went up the gallery steps in the sight of all Israel; and the doors opened right into the grave-yard, grassy, still and peaceful. Within and without everything was marked by stark plainness.[29]

The changing fortunes of Nonconformist progress began to centre on the Midlands in general and Northampton in particular. Blower had established in the town a tradition of intellectual and spiritual life, and to this influence was added the powerful personality of John Moore, the first minister of College Lane. For a brief period Castle Hill was pastor-less but in 1699[30] the Revd John Hunt became its minister. He was a man well able to steer the church through the dangerous waters of theological controversy which characterised the close of the seventeenth and the early decades of the eighteenth centuries. It was a period in which men were quick to point out heresy in each other and to label their fellows as Calvinist or Arminian, Arian, Sabellian or Socinian (see Appendix III).

It was clear that Castle Hill was torn with discord over the question of baptism as well as other matters. The Church Book (29 September 1698) records that it had given power to the minister to determine who was to preach at Castle Hill so that controversies could be avoided. Over the question of baptism six members transferred their membership to College Lane. Hunt ruled with a rod of iron and succeeded in minimising the effect of disputes on the Castle Hill Church. In May 1707 he abolished the office of Ruling Elder, a vestige of Presbyterianism, and propagated his own views in pamphlets and books: 'Since God hath set me a Watchman over this Flock, I think myself bound . . . to take all the Care of them I can, and to do my utmost to reduce such as are wandering, and to establish such as are wavering.'[31]

Such powerful leadership, which included evangelistic work in the villages around Northampton, considerably strengthened the church. Hunt left Northampton in 1709 after eleven years' work, having added a hundred new members to the church. He moved to Newport Pagnell in an exchange of charges with the Revd Thomas Tingey. While in Newport Pagnell Hunt published a volume of *Hymns and Spiritual Songs*, and in a later move to Tunstead in Norfolk he continued his literary and ministerial activities until his death, probably in 1730.

Tingey was inducted to the Castle Hill pastorate on 22 February 1709 being 'Solemnly ordained into the Pastoral office and charge of this Church of Christ'. Unlike his predecessors Tingey did not engage in controversy but preferred to preach with a warm and sympathetic earnestness. He preached much in Northampton and the local villages. At Pitsford he made the acquaintance of a young mystic, Mary Wills, who prophesied his removal from Northampton and early death. Philip Doddridge was later to meet this young mystic whose remarkably accurate predictions were taken with some seriousness by him. Tingey's ministry continued the steady build-up of the church which 'prospered in numbers, piety and zeal'. It was during this time that the trust deed of 'Castle Hills' (as it was then called) was drawn up, the name of Thomas Tingey being the first of the church's nineteen trustees. Tingey poured his energies into his work and began to suffer ill health. He resigned his pastorate at Castle Hill at the close of 1728, and within two months was ordained minister of a well-known London church. The *Northampton*

*Mercury* reported that on 5 March 1729: 'One Mr Tingey, a noted Independent Preacher, from Northampton, was ordained at the Meeting House in Fetter Lane (late Mr Bradbury's) by Dr Calamy, Dr Watts, Mr Brice and others, according to the Custom of People of that Perswasion, who allow of no Ordination but to a particular Congregation.'[32] Unfortunately he died on 1 November of the same year, enfeebled by his exertions.

Upon the removal of Tingey the church at Castle Hill procured the services of local ministers to conduct worship; Philip Doddridge preached at Castle Hill on several occasions, leaving behind him a growing conviction amongst his hearers that he was the man best able to fill their vacant pulpit. On 28 September 1729, the following letter was despatched by special messengers from Northampton:

> The Church of Christ in Northampton sendeth greeting:
> ... Sir we have had some taste of your ministerial abilities in your occasional labours amongst us, which gave a general Satisfaction to the Congregation, but the matter being so important, we humbly apply our Selves to you, that you would come to us and preach amongst us a month as a Candidate in order for whole Satisfaction; you being the first after Mr Miles that has been invited on such an account. We shall leave our Brethren that bring this to use what further arguments they think fitt with you, to accept of this Invitation, and shall recommend you to the Wisdom and Conduct of the divine Spirit and continue our Prayers and supplications to the Great God for our Direction and do Subscribe our names under written by the order and Consent of the whole Church

| Sept. 28: 1729 | Geo: Mason | Malory Weston |
| --- | --- | --- |
| | Wm: Bliss | Rich: Norton |
| | Edward Dunkley | Wm: Avery |
| | Richard Pendred | Wm: Manning |
| | Henry Bunyan | James Hackleton[33] |
| | Benj. Knott | |
| | Josiah Brine | |

Initially the invitation was turned down by Doddridge who felt keenly David Some's objection to his leaving the newly formed academy at Market Harborough so soon; Mrs Jennings, the widow of John Jennings and matron of the academy, also voiced her opposition. On 23 October 1729 Doddridge wrote to Some virtually promising to stay at Harborough, 'at least till the end of the course I have begun with my pupils', and revealing his distress at his friends' reactions: 'I cannot bear the thought of having given so much uneasiness.'[34]

Yet Castle Hill Church had other ideas and despatched William Bliss to enlist Clark's support in urging Doddridge to accept Northampton's call. Bliss must have had strong powers of persuasion as Clark subsequently wrote to Doddridge encouraging him to accept Castle Hill's offer; a large house would be provided for himself and the academy on generous terms, with some rooms furnished at the church's expense, and Mrs Jennings, whether she chose to come or not, would be handsomely reimbursed. In short, the people were set upon having Doddridge on any terms. Clark admitted: 'I am ready to think that God has some special work for you to do there.'[35]

Earlier in October Mr Some had travelled to Northampton in order finally to convince the good folk there to leave Doddridge to his duties in Harborough. At a full meeting of the vestry the wind was taken from his sails by the declaration that the father of William Worcester, one of Doddridge's students, was prepared for the youth to transfer to Northampton, 'by which I perceived they had been making interest with him'. Some was face to face with adamant and united feelings, and began to waver. He felt himself like 'Saul amongst the prophets' and had to admit to Doddridge 'I find myself in the utmost perplexity, and know not what to say or do. . . . The matter requires the closest consideration.'[36]

Nevertheless, Doddridge considered that he had to continue with his present responsibilities, and resolved to bury the matter once and for all when he next preached at Castle Hill at the beginning of November. Bolstered by an unequivocal text, 'And when he would not be persuaded, they ceased, saying, The will of the Lord be done' Doddridge entered the Castle Hill pulpit. But doubts flooded his mind: Clark's words of encouragement; Some's change of heart; above all, the earnestness of the Castle Hill people. There must have been a note of hesitancy in Doddridge's voice. After the service he was met with much kindness and entreaty. Upon reaching his lodgings in the house of Mr Shepherd in Gold Street, his thoughts were still 'tumbled up and down'; perhaps, he thought, his refusal was more lack of personal confidence in himself than anything else. Suddenly a remarkable thing happened; passing an open door he heard a child reading to his mother, as he had done so many times in his own infant years: 'As thy days, so shall thy strength be.' The words struck Doddridge with a force that laid bare his dilemma. He stayed for a few days in order to take the funeral of Mr Bunyan's father, and was met by a deputation of young people who urged him to come to Northampton. 'I was besieged by the friendly importunities of the congregation,' wrote Doddridge, 'I found my heart so much melted with their affectionate fervour, that I was no longer master of myself, and agreed to take the affair into consideration again. . . .'[37]

On 8 November Doddridge wrote to Isaac Watts: 'It is a very large Congregation, & tho their Sentiments be much narrower than I could wish . . . I am ready to hope I might have a comfortable Settlement amongst them.' He doubted that Northampton was an ideal place for an academy 'for provisions are very dear there, and many other Circumstances make it an inconvenient Scituation for young Students.' Nevertheless 'the Temper of the Dissenters in these parts . . . chearfully allows innocent Freedoms, which such young Students should not be denied'.[38]

On 6 December 1729 Doddridge penned his acceptance of Castle Hill's invitation:

> My dear Friends,
>     After a serious and impartial consideration of your case, and repeated addresses to the Great Father of Light for His guidance and direction, I can, at length, assure you that I am determined by His permission to accept of your kind invitation, and undertake the pastoral care of you, with the most ardent feelings of sincere gratitude and affection. . . .[39]

Doddridge continued by stating his faith in Divine guidance, although he was taking 'this important step in fear and trembling'. The work of a large congregation and an academy was a daunting prospect, he admitted, and he humbly asked his new flock 'to cover my many infirmities with the mantle of your love'.

On 23 December 1729 Doddridge wrote to Clark with details of his removal to Northampton: 'My Books are gone . . . & I follow them to Morrow, if God permit.'[40] He duly arrived in Northampton on Christmas Eve, conscious that an exciting chapter in his life was about to begin.

The period prior to his removal to Northampton was a distressing time for Doddridge because his friends in Harborough left him in no doubt that he had deserted them: 'I never spent any days in my life in such deep, bitter, uninterrupted anguish, as those which preceded my removal from Harborough,' he wrote.[41] Complicating his feelings was his fondness for sixteen-year-old Jenny Jennings who treated his amorous attentions 'with silent scorn and indifference'.[42] Accepting the £20 compensation paid by Castle Hill Church, Mrs Jennings decided not to remove with the academy to Northampton; thus Doddridge was spared the distress of having Miss Jennings close at hand. For several nights Doddridge had little sleep. It seems, however, that all parties involved in Doddridge's dramatic change of course were finally reconciled to the idea, and wished him well in his new responsibilities.

He stayed for several weeks at the house of a friend and made several journeys before organising his 'housekeeping' which he commenced on 13 January 1730. There was much to be done in starting his ministerial duties and preparing his new premises for the students who would soon be arriving. Doddridge's first house stood in Marefair at the corner of Pike Lane. From church rate books for 1731 we learn that he paid three shillings and eightpence tax for the maintenance of the Vicar of All Saints. Doddridge resided in Marefair for about ten years until he moved to a larger residence in Sheep Street, formerly owned by Lord Halifax of Horton, and still standing close to the Greyfriars bus station.

The extra nervous strain placed upon Doddridge in the early months of his new responsibilities led to a serious illness from which he had only partly recovered when the day of his ordination arrived.

> The afflicting hand of God upon me hindered me from making that preparation for the solemnities of this day, which I could otherwise have desired. However, I hope it hath long been my sincere desire to dedicate myself to Him in the work of the Ministry; and that the views with which I determined to undertake the office, and which I this day solemnly professed, have long since been seriously impressed upon my heart.[43]

Of the eight ministers present five were Presbyterians; Clark had travelled from St Albans to read the charge to the church,[44] and with his fellow ministers signed the Ordination Certificate:

> We whose Hands are hereunto Subscribed, do hereby certify all whom it may concern, that Mr Philip Doddridge of Northampton, having addressed himself to us Ministers of the Gospell, desiring to be ordained a Presbyter, we being sufficiently assured of the unblameableness of his Conversation and Proficiency in his Studies, proceeded solemnly to set him apart to the Office of the Ministry and the Pastorall Care of the Church of Northampton by the Laying on of Hands, with Fasting and Prayer, at the Town of Northampton aforesaid, on the Nineteenth day of March 1729-30.

And therefore esteem and declare him to be a lawful and sufficiently Authorised Minister of Jesus Christ, and heartily recom-
mend Him and his Ministry to the divine Blessing.

Presenting and Consenting:    Witness our Hands:
    J. Brogden (Wigston)      J. Norris (Welford)
    Robt. Dawson (Hinkley)    S. Clark (St. Albans)
                              Ja. Watson (Leicester)
                              Edw. Brodhurst
                                           (Birmingham)
                              Tho. Sa[u]nders (Kettering)
                              J. Drake (Yardley)
                                       [Hastings]
                              W. Hunt (Newport)
                              Danl. Goodrich (Oundle).[45]

Doddridge set about his new duties with determination, seeing himself as pastor, tutor, and student:

> I am sensible it will be difficult to unite them all. I apprehend my
> course in general must be this: I will usually rise at about five
> o'clock, and study till the time of morning prayer, which will be
> half-past eight. The forenoon will generally be employed in
> lectures. If I dine very moderately, I may secure a little time before
> I go out in the afternoon; but the business from two till six will
> be to attend upon my people. I shall generally read a lecture in
> the evening, and will retire as early as I can; but will take care to
> give the family prayer so soon, as to have a little retirement
> between that and bedtime.[46]

Doddridge continued by outlining an incredibly detailed set of objectives
which he hoped to complete by the next vacation; his list of personal
studies in Classics and Divinity that he set himself is quite amazing.

Yet something was wrong. He felt depressed, and in his private
meditations he lamented that he had 'perpetual reason to complain of
myself'. On 1 June 1730 he wrote in his diary:

> I have been extremely negligent in my conduct of late, never more
> formal in devotion, never more indisposed not only to secret, but
> to family and public worship. The Bible has been to me as a sealed
> book. . . . I have been under great temptation to doubt the truth
> of Christianity itself. . . . My passions have been exorbitant. . . .
> The Spirit of God seems to have deserted me, and to have left me

under blindness and hardness. . . . I condemn myself for it. I
resolve against it. . . . Lord, I am weary of such a frame. O
that my heart were enlarged! O that it were melted under a
sense of sin! . . .[47]

Reasons for such feelings are not hard to find because on the previous
day he had proposed marriage to Jenny Jennings by letter. Having
rebuffed him once before, she finally refused him; sensibly 'he magnanimously resolved to raise the siege, and to think himself happy in her
friendship'.[48]

It was good to get away from the pressing cares of Northampton
during the summer of 1730. Having resolved 'to spend this vacation well'
Doddridge rode out towards Worcester where, at the house of Mrs
Owen at Coventry he fell head-over-heels in love with a raven haired,
fresh complexioned, good humoured girl. 'Mistress Mercy Maris', like
Doddridge, was an orphan and living under the guardianship of an uncle,
Ebenezer Hankins; Mrs Owen was her great-aunt. Mercy was six years
younger than Doddridge, being twenty-two years old; she was born on
4 September 1709 into a family of Worcester bakers and maltsters. Her
mother's side of the family originated from Coventry where an uncle
named Pool, during the period of his mayoralty, had urged Doddridge
to accept the call to the church there.[49]

Upon returning to Northampton Doddridge quickly wrote to Mrs
Owen as a prudent preliminary to pressing his suit with Mistress Maris
herself:

> I discovered so many charms in the person and conversation of
> the agreeable lady I saw at your house last week, (and whom I was
> so happy as to meet there more than once before), that had I
> followed the impulse of a rising passion, I should immediately
> have offered her my services, and urged my suit with an impor-
> tunity as the circumstances would permit.[50]

Frank as usual, he continued by stating his inability to 'purchase' such
'a bright jewel', as his total income only amounted to £120 per annum
plus some possible future inheritances: 'You have here, madam, a plain
account of my circumstances, in which I have concealed nothing that I
apprehend disadvantageous to my pretensions. I had indeed much rather
lose the dearest blessing of life, by frankness and integrity, than gain it
by artifice and deceit.'[51] If Mrs Owen doubted his character, he added,
then his ministerial colleagues would vouch for him but 'allowance must

be made for what they say of me, as erring rather on the favourable hand'.

Doddridge's spirits were uplifted. Almost terrified of 'overloving' such 'a dear creature' he poured out his heart to Mercy in his letters. He stated that love meant bearing with his 'infirmities of temper' and 'follies' as well as delighting in mutual converse and friendship. To him marriage was a life-long bond. By October 1730 he was in a state of heightened emotion and excitement after Mercy had accepted him; 'Must three tedious weeks roll, or rather creep away, before I see you . . .?' he wrote on 22 November a month before their wedding at Upton-on-Severn. He was fearful of the news that smallpox had broken out at Worcester and wrote on 29 November: 'My heart, or rather that heart of yours which is lodged in this fond and faithful bosom, trembles at these thoughts; and I must entreat, and even charge you, by all the tenderness of our loves, that you will not expose yourself to unnecessary danger.'[52] On 22 December they were duly married. Doddridge considered his wedding day as the happiest of his life; writing on 5 January 1743 to Mercy he could say:

> I hope if any memoirs of my life be ever written, the world will be informed of that most happy part of my history which relates to your character and affection, and takes its date from December 22, 1730—and it probably will, if I should have the unsupportable calamity of surviving you, from which I verily believe God will graciously deliver me.[53]

Philip and Mercy Doddridge shared a deep and abiding love for one another. Mercy was his 'Dearest Dear of all Dears', and he her 'Dearest and Best of Men'. When they were parted during Doddridge's yearly visits to London, or away at the ordination of his students, they wrote numerous long and loving letters to each other. On 21 July 1731 Doddridge wrote from his sister's house:

> Think then, my charming creature, that when this comes to hand, I shall be with you in a few hours, at once to stop your pen and your mouth with warmer and fuller assurances than I can now give you of that inexpressible and transporting tenderness with which I am
>
> My dearest Creature
> Most affectionately and invariably your
> DODDRIDGE.[54]

Neither of them enjoyed robust health. In 1742 Mercy was sent to Bath in order to restore her vitality after a serious illness had reduced her to using crutches. Writing to her, Doddridge's passionate loneliness burst forth: 'I would trudge on Foot to Bath with all my Heart to bring you back half so well. . . . Every thing centers in you.'[55]

A cheerful optimism runs through Doddridge's correspondence. When taken ill in London in December 1740 he tried to make light of his ailments by describing to Mercy the masses of clothes heaped upon him by his hosts to sweat out the illness: 'Over my tunick and gown of state [he says he resembles the King of the Gipsies] I have, for an upper robe, a white quilt pinned under my chin, and a white handkerchief in like manner tied over my nightcap, with a beard like an antediluvian, & nails like a Chinese mandarin.'[56]

Mercy was not deceived by his making light of his frailty, and often warned him not to overtax his strength. His exhausting tours by coach or on horseback that took him hundreds of miles (see Appendix VI), the mounting correspondence plus his other duties began to take their toll; Mercy upbraided his 'wickedness' for preaching three times a day and entreated him to ease up for the sake of his health. He was, he said 'continually beating the hoof from place to place, and must live in such a rotation till I wheel back to that dear centre [i.e. Mercy] from which I set out . . .'.[57] Wherever he went he thought of Mercy; at the Tower of London the guns were fired at the mention of her name;[58] daily he drank her health with his friends, and thought of her over his green pease soup. He bought her presents; a fan, damask and kitchen utensils,[59] and sent her presents from other friends, notably 'a fine harlequin dog' from Mr Aikin and a white damask gown from the Prince of Wales.[60] Writing from London on 9 August 1748 he informed Mercy that he had slept 'in a fine Genoa Velvet Bed in a splendid Apartment yet fine & well aird & charmingly situated as it is I had a thousand Times rather have been with you in the old green Curtains of Stuff, within which I hope soon to incamp'.[61]

Some of Doddridge's friends spoke sternly to him, particularly John Barker, whose 'earnest desire [was] that you would take a reasonable care of yourself, and, like a dutiful husband, be absolutely ruled, managed, and governed by your wife! You need not fear living too long, doctor; and therefore, pray do not live quite so fast'.[62] It was a prophetic utterance.

In happier days Doddridge indulged his taste for humorous rhyming:

Resolved I will but little write
I take but half a sheet to-night,
Which is two quarters more than you
Would me by this night's post allow,
Though I'm but one, and you are two;
Yet I'd excuse it, could you tell
In your next letter, that you're well:
You may conclude that I am so
When this day's busy train you know.
At Little Creaton I have been
And happy cousin Perkins seen;
Married two months ago at least,
To his first mistress, and the best
Which he in twenty might have found;
He seems in all his wishes crown'd.
She's modest, courteous, young, and fair,
And not above domestic care,
Though worth three hundred pounds a year.[63]

During June and July 1742 Doddridge visited the West Country and had been to see the former estates of his family; at Mount Radford, the one time home of Sir John Dodderidge, he had seen the family coat of arms carved over the mantelpiece in the dining room: 'I assure you, my dear, I saw this without any regret; and I hope I have a much nobler mansion reserved for me in my Father's house above.'[64]

A few weeks later he wrote in Dorset dialect:

Lovee,
    Zince ch'a been in Downzhire and Zomersetzhire ch'alearnt zum-dthing o'th'Tongue, and zure, and zure, and double zure, ch'ood be glad to zhow ye all my zgollership. . . .[65]

Mercy's letters show a reciprocal affection. On 4 August 1742 she longed for his return from Essex: 'Friday sevennight is an age to a love and impatience like mine. . . . I hope you will not be late, as I shall watch every hour with the utmost anxiety till I see you. The dear children are well, and much rejoice to hear of dear papa's coming home;—they have made their bargain with me already, that they may sit up to see you. . . .'[66]

Their first child was born on 8 October 1731, and named Elizabeth. Little 'Betsey' or 'Tetsy' Doddridge was an engaging and lively character who even tried to teach the family dog his catechism. Everyone loved

*Submiſſion to Divine Providence in the Death
of Children recommended and inforced,*

# IN A
# SERMON

## PREACHED AT

# *NORTHAMPTON,*

### ON THE DEATH

Of a very amiable and hopeful
CHILD about Five Years old.

*Publiſhed out of Compaſſion to mourning* PARENTS.

## By *P. DODDRIDGE,* D.D.

*Neve Liturarum pudeat : qui viderit illas,
De Lachrymis faƈtas ſentiat eſſe meis.*  OVID.

## *LONDON:*
Printed for R. HETT, at the *Bible* and *Crown,*
in the *Poultry.*  MDCCXXXVII.

[ Price Six-Pence. ]

14. Title page of Doddridge's sermon on the death of his daughter
Elisabeth. Little 'Tetsy' Doddridge was born on 8 October 1731
and died on 1 October 1736.

her, she declared, because she loved everyone. But only a week before her fifth birthday Tetsy died of consumption. It was a shattering blow for the parents, who both drew on their personal faith to uphold them at such a tragic time. Heartbroken, Doddridge preached her funeral sermon composed with 'more Tears than Ink'[67] and partly written as he sat by her coffin. The sermon was published in 1737 under the title *Submission to Divine Providence* as an attempt by Doddridge to bring comfort to others in similar distress. He felt that part of himself had been placed in the grave beside her, and was deeply conscious of his own mortality. He prayed earnestly for the soul of his dead child; the following passage from his diary with its clipped phrasing shows his feelings:

> But God delivered her; and she, without any violent pang in the article of her dissolution, quietly and sweetly fell asleep, as, I hope, in Jesus, about ten at night, I being then at Maidwell. When I came home, my mind was under a dark cloud relating to her eternal state, but God was pleased graciously to remove it, and gave me comfortable hope, after having felt the most heart rending sorrow.[68]

There were other children: Mary, or 'Polly', was born on 7 May 1733, became the second wife of John Humphreys of Tewkesbury and lived until her sixty-seventh year (8 June 1799). Another daughter, Mercy, was born on 26 August 1734, and died unmarried at Bath on 26 October 1809. A son, Philip, was born on 6 August 1735, and died unmarried at Tewkesbury on 13 March 1785. Another daughter Anna Cecilia (Caelia)[69] was born on 3 July 1737 and also died unmarried at Tewkesbury on 3 October 1811. Then followed a period of miscarriages, premature births and sickly infants; a second boy, named Samuel after Dr Clark, was born on 30 April 1739, but died in the following year; twin girls Sarah and Jane were born on 22 April 1746, but lived for only two days; finally a son William, named after William of Orange, was born on 5 November 1748, and died on the 11th.[70]

Of the children that survived infancy there was frequent alarm because of the scourge of smallpox. In 1740 Doddridge noted in a postscript that 'The smallpox rages in the town, and depopulates the market, but not the meeting'. The following day (8 August) he wrote:

> As for the state of the distemper here, I am sorry to say, it grows every day more discouraging than before. At home, through mercy, we are well; and Master Shepherd, who was so bad, is

much better, and likely to get well through the trial; but several died; two were buried last night. . . .'[71]

In order to protect the children during such epidemics Mrs Doddridge and the children found a safe retreat at Delapré, the home of their friends the Collier family.[72] In the 1740 epidemic Mrs Doddridge was sent to London whilst the children, who were extremely ill with smallpox, were nursed by a kindly neighbour Sarah Dunkley and the Collier ladies. As the epidemic began to wane Doddridge warned his wife, 'You must not, on any Terms, come nearer than Delepree, my Country Seat, as my friends kindly call it'.[73] Although many families suffered greatly, the Doddridge children soon recovered sufficiently to be rattling around the house.

Philip and Mercy Doddridge were never wealthy. Doddridge's ministerial stipend of £70 was augmented with slender profits from the academy and Mercy's dowry of £400 was not an excessive amount. In 1730 they paid out £2.10s. (£2.50) for a quarter's rental on their Marefair house, fourteen shillings (70p) for two bedsteads and six shillings (30p) for an easy chair. We read in their domestic account books of Mrs Doddridge's 'pin money' for one year of six shillings and one penny, and a quarter's school fee for one child that amounted to three shillings and sixpence. A proportion of between one eighth and one tenth of their income was used to help the needy.[74]

On 3 July 1742 Mercy wrote to her husband who was at Blandford in Dorset during one of his summer excursions:

> Money very scarce at Northampton for I was forced to send this morning to four places before I could get the 20 pounds you was good as to order me, & at last had it of Mr Knight. I believe if you could send him an order for payment and settle before the end of the month it would be more agreeable to him, & at the same time if it would save you to add an additional order of 20 or 30 pounds or what larger sum you please Sir it would much contribute to the health of our coal house, & very much oblige her who is with the greatest esteem and affection
>
> My Dearest<br>Most Intirely yours<br>M. Doddridge[75]

In 1740 when they moved to the larger house in Sheep Street in order to accommodate the rise in student numbers, they paid a substantial rental of £40 a year. Seven servants were needed to keep the establish-ment running and their combined wages amounted to £20 a year. In the Doddridge living room there were no ornaments 'save six or seven family portraits on the panelled wall, and the framed family arms with the motto, "Dum vivimus, vivamus". There were no carpets, for even in the houses of the nobility, these were only laid down on state occasions'.[76] The only luxury that Doddridge seemed to have indulged in was 'pipes and tobacco' and a glass of wine. He often enjoyed a game of cards, humorously referring to it as 'a chapter in the history of the four kings'.

Yet in spite of few material possessions, they shared a deep family intimacy. Writing from London on 27 July 1749 Doddridge could comment to the female members of his family about the latest fashions:

> Poor Mrs Roffey looked dreadfully, in consequence of the abominable manner of dressing the head, which some evil demon has introduced to destroy the works of God. The foremost plait of the fly cap is nearer the back of the head than the forehead; the hair on the forehead and sides of the face is all combed up straight, and that behind is tucked up under the cap; and the wings of the fly are pinned back, and stand up, that it may seem as if the wind has blown the cap off, or at least turned it quite back; and poor Miss Roffey was in the same monkey form. May you, my dear, and my sweet girls, be preserved from the detestable fashion, though all the rest of your sex should be corrupted with it.[77]

An essential ingredient of such intimate family life was a profound seriousness on the part of Doddridge for the spiritual welfare of all his family. Writing to his 'lovely girl', Mary, on 31 July 1749 he assured her of his 'tenderest love' and 'great joy that you are, through the divine goodness, so well recovered' [from an illness]. He continued: 'the life of either of my children and such a child, is more to me than the treasures of a kingdom. [Like] your dear mama . . . learn every thing that can, in private life, adorn religion, and make those around us happy.'[78]

It was an aim that Philip Doddridge constantly strove to achieve throughout his life.

# Doddridge the Minister

> When the hour of worship struck, punctual to the moment, the
> Doctor, in rolling white wig and dark blue Geneva gown, would
> step into the pulpit and hang his triangular hat on a peg behind
> him. There would be a solemn hush, and a short, solemn prayer;
> then he would read—oh, how reverently!—a short psalm.[1]

Stanford leaves us with this vivid picture of Doddridge in action as
minister at Castle Hill. Doddridge's clear loud voice was easily heard in
all corners of the meeting house, and as he preached he gesticulated with
'nervous violence' and spoke with 'earnest tenderness'. Usually the
building was filled with people who represented a cross-section of society:
shopkeepers and tradesmen from the town, farmers, farm workers and
villagers from a wide radius around Northampton, soldiers temporarily
stationed in the town, local gentry and intelligentsia.

The pattern of worship on the Lord's Day at Castle Hill involved a
crowded service during the morning, and during the afternoon Doddridge usually preached to an equally large and attentive congregation.
Before this second service he catechised the children, being greatly
encouraged by the large numbers who began to attend accompanied by
their parents. Usually there was no evening service except once a month
when the celebration of the Lord's Supper was held. The dates varied
according to the phases of the moon, a very practical consideration as
many worshippers came from the countryside, moonlight diminishing
the hazardous nature of the waggon tracks that served as roads. At other
times special lectures on religious subjects were given by Doddridge
during the Sunday evening. From time to time senior students from the
academy would be asked to preach. Writing in February 1735 in his diary,
Doddridge expressed admiration for his student Wilkinson who delivered
'perhaps the best sermon I ever heard, undoubtedly one of the best on the

Notes and references for this chapter begin on page 159

16. Philip Doddridge
in later life.

15. Philip Doddridge
as a young minister.

17. The church at Castle Hill, founded 1695. Water-colour of the original building by Ellen Phipps Robinson in 1870, inscribed 'after Cooking 1805'. The tower of St Peter's Church is in the right background.

18. Doddridge and Commercial Street United Reformed Church (Castle Hill) in 1979. The church was renamed 'Doddridge Chapel' in 1862, and amalgamated with the Commercial Street Church in 1959.

duties and privileges of the children of God: a subject from which I had preached a sermon that I thought laboured: but when I saw the vast disproportion between the two discourses, and how much superior to almost anything I ever produced, it shamed and humbled me; and yet I bless God it did not grieve me. If any stirrings of envy moved, they were immediately suppressed'.[2]

Doddridge was realistic enough to know that he had little enough time to spare in composing sermons. The vast knowledge he had built up, plus a developing gift in extempore speaking, served him well. Job Orton noted that Doddridge's sermons were 'more admired for the direct assistance they furnished than for literary excellency'.[3] Knowing his people and their particular needs gave Doddridge much material for his sermons; 'he came home to his hearers' bosoms', wrote Orton, 'and led them to see their real characters, wherein they were defective, and how far they might justly be comforted and encouraged.'[4]

In his early years as a minister Doddridge carefully composed his sermons but later, Orton tells us: '. . . he sometimes only wrote down the heads and leading thoughts of his sermons, and the principal texts of scripture he designed to introduce. But he was so thoroughly master of his subject, and had such a ready utterance and so warm a heart, that perhaps few ministers can compose better discourses than he delivered from these short hints.'[5] Kippis however recalls one occasion when a number of the students complained that 'though their revered tutor's academical lectures were admirable, they had not in him a sufficiently correct model of pulpit composition'.[6] Doddridge received the criticism with good grace, and made efforts to prepare his sermons more thoroughly.

In the main his sermons were based upon scriptural texts from which he discoursed with pleasing variety. He was anxious not to confuse preaching with lecturing, and desired to 'speak and write of divine truths with a holy fervency'.[7] Doddridge often made reference to public matters affecting his congregation, and to wider issues in both the town and the nation; uncommon occurrences in nature, the changing seasons, especially harvest-time, and the importance of family religion were all part of his homely sermon material. Stoughton neatly summarises Doddridge's aims as a preacher: '[he] entered the pulpit not to dazzle, but to teach; not to amaze but to convince; not to gratify, but to reform; not to be thought great, but to do good.'[8]

If his sermons were at times less edifying than people expected, he could rise to heights of eloquence when necessary. The poet, Mark Akenside, settled in Northampton for a while hoping to establish a

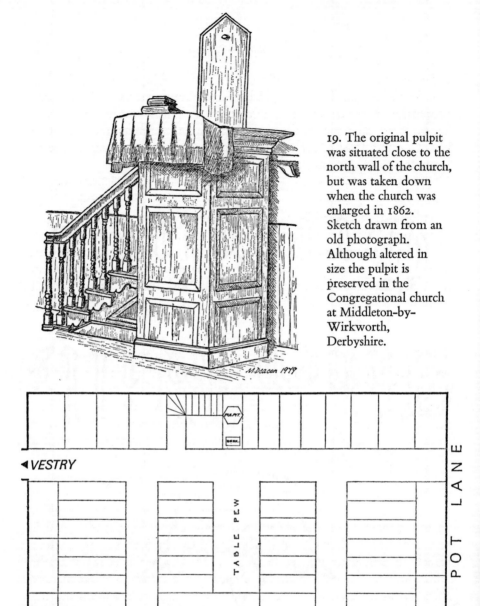

19. The original pulpit was situated close to the north wall of the church, but was taken down when the church was enlarged in 1862. Sketch drawn from an old photograph. Although altered in size the pulpit is preserved in the Congregational church at Middleton-by-Wirkworth, Derbyshire.

◄ VESTRY

TABLE PEW

QUART POT LANE

20. Plan of the original chapel drawn by Thomas Grundy in 1826. The positions of the box pews are shown; the students from the academy sat in the table pew, where they made their notes on the sermon and the conduct of the service.

medical practice. Being visited by some relatives who were Dissenters, Akenside thought it worth while to go to hear the Doctor preach at Castle Hill. Aware of the visitors' presence Doddridge 'roused his faculties', reports Kippis who was also present, 'and spoke with such energy, variety, and eloquence as excited my warmest admiration, and must have impressed Dr Akenside with a high opinion of his abilities'.[9]

As early as 1724 Doddridge remarked that theologically he was 'in all the most important points a Calvinist',[10] a position which he maintained for the whole of his ministry. Doddridge's Calvinism was not of the repressive, gloomy variety that stressed eternal damnation; but vigorous, optimistic and cheerful, and looked to Heaven as the ultimate goal of the faithful. Yet Doddridge did not hide the essential note of judgement inherent in the Gospel; 'like John Calvin himself', writes Routley, '[he] is awed by the thought of what he has been redeemed from' (i.e. Hell).[11]

When Doddridge started his ministry in Northampton, congregational hymnsinging was still in its infancy. Before the *Toleration Act* of 1689 Dissenters had had little desire to advertise their presence by singing hymns. Yet there were more fundamental reasons why hymn singing was unpopular; following Calvin, Anglicans and Dissenters alike considered such innovations in divine worship as carnal and worldly; women were especially forbidden to sing in church as it was considered contrary to scripture. The first English hymn-book had been published by Miles Coverdale, but Henry VIII had banned it; during the seventeenth century sporadic attempts had been made to introduce hymns, but this led to fierce dissension within congregations. Richard Davis of Rothwell published one hundred and sixty-eight *Hymns composed on several subjects and on divers occasions* in the 1690s, and one of Doddridge's predecessors, Thomas Shepard, had published his *Penitential Cries*. But these had only limited influence. It was not until after the publication of Isaac Watts's *Hymns and Spiritual Songs* in 1707, and *The Psalms of David imitated in the language of the New Testament* in 1719, that congregational hymn singing became acceptable to most Dissenters.[12]

Doddridge's Calvinism pervades his hymns, which were written to reiterate the main points of his sermons. The congregation, unaccompanied by the familiar organ of later times, would repeat each line or couplet in the technique of 'lining out'. This meant that each line or couplet had to be a complete unit containing its full sense. As Doddridge was tone deaf and 'could never change two notes',[13] and lacked the assistance of a choir, the singing was led by the clerk.

Doddridge's hymns are essentially the outpouring of a hard-working minister. Each one is prefixed with a scriptural text from which the hymn is derived. *Hark the Glad Sound*, one of his best known hymns, is typical; its theme is taken from Luke IV verses 18 and 19, and the whole texture of the hymn is rooted in the scriptures:

> He comes the prisoners to release
> In Satan's bondage held;
> The gates of brass before him burst,
> The iron fetters yield.[14]

Perhaps 'the most remarkable single contribution made by Doddridge to hymnody,' writes Routley, is 'his invention of the hymn, now a common enough kind, upon the social implications of the Gospel'.[15] In *Hark the Glad Sound* the coming of Christ has direct impact for those imprisoned by their sins, the blind, the broken-hearted and the poor. Many of the hymns were composed for special occasions such as bereavements, 'national sins', re-dedication at New Year, fasts and thanksgivings, and deliverance from war and natural disaster. In no. 369, composed for a fast day in time of war, there is a powerful plea for national righteousness:

> Forgive the follies of our times,
> And purge our land from all its crimes:
> Reform'd and deck'd with grace divine,
> Let princes, priests and people shine.[16]

Doddridge's hymns ring with tremendous confidence and expectation. God is seen as mighty and omnipotent, and worthy of the thankfulness of his people for his continuing goodness and faithfulness:

> O God of Jacob, by whose hand
> Thine Israel still is fed,
> Who through this weary pilgrimage
> Hast all our fathers led.[17]

Doddridge's optimism constantly breaks forth even in times of trouble and grief:

> In scenes exalted or depress'd
> Thou art our joy, and thou our rest;
> Thy goodness all our hopes shall raise,
> Ador'd through all our changing days.[18]

The reason for such confidence lies in the belief that God protects his people, feeding them by his 'incessant bounty' and leading by his 'unerring counsel'. Such a view of life leads to a triumphant death, and Doddridge's hymns bring the Christian's earthly pilgrimage to its ultimate goal:

> My grateful soul, on Jordan's shore,
> Shall raise one sacred pillar more:
> Then bear, in his bright courts above,
> Inscriptions of immortal love.[19]

The monthly celebration of the Lord's Supper was of immense importance to Doddridge, who wrote meditative reflections in his diary on the content and manner of his conduct at each sacrament. On 1 April 1733 he commented on his thirty-fourth sacrament since coming to Northampton: 'This has been a delightful day. God gave me freedom and boldness in delivering his word from the pulpit, and sweet enjoyment in meditation at his table. . . .'[20] He took delight in discoursing on scriptural texts in order to give added meaning to the sacrament.

Orton refers to Doddridge's 'extraordinary gift in prayer' which he 'cultivated with great diligence'.[21] Doddridge often spent three, four or even five hours at a time in fasting and prayer, reviewing his own spiritual state, as well as the welfare of his congregation and students in the academy. He would frequently retire to his vestry, away from the noise and bustle of the academy in busy Sheep Street. On 2 March 1751 he reached his 'asylum', the vestry, at about eleven in the morning and by two o'clock had 'recommended my flock, pupils and children by name to God'. Prayers for wider interests followed: the nation, the Protestant interest, for Jews and Gentiles, and 'in conclusion, I adored God for the enjoyment of the day, registering the following purposes;—of visiting in the congregation as much as I can, keeping some history of it; of talking on practical religion with as many pupils as I can in an evening, and with the servants . . .'. Resolutions on praying before writing his letters, and really getting down to answering the most important and urgent of his voluminous correspondence, as well as plans for the subject of his next devotional day (which was to centre on increasing the membership of the church), completed this period of prayer. 'Thus I left the place at nearly half an hour past two, with some cheerful persuasion that my prayers were heard, and that I shall see the outgoings of my God and king in the sanctuary.'[22]

Such care for his responsibilities marked Doddridge's ministry in Northampton. In his diary he often lacerated himself for failing to visit his people sufficiently, and at the end of each year he objectively reviewed his failings and resolved to improve in the future. In 1729 when Doddridge commenced his ministry there were 342 members in communion with the church but by 1749 the number had dropped to 239. Deeply conscious of this numerical decline, which was partly a symptom of a general lassitude towards religion in society, Doddridge strove hard to redress the balance. In the Church Book we can still read Doddridge's notes:

> May 2 1748 I reviewed the List of the Church from the Beginning & found that from 1694 when it was gathered i.e. within the compass of 54 years 784 Members have been admitted i.e. one year with another more than 14 members each year of which 240 only continue alive & reside still among us of which 58 were admitted before my Settlement with the Church & as I have admitted 299 that shows that 117 who have been admitted since that Time are either removed or dead; besides many others who were admitted before N.B. 78 have been my Pupils.[23]

On another occasion he cheered himself up after discovering that three members had not been accounted for in his reckoning thus making 'the state of affairs' less 'melancholy'.[24]

Many of his flock came from surrounding places such as Duston, Piddington, Harpole, Kislingbury, Houghton, Hardingstone, Kingsthorpe, Blisworth, Billing, Moulton and Althorp. Anxious to maintain his pastoral contact, Doddridge visited each village at least twice a year in order to preach among the people, and visit the sick and infirm who could not travel into the town. Orton recalls: 'When any of them died, he chose to preach their Funeral-sermons in the villages where they had lived, that their neighbours and acquaintance might have the benefit of them.'[25]

Doddridge was greatly concerned with the needs of the rising generation, and did all in his power to ensure that the young were brought up within the Christian faith. Addressing himself to every 'Master of a Family' Doddridge circulated a printed sermon . . . *on the important Subject of family-religion.* Acknowledging how time-consuming pastoral visitation was and how long it took to 'progress through large congregations', he appealed to his people to give him serious attention: 'I therefore take this method of visiting you while alone, and of addressing you on the very important Subject of Family Religion. For your own Sake, and the Sake of those dearest to you, I intreat you to give me a calm attentive Hearing.' Urging the head of each household seriously to consider his responsibilities to all, including the servants, Doddridge stressed the vital nature of Christian duty in the home:

> What I desire and intreat of you is, that you would honour and acknowledge God in your Families, by calling them together every Day, to hear some Part of his Word read to them, and to offer, for a few Minutes at least, your united Confessions, Prayers and Praises to him.[26]

Doddridge encouraged his young people to come to commit themselves to the Christian way of life. In his sermon *The Young Christian invited to Communion* there is an impassioned plea copiously argued 'that when you weigh all I have been saying, and compare it with whatever can be objected against it, you will be convinced of your duty, and engaged to an immediate compliance with it'.[27] As has already been noted, weekly catechism of the young was held on Sunday afternoon; in addition lectures in the form of catechisms were given from time to time. In the Church Book are neat lists of children's names together with an account of which catechism, sermon or Bible they had been given to study. Evidently Doddridge was in receipt of literature from a charitable source as he notes:

> Recd from Mr Coward's Trustees Jan. 16 1741/2
> 40 First ......................................... ⎫
> 40 Second Catechisms ⎬
> 40 Songs for Children ⎭
> 1 Book of Catechisms for myself.
> 20 Assemblies Catechisms.[28]

Doddridge also encouraged meetings of various kinds within the church, 'especially religious associations among the young persons of the congregation, who used to meet weekly for reading, religious discourse and prayer'.[29] One group of young men, including several of his students, met weekly to debate problems posed by Doddridge; he took note of their conclusions and often made them the basis for one of his Friday evening lectures. For several winters he taught on Thursday evenings at College Lane meeting, usually obtaining large audiences. On 12 December 1742 in a letter to Mercy, he mentioned lectures on Tuesday or Wednesday evenings 'somewhere in the country'.[30]

Throughout his ministry Doddridge maintained his interest and care for his people. He often felt guilty that other pressing concerns kept him from serving his flock more fully. Even when he was away from Northampton on his annual summer visitations he could not forget them; writing to his wife from Dedmarton ('12 miles short of Bath') on 9 June 1742 he says: 'Remember me most affectionately to all my friends at Northampton, especially the afflicted, whom I bear most tenderly on my heart, and long to hear how they do.'[31] Even though there were requests for him to accept larger and more lucrative pastorates in London and Nottingham, Doddridge remained loyal to his responsibilities in Northampton.

In order to deal with his heavy pastoral load, Doddridge proposed the restoration of the office of elder. This had been dispensed with in 1707 during the pastorate of the Revd John Hunt. Accordingly, the Church Book recalls the unanimous choice of 'the Revd Mr Job Orton and the Revd Mr John Evans as also of Mr John Browne for Elders to assist the pastor in his care of this Society and having also desired Mr Samuel Hayworth by Divine Providence resident amongst us tho' a member of the Church at Rowell to assist by his Counsels and Labours in the same office they were solemnly recommended to God by Prayer at the Church Meeting on our preparation day Feb. 26 1740/1 having then signified their acceptance of the Call'.[32]

Upon request Doddridge prepared a written set of 'Counsels' to his elders assuring them of his esteem and friendship: 'I, who also am an Elder, and your Companion as well as your leader in the Service of our common Lord, have thought it highly incumbent upon me to comply with this your Request, and in doing it I shall use great plainness of speech, humbly hoping that He, in whose Name I set about this Work, will assist me to write what may be as a nail fixed in a sure Place, and may be made useful to others as well as to yourselves.' The elders were urged to visit the people as a duty of the highest importance 'for without that [care] it will hardly be possible to judge thoroughly of the state of things amongst them'. Doddridge recommended the elders to adopt his own practice of making a list of heads of families and periodically reviewing it. When visiting, the elder should 'call the Heads of Familys apart, inquire of them how it fares with them and their Familys as to their religious Concerns, give them such Exhortations, Instructions and Admonitions, as you judge proper and especially endeavour to engage them to a strict observation of Family Worship, and a care of Children and Servants'.

The 'counsels' are a model of wise and sound advice. The elders were encouraged to note the provision of 'good books' especially Bibles in the homes visited. Together with the deacons, the elders should regularly visit the charity school. They were also to keep a careful watch for those in any kind of distress, trouble or sickness, encourage those on the threshold of Christian commitment, and use their diplomacy in dealing with quarrels and disorderly behaviour, attempting to solve problems before they grew out of proportion.

'But as for cases of Publick Scandal,' wrote Doddridge, 'I think the Offender ought to be publickly admonished, and if he does really repent I apprehend that he ought to express that Repentance by such Confession and Humiliation as may be satisfactory, not to the Elders alone, but to the Church in general; till he has done which I cannot be free that such a Person should sit down with us at the Table of the Lord. This I take to be the regular Method of proceeding with Offenders, yet must add, that I think it proper the Elders should examine the Case and perhaps deal with every Offender privately, before publick admonition is solemnly given.'[33]

Doddridge had particular cases in mind when he penned this last statement; a minority of church members were bringing the name of the church into disrepute. Apparently private admonition failed, because within six weeks of taking office the four elders, supported by the six deacons, issued a strongly worded letter to the whole congregation. The letter was read out at the Lord's Table on 5 April 1741, and in the following church meeting on the 16 April seven cases causing scandal to the church were reviewed. Three men were censured for drunkenness, and one who swore profanely and who showed 'proud contempt of the admonitions which had been given him' was excluded from membership. Families who had quarrelled with each other were reconciled. Another man who frequented alehouses, thereby neglecting his trade and family, and getting into debt was 'exhorted to Repentance, Humiliation and Reformation'. Others who had become bankrupt and had caused grave distress to creditors were severely censured and excommunicated. On 1 May under the signatures of Doddridge and the elders the following statement was issued:

> It is the unanimous Judgement of this Church that frequent Acts of Bankruptcy which have happened in Dissenting Congregations, as well as elsewhere, have brought so great Dishonour on Religion & occasioned so much Mischief & Reproach that we think our selves obliged in Duty to enter our publick protest and Caution on this Head. And we do hereby declare that if any person in stated Communion with us shall become a Bankrupt or as it is commonly expressed fail in the world, he must expect to be cut off from our Body, unless he do within two months give to the Church by

the Elders either in word or writing, such an account of his Affairs as shall convince us that his Fall was owing not to his own Sin or Folly but to the Afflicting Hand of God upon him. In which case far from adding Affliction to the Afflicted, we hope that as God shall enable us we shall be ready to vindicate, comfort and assist him as his Friends and Brethren in Christ.[34]

It appears from the entries in the Church Book that Doddridge's attempts to retain the honour and purity of the church were successful. On 1 May to Doddridge's delight two men had expressed their repentance, although others still behaved 'in a very haughty and indecent manner'. The final entry on the sad episode is dated 1 October when two men were 'cut off' from the church's communion for relapsing into 'the sin of drunkenness'; one woman was also dismissed from membership 'For the same Crime & that of keeping a very disorderly House as well as other great Scandals of Behaviour testified before the Church'.[35]

It is clear from his correspondence that Doddridge found such disciplining distasteful yet necessary. Writing to Clark a few years earlier he expressed his pleasure at the 'prudent and honourable' way in which the church was dealing with an inter-family feud, possibly the same dispute that ended in reconciliation at the church meeting in April 1741.

Nothing can better illustrate Doddridge's care for his people than the detailed instructions which he left in his will. He made provision for his wife and children and left bequests to a number of his particularly close friends to purchase rings as tokens of remembrance. His flock were also remembered, for they were 'as serious, as grateful, and as deserving a People, as perhaps any Minister had ever the Honour and Happiness to serve'. To each of the elders Doddridge willed a guinea to buy a ring, and the deacons were to receive 'such a Volume of my Sermons as they shall choose, handsomely bound in Black Calf and lettered'. To the congregation he asked that £20 be distributed by the deacons in amounts varying from five to twenty shillings 'among such poor Christians as statedly attend Ordinances among us, desiring their prayers (which living I have greatly esteemed) may be continued for the afflicted Remains of my dear Family, which will not I am perswaded be upon the whole the poorer for this little Kindness to those whom I hope they will consider as the Friends of Christ, and will delight as they can, in doing them good'.[36]

Doddridge's pastoral care went beyond the confines of his own church. In another letter to Clark dated February 1739 he wrote: 'I have brought almost all the Ministers in our County into a Contribution to the Society for relieving the Widows & Children of necessitous Dissent [ing] Ministers.' A month later a correspondent acknowledged the receipt of twelve guineas 'as Money Coll[ected] by you, among your Friends in and about Northampton'.[37]

We catch another glimpse of his wider responsibilities from a letter written on 21 February 1741 also to Clark:

> Welford is likely to be vacant again; the young minister who settled with them for the winter, being deficient either in orthodoxy or prudence, or both; several neighbouring congregations, especially Ashley and Harborough, which continue vacant, increase my care. . . . The ministers in these parts have, at my request, agreed to preach on family religion, on the third Lord's day in April.[38]

Problems concerning individual families touched him deeply, particularly when the deaths of children occurred:

> . . . I have just heard of the calamity of a very friendly and generous family at Olney, who, after having buried ten children, some of them very amiable and at engaging ages, have now lost by a fever the only surviving child, a beautiful and lovely daughter of about nine years old, for whose life they have been trembling ever since she was born. It touches me very tenderly. May we be sensible of the divine goodness in having built up our families and in continuing our children around us, and may they grow up to religion and usefulness.[39]

Sometimes Doddridge's interest in the churches of the locality was decisive. The church at Newport Pagnell found itself in difficulties over ownership of the land upon which the church was built. Doddridge intervened, paid the necessary price from his own pocket, and ensured the continuance of the church.[40] As is mentioned elsewhere, relations with the Baptist church in College Lane were extremely cordial; Doddridge loaned his vestry for candidates for adult baptism, although he himself believed in infant baptism. Dr Ryland of College Lane recalls Doddridge's acceptance into membership at Castle Hill, of people baptised by total immersion:

> I have heard several aged people mention it as a well known instance of Dr. Doddridge's candid spirit that he once was present at the river side when Mr Rodgers Baptised and that when Mr

Rodgers came out of the water the Doctor pulled off his own cloak which he usually wore on the Lord's day and offered to put it on Mr Rodgers observing at the same time in the audience of all the spectators that it was a very solemn ordinance.[41]

During his Kibworth days Doddridge had refused to 'subscribe' to any form of words that attempted to define theological truths. In his Confession of Faith upon entering the ministry at Castle Hill in 1730, he cautiously avoided any detailed reference to the most vexed controversies of the period, those of the nature of the Trinity and the person of Christ, attesting his belief in 'the great doctrine of a TRINITY of persons in the unity of the Godhead'. Doddridge stated his view that such a concept was 'an awful mystery which, being matter of pure revelation, I apprehend I should only obscure by attempting fully to explain it'.[42] Indeed it seems clear that Doddridge regarded the human mind as not being fully capable of expressing the wonder of the Godhead. In one of his lectures he stated 'If it be asked, how these divine persons are three, and how one; it must be acknowledged an inexplicable mystery: nor should we wonder that we are much confounded when enquiring into the curiosities of such questions, if we consider how little we know of our own nature and manner of existence'.[43] Perhaps, he continued (in reviewing the many divergent viewpoints on the matter) the whole question was 'not fundamental to religion' anyway. All his lectures and sermons were based on the principle that 'matters of abstruse speculation and laborious inquiry, are not, even to Theological students, the one thing needful, though they may be important in subordination to it'.[44]

Although Doddridge carefully avoided theological statements that would cause offence, he himself became the object of much criticism. It was 'a time when the trend amongst Presbyterians was towards Arianism and the trend amongst Independents [was] towards a militant Evangelicalism'.[45] To some he was too orthodox, and to others far too liberal. Writing to his wife from London on 21 June 1734, he joked about sharpeared critics ready to pounce upon his words:

> I had several orthodox spies to hear me this afternoon, and they observed, with great amazement, that I urged my hearers to endeavour to get an interest in Christ. This, it seems, is Arminianism.[46]

Even within his own Northampton congregation there were those who criticised him for allowing a professed Arian to come to the Lord's Table. Kippis comments 'the Doctor declared, that he would sacrifice

J. H. N.    "Idea of a University"
    Dessain    pp. 103 & 105.


Doddridge  —  Nuttall Eval.
    chap 5.  Educ.  —  A. V. Murray
                pp. 102 &-118.  55

Priestley — "parliamentary religion"

Taylors charge.

0942 30893.

Limbitrol treats anxiety first
then combats the underlying depression.

<br>

his place, and even his life, rather than fix any such mark of discouragement upon one, who, whatever his doctrinal sentiments were, appeared to be a real Christian'.[47]

Financial support for the academy from the Coward Trustees was something of a mixed blessing; Doddridge was subjected to pressures to ensure orthodoxy among his students; it has been suggested that the practice of ensuring that the students took down their lectures in shorthand enabled any controversial points to remain hidden from the eyes of scrupulous heresy hunters. The encouragement of 'piety and catholicism' through free enquiry that pervaded Doddridge's academic lectures were the principles that governed every aspect of his life. It took courage to tread the middle road, but Doddridge struggled to maintain his advocacy of toleration:

> Indeed, the Gospel is a great thing, or it is nothing. I am more and more convinced of the importance of keeping to the good old evangelical and experimental way of preaching; and look on most of the new fashioned divinity, of which some persons in different extremes, are so fond, as a kind of quackery, which bodes ill to the health of the soul and of the church in general.[48]

In 1737 Doddridge seems to have acted uncharacteristically by denying his pulpit to the controversial London preacher James Foster.[49] It was a time when Doddridge was struggling against criticism of the academy, and did not want to be suspected of harbouring unorthodox views similar to those of Foster. Doddridge received a mild rebuke from Clark:

> I think we cant be too careful not to give any Countenance to that narrow Spirit, which has done so much Mischief in the Christian Church. And what Confusion would it breed amongst us, if those who were suppos'd to be of differing Sentiments either in the Trinitarian Calvinistical or other Controversies, were to be on both sides excluded from each others Pulpits?[50]

Such words must have struck Doddridge with irony; henceforth he became less conciliatory towards the feelings of his critics, and more determined to stick to his principles.

Controversy raged over Doddridge's friendships, particularly his relationship with George Whitefield. The latter, who with the Wesley brothers was one of the leaders of the emerging Methodist movement, had been denied every pulpit 'in City or Suburbs' and was regarded with distrust by most Dissenters. Whitefield had preached in May 1739 from the

Weighing Chair on Northampton Racecourse (referred to by contemporaries as the Horse Course).[51] Many Dissenters looked askance at the developing friendship between Doddridge and Whitefield, particularly in July 1743, when Doddridge preached at Whitefield's Tabernacle at Moorfields in London. Watts and others were outraged when news broke that Doddridge had reciprocated by welcoming Whitefield to the pulpit at Castle Hill in the following October. So many people came to hear Whitefield that the two north windows of the church had to be removed so that the crowd outside could hear him preach. A stream of criticism and abuse inevitably descended upon Doddridge. Nathaniel Neal, writing from the Million Bank in London expressed his own and the Coward Trustees' views:

> It is with the utmost concern that I received the information of Mr Whitefield's having preached last week in your pulpit, and that I attended the meeting of the trustees this day, when that matter was canvassed, and that I now find myself obliged to apprize you of the very great uneasiness which your conduct herein has occasioned them.[52]

Although there was a hint of an apology from Doddridge, he remained basically unrepentant. On 7–8 May 1750 Whitefield returned to Northampton where he met Doddridge, Dr Stonhouse, the Revd James Hervey[53] of Weston Favell, and the Revd Thomas Hartley, Vicar of Winwick in Northamptonshire and an advocate of Swedenborgianism.[54] Such a meeting, which probably took place at the Earl of Halifax's home at Horton, vividly displayed Doddridge's determination, tolerance and ecumenical spirit. On the second day of his visit Whitefield was entertained by Doddridge after preaching at the academy during the morning.

After preaching to his ministerial brethren at Creaton in 1750, Doddridge published his sermon under the title *Christian Candour and Unanimity stated, illustrated and urged*. It was dedicated to the Countess of Huntingdon who, as an ardent Calvinistic Methodist like Whitefield, greatly admired Doddridge, considering him 'a polished shaft in his [i.e. the Lord's] quiver'.[55] The feeling was reciprocated and they remained great friends, the Countess frequently asking for copies of his sermons (on one occasion a hundred). We find her urging Doddridge to look out for a suitable curate for her, and in her letters to him she gives details of her successful evangelistic efforts within the aristocracy. John Wesley the Arminian Methodist was also Doddridge's friend, and came to Northampton on 5 September 1745: 'It was about the hour when he was accustomed to expound a portion of Scripture to the young gentlemen under his care,' wrote Wesley and added, 'He desired me to take his place.' Nuttall comments 'It showed no small breadth and independency for a Dissenting minister thus to be Wesley's friend and to admit George Whitefield to the pulpit at Castle Hill.'[56]

Such friendships showed Doddridge's preoccupation with the essentials of Christian living; every facet of his ministry displayed his passionate belief in toleration. Not only did he 'obliterate old party lines' and 'unite Nonconformists on a common religious ground',[57] Doddridge set an example to all subsequent generations of Christians of personal integrity and unselfish dedication to his Master.

# Doddridge the Teacher

Early in 1730 Doddridge commenced the task of establishing the academy at his house on the corner of Pike Lane and Marefair.[1] Forty students arrived and lectures commenced in earnest. In August 1733 Doddridge wrote to his friend, John Barker, who had requested that he take in another promising youth, 'I shall be very willing to take him under my care. . . . For the present he cannot possibly be in my house, that being so full that I have three gentlemen already lodging abroad, who wait for places in it. A fourth place will, however, be vacant by Christmas; and, in the mean time he may reside with a sober family in the neighbourhood, where I believe he will be well accommodated.'[2]

The enterprise rapidly expanded, and so overcrowded did the premises become that Doddridge found it necessary to look for more spacious accommodation. A large town house in Sheep Street belonging to Doddridge's patron, the Earl of Halifax, seemed a suitable building. Doddridge negotiated the rental which was fixed at £40 per annum. In August 1737 he requested that the walls be pierced in order to let in more light to some of the dark rooms. In 1740 the entire academy moved into the new premises, and by 1743 there were sixty-three students receiving tuition. The academy was thus situated in a prominent position in one of the busiest parts of the town surrounded by inns, shops and houses. It is believed that the building dates from after the fire of 1675[3] and served as an inn before coming into the possession of the Earls of Halifax.[4]

'As for my terms,' wrote Doddridge, 'they are sixteen pounds a year board, and four pounds teaching. But when persons have any assistance from charitable contributions to support the charge of their education, I board them for fourteen pounds a year. . . .

When pupils enter the Academy they pay a guinea each for a closet, and bring a pair of sheets. They find their own candles, and put out their washing.'[5]

Notes and references for this chapter begin on page 162

21. Doddridge's vestry, exterior view.

22. Doddridge's vestry, interior view. In this room Doddridge spent many hours in prayer, and in the work of the church.

23. A fragment from Mercy Doddridge's white damask dress embroidered in silk, given by the Prince of Wales, and worn at a ball given by George II.

24. A pair of Mercy Doddridge's shoes with latchet ties, not buckles; approximately size 3. The heels are nearly 5cm high and are covered with black silk. The style and material suggest the 1770s or 1780s.

Fees remained stable for some years but eventually rose to £26 per annum in 1747. The number of students fluctuated, dropping to twenty-nine in 1747–8. Stanford records the lowest number in any one year as thirteen.[6] In all over two hundred students passed through the academy in its twenty-two years of existence at Northampton, of whom one hundred and twenty became ministers of the Gospel. Many were assisted by the Presbyterian and Congregational Fund Boards established after the Revolution of 1688, and others were sponsored by the trust set up by the London merchant William Coward upon his death in 1738.[7] Dodd-ridge was extremely generous to his students, and paid from his own pocket to support them. Young Samuel Mercer who entered the academy in 1750 at the age of sixteen wrote to his father that the Doctor had 'provided me a tutor last year, and I do not know whether he will be paid for it'.[8] Doddridge's diary records Samuel and three other students as benefiting from 'more than one-tenth' of his total income. Samuel's father was a farmer and cheese factor, and it is not surprising that the son should ask that 'a couple of Cheshire cheeses, not strong but mild and fat' should be sent to the Doctor as a gift to mark his appreciation.

Job Orton (Doddridge's biographer, first assistant[9] at the academy and elder at Castle Hill), recalls the demands on the students:

> . . . it was an established law, that every student should rise at six o'clock in the summer, and seven in the winter. A monitor was weekly appointed to call them, and they were to appear in the public room, soon after the fixed hour. . . . Their tutor set them an example of diligence, being generally present with them at these early hours. When they were thus assembled, a prayer was offered up, suited to their circumstances, as students, by himself when present, or by them in their turns. Then they retired to their respective closets till the time of family worship.[10]

The students met again for family prayer at eight o'clock during which a chapter from the Old Testament was read in Hebrew by a senior student, and Doddridge expounded upon the text; in the evening prayer at seven o'clock he did likewise, with a chapter from the New Testament read in Greek. 'By this method of conducting the religious services of his family, his pupils had an opportunity, during their course, of hearing him expound most of the Old Testament, and all the New Testament more than once, to their improvement as students and christians.'[11]

Breakfast followed family prayer and had to be concluded by five minutes to ten. After the blessing was spoken by a senior pupil the students could attack their meal with relish:

> They that chuse Tea in the Morning may either breakfast with the Tutor in his Parlour or at the other Tea Board in the great Parlour, Each in that Case providing his own Tea & Sugar in a just proportion as the Company shall agree.

The making of 'Toast & Butter & Toasting Cheese' was disallowed owing to the expense 'except by the Parlour Boarders'.[12]

The kitchen obviously had its attraction for hungry students:

> That the servants may not be hindred in their Businessn-one of the Students are on the Penalty of forfeiting an half Penny each Time to be in the Kitchen before Morning prayer, nor from twelve at Noon till the Dinr is served up, nor from seven in the Evening till supper is intirely carried into the little Parlour. And during these Seasons of Exclusion the Kitchen Door shall be bolted whenever the Cook shall think fit.

Supper followed evening prayer and had to be eaten by nine o'clock 'after which the Table is to be cleared'. At ten o'clock every night the gate was locked, latecomers being fined twopence. Indeed, fines were an essential part of the academy's discipline; 1d for neglecting the rules relating to the return of library books, 1d for lateness at prayers, 6d [2½p] for not pursuing an allotted duty at prayer time, 2d for lateness at lectures and 6d for 'failure in preparing a set exercise'. The activities of the students when outside the academy were also controlled:

> No student is to go into a Publick House to drink there on Penalty of a publick Censure for the first Time, & the Forfeiture of a shilling the second. . . . If any one spread Reports abroad to the Dishonour of the Family or any Member of it he must expect a publick Reproof & to hear a Caution given to others to beware of placing any Confidence in him.

A degree of democracy was exercised in the conduct of the academy, the students being consulted on various matters. At the end of each year votes were taken as to the disposal of money accruing from 'the small Pecuniary Fines':

> Six Pence is to be allowed from the Box weekly toward the Support of the Charity School & the Remainder of the Cash (excepting only twenty Shillings to be reserved in Bank) at the End

of every year shall be disposed of in Books or Instruments for the apparatus according to the Vote of the Society to be determined by the Majority of Votes, in which every one who is ending his second year shall have two Votes & the rest but one. This Distribution to be made at the Beginning of the next long Vacation.

Annexed to the academy's rules dated 10 December 1743 (written in Doddridge's handwriting) are signatures of himself and his assistant Thomas Brabant, as well as fifty-one students who 'hereby Declare our Acquiescence in these Constitutions, Orders & Rules as the Terms of our Respective Admission into or Continuance in the Academy at Northampton'. Amendments were made from time to time and the signatures of new students added (see Appendix IX).

Occasionally Doddridge had to expel a student who had persistently failed to take notice of his admonitions. Such expulsions saddened him, probably more than the students; on one occasion he wrote:

> A very melancholy scene opened this day. We had some time spent in fasting and prayer, on account of an unhappy youth, whose folly and wickedness hath obliged me to dismiss him. I pronounced the solemn sentence of expulsion upon him before the whole academy.[13]

Orton complained that when he was assistant tutor too much of the academy's affairs were left for him to deal with; he also felt that Doddridge was too lenient with the students. Doddridge was conscious of the fact and mentioned it to his friend William Warburton, later Bishop of Gloucester, as 'a want of government' in the academy. He admitted that he had too mild and gentle a nature, and could be deceived by students' appearances of penitence and promises of more responsible behaviour. Doddridge certainly gave some deference to rank, and the presence of sons of aristocratic blood in the academy posed problems. John Fergusson, son of Lord Kilkerran, became 'tenderly dear' to his tutor, but a period of laziness in which the young man rose late from his bed, impertinently burned an essay and preferred 'sauntering' to 'business' convinced Doddridge that he had been insufficiently firm with him.[14]

There was a strong bond of real friendship between Doddridge and his students. In 1736 when news broke that their tutor had been awarded an honorary Doctorate of Divinity by the two colleges of Aberdeen University, Marischal and King's, all the students gathered to express their congratulations. In reply Doctor Doddridge thanked them for their kindness and told them that the greatest honour he could have would be their growth in piety and learning, and usefulness in the world.

The affection between the students and Doddridge was strengthened by shared afflictions. A number of students died during the course of their studies; on 23 January 1744 Doddridge wrote to Clark:

> God has deeply afflicted me with the death or hopeless illness of four dear and excellent pupils within five months. Mr Joseph Marshall was the only one who had finished his course. Two got their deaths in the last vacation, the other brought a constitution greatly shattered by a fever last year, and is sinking in a consumption amidst all the anxious and tender cares that can be taken to prevent it. You will easily believe that these things must wound me in a very tender part, but I would submit to infinite wisdom.[15]

The last student referred to by Doddridge was John Gibbs who wrote several letters to his tutor from Stratford upon Avon. His father had already died from consumption a short time before Gibbs himself succumbed to the disease. Gibbs requested that Doddridge should preach a funeral sermon for him:

> Oh, Sir, many things concur to render this world insipid to me: my own corruption, my afflictions, and, can I write it! the death of my dear father. I have none now to call father; but blessed be God! though I am fatherless, I am not friendless; and I believe, never shall be while dear Dr Doddridge lives.[16]

Gibbs' sister, Frances, writing on 9 January 1744 before her brother's death, told Doddridge, 'I believe its impossible for a pupil to Love His Tuter with a stronger affection than he dose you'.[17]

One of Doddridge's most promising pupils was the Revd Thomas Steffe, son of a Suffolk clergyman. He too died very young, and as a tribute to his pupil, Doddridge published his life and character as a preface to a volume of Steffe's sermons.

The academy was an open institution with no tests of religious belief exacted upon its members. One student was intended for the Church of England ministry, and the sons of Anglican families came to the Northampton academy in preference to the universities of Oxford and Cambridge. Students came from virtually every region of England as well as Scotland and Holland. Although the majority trained for the Nonconformist ministry, the others entered a variety of trades and professions. 'None of the pupils turned out great scholars or thinkers, but among them were men of superior attainment and a large number of useful ministers.'[18] John Aikin, Samuel Merivale, Caleb Ashworth, Andrew Kippis and Stephen Addington became distinguished tutors of academies. James Robertson became Professor of Oriental Languages at Edinburgh, and Hugh Farmer an influential theological writer.

Students studying theology stayed for five years, and lay students three. Their 'academical exercises' reflect the rigorous standards of their tutor whose voracious appetite for study set them a powerful example. Doddridge encouraged his young men to read widely and make critical annotations as they did so. The students were required to have good standards of Latin upon entrance, as Doddridge did not have the time to devote to the teaching of classical languages. Towards the end of his life the prospect of a second assistant opened up the possibility of 'educating lads not yet ripe for academical studies' as an attempt to ease the shortage of ministers. Senior students were appointed to teach any who showed weakness in their mastery of Greek, and all students were given the option of studying French. Doddridge was practical enough to realise that full mastery of Latin and Greek might not be possible for some students, and consequently he allowed entrance to several 'serious young men' in their early twenties who 'might be useful in plain country congregations'.[19]

The students were required in their first year to make translations from Latin into English, and vice versa. By the conclusion of the fourth year a student was required to have exhibited at least six 'Orations, Theses or Dissertations'. Disputations on a variety of subjects were held, with respondents and opponents being expected to have prepared their arguments adequately. Two sermons on given subjects had to be composed by a theological student in his eighth half year, and having been read in class were to be preached to 'the assembled student-body or to the public before he left the academy'. Six other sermons had to be carefully planned. In the fifth year two major theological theses had to be prepared and defended, in addition to the preparation of sermons and other exercises. From the second to the eighth half-year, theological students had to make notes on sermons preached at Castle Hill on pain of 'a proper Fine'. In addition:

> Four Classicks viz One Greek & one Latin poet, one Greek and one Latin prose writer as appointed by the Tutor are to be read by each Student in his Study, & Observations are to be written upon them to be kept in a distinct Book & communicated to the Tutor whenever he shall think fit.

Doddridge's epistemology was essentially simple; he believed passionately that all knowledge was interrelated. To him there was no contradiction between scientific and theological conceptions of the world; all knowledge pointed to an ultimate Deity. The course therefore was wide ranging with lectures on Watts' logic, rhetoric (based upon Jennings' lectures), geography and metaphysics. The students were referred to numerous books which they could borrow from the academy's extensive library.[20]

Andrew Kippis, remembering his student days at the academy, wrote of the lectures on algebra and geometry 'which, besides their intrinsic excellence, were happily calculated to form in the young men a fixedness of attention, and a habit of rightly discriminating, and properly arranging their conceptions. When these branches of science were finished, the students were introduced to the knowledge of trigonometry, conic sections, and celestial mechanics; under which last term was included a collection of important propositions, taken chiefly from Sir Isaac Newton, and relating especially, though not solely, to centripetal and centrifugal forces. A system of natural and experimental philosophy, comprehending mechanics, statics, hydrostatics, optics, pneumatics, and astronomy, was likewise read, with references to the best authors on these subjects'.[21]

Lectures on ecclesiastical history and Jewish antiquities as well as natural and civil history added to a very full timetable. Anatomy of the human body was also studied which was 'well calculated to inspire the young men with the sentiments of veneration and love for the supreme Artificer.'[22]

Not only did Doddridge work hard to build up the academy's library, he constantly sought to add to the collection of scientific apparatus. In 1731 Lady Russell sent him a pair of globes and Dr Beard donated a handsome microscope. In July 1733 Doddridge was in London selecting new equipment in readiness for the next academic session.

In some ways Doddridge retained aspects of the medieval conception of education; to him theology was still queen of the sciences sitting at the summit of knowledge. His two hundred and thirty divinity lectures were the backbone of the entire academic course. In true scholastic tradition he retained a method of teaching inherited from Jennings, but stretching back to Aquinas and even further to Abelard. Every lecture was set out with mathematical precision, a method upon which Doddridge was criticised on the grounds that theological and moral truths are not necessarily compatible with such an ordered presentation.[23]

In lecture 163, for example, Doddridge assesses contemporary English theological writings on the doctrine of the Trinity, a topic fiercely debated at the time. The body of the lecture is a 'demonstration' that neatly summarises and compares writers on the subject. As a 'corollary' the student is required to consider a statement that if so many divergences are expressed by so many 'excellent characters' then perhaps they 'are not fundamental to religion'. As a second 'corollary', advice is given to be careful of uttering 'unscriptural niceties in expressing our conception of this doctrine'. Two 'scholia' follow giving fuller explanations referring the students to classical writers and other statements, and leaving the student with a further statement to consider and references to follow up.[24]

Doddridge's divinity lectures, published posthumously in 1763, were entitled *A course of lectures on the Principal Subjects in Pneumatology, Ethics and Divinity*. The modern equivalent for 'pneumatology' is psychology, and it is significant that Philip Doddridge was one of the first to introduce the subject as part of an academic course. Equally revolutionary was Doddridge's insistence that his lectures should be delivered in English and not the traditional Latin. Students were free to ask questions during the lectures, and to voice objections. Always open-minded, Doddridge tried to present both sides of an argument; in writing to John Wesley, who had asked his advice on a booklet for young preachers, Doddridge stated 'in order to defend the truth, it is very proper that a young minister should know the chief strength of error'.[25]

Doddridge divided his students into classes and usually lectured to each group in the mornings except on Thursdays, which were free periods. Students were required to spend time in checking references given during the lectures, and much effort was spent by Doddridge and his assistant in tutorials and extra coaching of individuals. In order to facilitate note-taking and composition, Doddridge insisted that every student in his first year at the academy mastered shorthand. Doddridge himself had used shorthand from the age of fourteen. He prepared lectures and sermons, made notes and wrote letters in a minute and neat shorthand which he had simplified from the system of Jeremiah Rich.[26]

Part of the theological students' curriculum was to have preaching experience; Doddridge took some of them with him on his excursions, and they were sent out to congregations in the local villages where they were allowed to preach certain selected model sermons ('repetitions'). On 21 October 1736 an extraordinary event occurred at Brixworth involving one of his students, Risdon Darracott, who was about to lead a service of worship in the cottage of William Beck. Trouble had started on the previous Sunday, and before the service could begin an anti-Dissenting mob stormed the house, smashing the windows and threatening Darracott's life. The *Northampton Mercury* records that William Beck was pelted with dirt, stones and sticks before being thrown several times into deep mud, 'in which considering the Darkness and the Crowd, he apprehended himself in Danger of being smothered. After this, some of them, who swore they would take his life, dragged him through a Horsepond and tore a great Part of his Coat from his Back'. Darracott escaped by clambering out of Beck's back window.

Doddridge was outraged by the incident but even more so by the lack of justice meted out by those in authority. The account in the *Northampton Mercury* ends with a communiqué apparently from Doddridge: 'the Last Scene of Riot pass'd in the Yard of the George Inn, where the Constables and other Magistrates of the Town were met at a Court-Leet; but, though they were too busy to interpose for Beck's Deliverance, it's hop'd that Persons of a much superior Character, to whom proper Application is made, will consider the Enormity of the Offence, and how much the Liberty of the Subject and the Public Safety are concerned in it.' Doddridge obtained a warrant for the arrest of four of the ring leaders: they were duly brought before Mr William Wykes J.P. of Haselbech,[27] who 'treated Beck as if he had been a Felon . . . & at last allowed him 2 shillings [10p] Damages besides 2 more to mend his windows, & 2 for the Warrant'.[28]

Doddridge was angered by this injustice, and initiated an action in the King's Bench against Wykes and nine of the rioters. Again the anti-Dissenting 'Tories' united to see the rioters acquitted. Finally Doddridge appealed to the Duke of Montagu, Lord Lieutenant of the County, and in the end 'some justice was done', although there is no record of what or how.

Doddridge thus learned by bitter experience the necessity of defending civil and religious rights. In June 1732 the Revd James Wells,[29] a curate to the Revd Richard Reynolds, Rector of Kingsthorpe, wrote to Doddridge complaining that he had preached 'in a certain barn' in Kingsthorpe. Doddridge was summarily forbidden to repeat his activities in the village. Doddridge wrote back civilly but with no intention of giving way:

> As for my preaching occasionally at Kingsthorp, and the neighbouring villages, I know it is a liberty which the law permits, and I cannot imagine that either you or any of your brethren can reasonably resent it.[30]

But Wells did resent it, and both men indulged in angry correspondence. Within a few weeks Reynolds informed the churchwardens of All Saints, Northampton that 'there is a fellow in the parish who taught a grammar school' and instructed them to summon Doddridge to appear at the Consistory Court at All Saints 'to answer to certain Articles or Interrogatories to be objected and administred to You concerning Your Soul's health and the Reformation and Correction of Your manners and excess And especially Your teaching and instructing Youth in the Liberal Arts and Sciences not being Licensed thereto by the Ordinary of the Diocese touching either Your Learning and Dexterity in teaching or Your right understanding of God's true religion or Your honest and sober Conversation . . .'.[31]

Doddridge was promised a licence if he would apply, but he looked upon the measure 'as a very artful scheme, to bring us under ecclesiastical inspection more than we have ever yet been'.[32] It was plain that much more was at stake than Doddridge's fitness to teach or the continuation of the Northampton academy; here was an issue of importance to all Nonconformists. Doddridge secured the support of the London committee of Protestant Dissenters and refused to apply for a licence. The Earl of Halifax enlisted the services of Sir Robert Walpole and the Attorney General, and the case went to Westminster Hall where Doddridge ably defended his rights. In the meantime an anti-Dissenting mob attacked his house in Marefair and stoned the windows. On 31 January 1734 the Judges supported Doddridge by granting a prohibition of the proceedings, but Reynolds re-opened the case in the following June by declaring the prohibition illegal. By now the case had excited wide interest and had reached the ears of George II who intervened by reiterating his earlier declaration 'that in his reign there should be no persecutions for conscience sake'. It was not only a personal victory for Doddridge whose work in the academy received widespread publicity; the outcome of the dispute resulted in progress towards equality in education for every Dissenter. In June 1734 the question of Nonconformist liberties was raised in parliament so that Doddridge wrote hopefully of 'a Design on Foot to secure our Schools by an Act of Parliament next Year';[33] indeed it was a measure of the significant progress the affair had produced.

Doddridge was not without his critics, but he took comfort in the mass of compliments and good-will that people paid him. 'Some of the rudest as well as the most contemptible things have been said of my character,' he wrote in 1733, 'especially as a tutor; and my Academy has been even represented as a nursery of error and heresy.'[34] Some disliked

A
SYSTEM
of
LOGICK,
RULES on Behaviour
and
SHORT HAND;
drawn up at
NORTHAMPTON

By P. DODDRIDGE, DD
VOL. IV.

J.H. Sculpf.                    T.B. Scripf.

---

12    Chap.    Of the Abbreviation of Sentences

The Cause of God                The Office of Christ
The Curse of God                The Peace of God
The Church of God               The People of God
The Glory of God                The Gospel of Christ
The Glory of Christ             The Praise of God
The Grace of God                The Raign of Christ
The Gift of God                 The Righteousness
The House of God                The Spirit of God
The Joys of Heaven              The Spirit of Christ
The Kingdom of Grace            The Ways of God
The Kingdom of Glory            The Ways of Christ
The Kingdom of God              The Will of God
The Kingdom of Christ           The Will of Christ
The Kingdom of Heaven           The Wisdome of Christ
The Kingdom of Satan            The Word of God
The Life of Grace               The Word of God
The Life of Faith               The Work of Faith
The Life of Christ              The Work of God
The Same of God                 The Work of Grace
                                The Works of God

Finis.

his methods of allowing the students to judge for themselves; he was alleged to be too undogmatic, too ingenuous and too catholic. Doddridge defended himself and resisted attempts to impose 'subscriptions' of faith upon his students. He also parried criticism that he was not supplying sufficient ministers for London churches, by pointing to the equal needs of the local churches in Northamptonshire and Leicestershire.

Doddridge's educational interests were not confined to the academy. In 1738 he persuaded his congregation to support him in establishing a charity school. The inspiration had come from Clark who had founded at St Albans the first Dissenting charity school outside London; at this institution, which was paid for by voluntary subscriptions, thirty boys and ten girls were instructed in reading, writing and arithmetic. Doddridge did likewise, raising sufficient money from his congregation and friends. The venture was successful from the beginning, and twenty boys were 'put under the care of a pious skilful master [John Browne] who taught them to read, write and learn their catechism, and brought them regularly to public worship'.[35] The boys were also provided with clothes. An anniversary sermon was preached and a special collection was made for the school, the academy also provided 6d (2½p) per week from the fines' box, and benefactors sent money, books and bibles. Doddridge 'often visited the school, to support the master's authority and respect, to examine the proficiency of the children, catechise, instruct and pray with them; and the trustees visited it weekly by rotation, to observe the behaviour and improvement of the children, and to receive the master's report concerning them'.[36] The exact location of the school is something of a mystery, and many other details are lacking. Doddridge wished to add girls to the school but there is no record of this being done. The school was probably closed in 1772, but it certainly influenced the establishment of similar institutions in Leicester, Hinckley and elsewhere.[37]

Early in Doddridge's ministry in 1730 an anonymous publication *An Inquiry into the Causes of the Decay of the Dissenting Interest* caused considerable uproar. The writer was Strickland Gough, a young Dissenting minister who later conformed to the established church. Doddridge was stung into publishing a reply, *Free thoughts on the most probable means of reviving the Dissenting Interest* by 'a minister in the country'. Doddridge stated that the number of Dissenters in his own locality had actually risen. He pointed to the central problem facing Dissent, namely its inclination to subdivide into numerous sects each dogmatically opposing the other. It was essential that Nonconformity should become united by an evangelical ministry that attacked bigotry with subtlety rather than crude antagonism. A united Nonconformist body was politically vital, too, with its hold firmly retained in all sections of society. Doddridge pierced the core of the whole problem: 'If we find, upon inquiry, that this our glory is departing, it surely deserves to be mentioned as one cause, at least, of the decay of our interest; and that all who sincerely wish well to it, should express their affection by exerting themselves with the utmost zeal, for the revival of practical religion amongst us.'[38] It was a call to action that received much praise.

In this, his first sortie into the printed word, we may discover the key to the whole of his ministry. In everything he said, did, or wrote the objective was to 'revive, strengthen, and develop spiritual life'.[39] Doddridge knew how important a dedicated and respected ministry was in holding the people to Dissent. In his twenty-five *Lectures on Preaching and . . . the Ministerial office*,[40] there is a mine of information acquainting his students with contemporary theological writers in both Dissent and the established church, advice on how to construct and deliver effective and public addresses, how to administer the sacraments, visit the sick and behave with proper ministerial, yet human, dignity. Always practical and realistic, he urged his students to be distinct when preaching:

> Take care of running your words into one another,—and of sucking in your breath,—or dropping your voice at the end of a sentence.—Make pauses in proper, and avoid them in improper places.—Let the accent be laid right,—but avoid too much, lest it seem affectation.[41]

His work in the academy was directed at producing a well educated generation of ministers who had eclectic tastes and wide sympathies but, above all, who had a burning passion to win souls for Christ. In his sermon *Christ's Invitation to thirsty Souls* published in 1748 but actually written in 1729, we see his passionate and consistent desire to win the unconverted. It is evangelism which is 'the thread on which his multi-coloured life was strung. It was for this above all that he wrote, preached, corresponded and educated his students in the Academy'.[42]

If Doddridge desired a dedicated and educated ministry within Nonconformity, he saw as equally vital the need to teach theological truths and encourage piety. He worked with tremendous dedication, often in the early hours before breakfast, at two major works which were to have enormous influence. In December 1743 Doddridge wrote: 'I am hard at work on my book the Rise and Progress of Religion, which Dr

Watts is impatient to see, and I am eager to finish, lest he should slip away to Heaven before it is done.'[43] Watts had planned the work and, conscious of his failing health, had urged Doddridge to complete his design.

Doddridge did not fail Watts' confident expectations, *The Rise and Progress of Religion in the Soul* (1745) shows Doddridge's religious genius at its greatest. Like Bunyan's pilgrim, the Christian has to traverse the difficult path of faith awakening to his sin and his utter helplessness before God, accepting the 'Good News', facing doubts, controlling emotions, enduring afflictions, holding fast to his personal relationship with God and finally, rejoicing in the prospect of eternal life. Unlike Bunyan, Doddridge does not use allegory; his style is a straight-from-the-shoulder personal appeal to the spiritual conscience of every reader.

> He [the author] entreats, that these addresses, and these medita-
> tions, may be perused at leisure, and be thought over in retire-
> ment; and that you would do him and yourself the justice to
> believe the representations which are here made, and the warnings
> which are here given, to proceed from sincerity and love, from a
> heart that would not designedly give one moment's unnecessary
> pain to the meanest creature on the face of the earth, and much
> less to any human mind.[44]

Every chapter concludes with prayer, and is interwoven with quotations taken from every part of the Bible. Doddridge's *Rise and Progress* emanated from a mind pre-occupied with the realities of reaching people both within the Christian church and throughout society.

The book immediately became popular and was translated into many languages including Tamil and Syriac. Doddridge wrote, 'This is the book which, so far as I can judge, God has honoured for the conversion and edification of souls more than any of my writings'.[45] The Princess of Wales sent her personal appreciation of the work. William Wilberforce was profoundly affected by it, as was Sir James Stonhouse, 'a most abandoned rake and an audacious deist';[46] the latter changed his way of life, founded with Doddridge the infirmary in Northampton, and eventually took holy orders in the established church. *The Rise and Progress of Religion in the Soul* is a lasting monument to Doddridge's greatness.

When Doddridge was still at Kibworth he wrote: 'I am drawing up, but only for my own use, a sort of analytical scheme of the contents of the Epistles of the New Testament.' Twelve years later in 1736 this idea had developed into a major work; he wrote to Samuel Clark:

The intended work, at which I hinted when I wrote last, is what I shall call *The Family Expositor:* a fresh translation, with paraphrase interwoven, and references to the most considerable writers, to be published in octavo, the first two volumes containing the Harmony of the Evangelists and perhaps Acts.[47]

The first volume appeared in 1738 and was dedicated to the Princess of Wales.[48] In total Doddridge laboured for twelve years to complete it; fearing that his life might end before he had finished, he worked daily on the text, snatching every minute he could between his 'multiplicity of business'. In June 1750 tragedy almost struck. Thinking that he had extinguished a candle used for sealing letters, Doddridge was summoned by a neighbour who had noticed flames coming from his study:

When I came up, I found my desk, which was covered with papers, burning like an altar . . . surrounded with flames, and drenched in melted wax . . . and yet, so did God moderate the rage of this element, and determine in his Providence the time of our entrance, that not one account is rendered uncertain by what it suffered, nor is one line which had not been transcribed destroyed in the MS . . . Observe, my dear friend, the hand of God, and magnify the Lord with me.[49]

Doddridge did not live to see the sixth and final volume published in 1756, but the success of the earlier volumes allayed his fears that his work might 'disappoint the world'. The first issue was quickly sold out. A wide spectrum of subscribers including 'squires, peers, peeresses, bishops, dons and Anglican clergy'[50] ensured the book's financial success. Subscribers were spread far and wide, predominantly from provincial and rural society.[51] Doddridge's translation of the New Testament from the original Greek, juxtaposing the four Gospels with commentaries and devotional exercises, was the first work of its kind designed to give to the public an opportunity of studying the scriptures with open and alert minds. *The Family Expositor* retained its popularity for well over a century. The Revd Richard Pearsall wrote to Doddridge: 'there is no one whose works have been translated into such various languages, and have had so wide a spread'.[52] William Carey made use of it when translating the first Bengali version of the New Testament from Greek. Together with others of Doddridge's writings, *The Family Expositor* had a marked influence on the reformation of family life, playing a considerable part in the extraordinary idealization of domestic life during the late eighteenth and nineteenth centuries. Everitt writes 'The reference to heaven as the

# THE

# PRINCIPLES

## OF THE

## Chriſtian Religion,

Expreſſed in

Plain and Eaſy VERSE,

And divided into ſhort LESSONS for
the Uſe of little CHILDREN.

*By* P. DODDRIDGE, *D. D.*

JESUS *ſaid unto* Peter,——*Loveſt thou me?*——*Feed*
*my Lambs.* John xxi. 15.

## *L O N D O N:*

Printed, and Sold by M. FENNER, at the *Turk's*
*Head* in *Gracechurch-ſtreet.* MDCCXLIII.
[ Price 4 *d.* ]

27. Doddridge understood the importance of religious education;
influenced by Isaac Watts, he published verses 'for the use of
little Children'.

*home* of the exiled human spirit does not seem to become general in England till the time of the great Nonconformist Philip Doddridge in the 1730s and 40s.'[53]

Doddridge placed great emphasis upon the family as the unit of religious education. In 1732 he published four *Sermons on the . . . Education of children* in which there is much good advice to all parents on the upbringing of their children. On the question of discipline, for example, he writes, 'Take heed—that your corrections be not too frequent,—or too severe—and that they be not given in an unbecoming manner . . . .'[54] Doddridge urged a duty upon all parents for the religious education of their children; nothing else was more important because 'there is nothing in which the comfort of families, the prosperity of nations, the salvation of souls, the interest of a Redeemer, and the glory of God, is more apparently and intimately concerned'.[55]

He was anxious that contemporary children should become 'a seed who shall serve the Lord' in future years. In 1735 he published seven *Sermons to Young Persons* which became extremely popular and widely read. Dedicated to 'the young persons belonging to the Dissenting Congregations at Hinckley, Harborough and Kibworth in Leicestershire, and at Ashley, and Northampton' the sermons make a strong evangelistic appeal emphasising approaching judgement. Above all, Doddridge's message is clear: 'While you are yourselves instances of the happy consequences which attend a religious education, I hope you will be singularly careful, that your descendants may share in the like advantages.[56] It is the same theme that prefaced his *Rise and Progress*, a desire that his words would carry over to future generations and thus strengthen the Christian cause. The same concern motivated his *The Principles of the Christian Religion, . . . in . . . verse . . . for the use of little Children* which appeared in 1743. Watts' verses to children had served as a prototype. Doddridge's friend the Revd John Barker wrote in November 1743: 'I am glad to hear your Poetry will be admitted into the Royal House. May [it] do as much good there as in cottages. . . .'[57] Dr Francis Ayscough, tutor to the royal children, corresponded with Doddridge and asked his advice on educational matters; on one occasion he told him that young Prince George (the future George III) had been learning his verses by heart.

Doddridge had wide contacts in this country, and his correspondence shows the multiplicity of his educational interests. He furnished John Wesley with an extensive booklist for his preachers, and there is little doubt that the work and reputation of the Northampton academy directly influenced Wesley's founding of Kingswood school, which was

29. Selina Hastings, Countess of Huntingdon, was noted for her piety and evangelical fervour. She often wrote to Doddridge, and during his final illness provided one hundred pounds to help pay his passage to Lisbon.

28. Isaac Watts D.D. was a popular writer on theological subjects, and became famed for his hymns. Doddridge was greatly influenced by him, and was co-editor of Watts' works after his death in 1748.

30. Doddridge Chapel (Castle Hill) in 1887.

31. Doddridge Chapel (Castle Hill) in 1894, showing the vestibule added in 1890 and the palisade and gates donated by All Saints Church in 1893.

32. Doddridge and Commercial Street United Reformed Church (Castle Hill) in 1979; interior facing north. This half of the church was added in 1862. The memorial to Doddridge is situated above the pulpit.

33. Doddridge and Commercial Street United Reformed Church (Castle Hill) in 1979; interior facing south. Under the gallery to the west is the entrance to Doddridge's vestry, which marked the north-west extremity of the original building until 1862.

34. George Whitefield, the fiery
Methodist preacher. When he came
to Castle Hill in 1743, the north
windows were removed so that the
crowds outside could hear him
preach.

35. James Hervey was Vicar of
Weston Favell, a popular writer, and
friend of Doddridge.

organised as an academy open to boys between the ages of six and twelve. Doddridge was greatly respected at both the Universities of Oxford and Cambridge; at the latter Dr Conyers Middleton showed him 'the fine university Library & some of the most curious Manuscripts in the World'.[58] In 1744 the Principal of Hertford College, Richard Newton, requested to see Doddridge's plan of education and enclosed a pre-publication copy of the college's statutes for Doddridge's perusal. Other correspondents from Oxford were Thomas Hunt, the eminent orientalist, and George Costard a writer on astronomy.

Doddridge's influence and interest in education was not confined to England. He corresponded with David Fordyce, Professor of Moral Philosophy at Aberdeen. In 1745 Doddridge was elected as a corresponding member of the Scottish Society for the Propagation of Christian Knowledge. Across the Atlantic great interest was shown in the Northampton academy. Through the Revd Daniel Wadsworth who was a trustee of the Yale College, Connecticut, Doddridge sent copies of his books for the college library. He was interested in the foundation of New Jersey College (now Princeton University) and was requested to send a letter of advice to the students. Doddridge also involved himself in a dispute over religious intolerance in Virginia, and corresponded with the Bishop of London under whose authority the colonies came.

Doddridge was realistic enough to hope that the results of much of his work would be seen in later generations. At times he became acutely depressed, considering himself an 'unworthy and unprofitable creature'. However, assisted by cheerful friends his essentially buoyant optimism would soon return. As late as May 1751 with the ravages of consumption becoming increasingly apparent, he was still making plans for a major scheme to ease the shortage of Dissenting ministers. In the previous September he had begun sending out 'circular letters to engage all the ministers in the country' in his 'Youths' scheme' which he considered a necessary 'sheet anchor' for the future of the churches. To the very end he poured forth his considerable knowledge and experience, using what failing strength he had left, in the service of his Lord.

## ☙ 6 ❧

# A Man in His Time

The Northampton to which Philip Doddridge came had greatly changed from the town of the late Stuart period. Between 1500 and 1700 virtually every major English town suffered some destruction by fire, and in 1675 Northampton was largely destroyed by a massive conflagration. The town had long experienced traffic congestion with horses, waggons and pedestrians crowded into the narrow streets, especially on market days. Thus 'the townsmen actually made a virtue of necessity and used the opportunity of the fire to rebuild parts of the town in a grander style with wide streets and brick houses, in order to attract the patronage of the gentry and professional men'.[1] It was to this changed urban scene that Doddridge ministered, seeing daily the stone-built houses and tiled roofs that emulated the fashionable buildings of London, instead of the timber and thatch constructions of earlier generations.

With a population of between four and five thousand, Northampton was a typical regional centre which provided a focal point for the social and political life of the gentry, and for the operation of the local economy. The town manufactured footwear and textiles, and was a centre for the distribution of agricultural seed in the Midlands, and an important market for horses. Linked with other major towns in the intricate network of carrier routes, Northampton boasted no fewer than sixty-two inns and numerous alehouses. Some establishments like the *George*, *Peacock* and *Red Lion*[2] were gallant and stately structures; others, situated in the suburbs of St James' End and Cotton End were well placed to serve the drovers' trade that existed along ancient routeways. In all, there was stabling for no fewer than five thousand horses in the town.

During every third week of September the town was thronged with those who came for the annual horse races. In October there were public breakfasts and card parties for the gentry; from December to February the three principal inns were the venue for the Northampton assemblies.

Notes and references for this chapter begin on page 166

Cock fighting was a popular pastime and the annual Florists' feasts, Carnation feasts and Gardeners' Society meetings drew large crowds from all social classes. Prize fights, wrestling, pugilistics, swordsmanship, concerts, plays, exhibitions and musical and literary activities were all part of Northampton life.[3] Although Doddridge was critical of some aspects of urban life he could not help but be involved in the cultural, social, and political life of the community.

He was a man of sincere Christian conviction, showing a genuine warmth to all with whom he spoke or corresponded. He became a familiar figure in the streets of Northampton, and his church and academy were well-known landmarks. He also dispensed money that others had entrusted to him for charitable purposes.[4] Orton tells us that he had 'great compassion for the industrious poor, visited their families, enquired into their circumstances and . . . gave away a great number of his smaller pieces, among the poor of the town and neighbourhood where he lived, without distinction of parties'.[5]

Orton also recalls that 'His temper was unsuspicious, mild and sweet; and in his tongue was the law of kindness. . . . His candour led him to think more favourably of some persons than they deserved'.[6] The Revd John Barker, one of his most affectionate yet outspoken correspondents wrote:

> I love you beyond expression . . . and yet I often Make My-selfe Merry with your Character & Conduct. . . . [You] are so perfectly Made Up of Civility candour and good nature, that a pious Enthusiast, or a godly Dunce, or an upright Arian &c. is Welcome to your table arms and heart. You are so good yourselfe that you thinke every Body ten times better than they are.[7]

Doddridge certainly seems to have been guileless, and believed many tall stories especially those couched in overtones of piety. In 1741 he became involved in a sensational murder trial in Northampton. An Irish Roman Catholic, Bryan Connell, was found guilty at the assizes of savagely murdering a Weedon butcher by the name of Richard Brimley on 4 April 1739. Connell was said to have inflicted on Brimley fourteen or fifteen vicious wounds and had 'cut off his Head, so that it hung only by some Sinews'.[8] Doddridge visited the condemned prisoner in order to give him what spiritual comfort he could; two of the students, John Olding and John West, also visited Connell, who protested his innocence and claimed that he had been the victim of perjury. Doddridge became 'so struck with the affair that I obtained time of the Under-sheriff to make Enquiry into the Truth of what he had told me'. Earlier, Doddridge had written to Clark of 'the conviction of the inhuman wretch Connell, by whom an honest neighbour of ours was butchered two years ago'. Now he applauded 'the singular interposition of that God who brings to light the hidden things of darkness'.[9] Doddridge acted fast to ascertain what truth he could. One of his students, Benjamin Fawcett, was despatched to Chester to collect further evidence; testimony was obtained from five creditable persons that Connell had been many miles away from the scene of the murder at the time it took place. But in spite of Doddridge's valiant efforts to re-open the case, Connell met his fate on 3 April 1741 two years after Brimley's murder. Doddridge wrote with feeling, Connell 'wished he might before he died have leave to kneel down at the threshold of my door, to pray for me and mine; which indeed he did in the most earnest manner, on his knees, just before he was taken out for execution.'[10]

Few had sided with Doddridge in his efforts to obtain Connell's freedom, and some uncharitably charged him with being a secret Papist. Two years later Doddridge was involved in a similar case at the Northampton Assizes. After a fight at the *Blackamoor's Head* in Kettering in which Benjamin Meadows was murdered, two men William Porter and William Attenborough, were found guilty. Doddridge visited them regarding their 'eternal concerns' as he had Connell, and was impressed by the story Attenborough told him of his innocence. Doddridge managed to gain a stay of execution for fifteen days, but both were hanged in March 1743.[11]

The mystical outpourings of Mary Wills of Pitsford intrigued Doddridge. Claiming to have oracular powers she foretold Doddridge's coming to Northampton and even detailed the text on which he would preach; she divined many of his private thoughts and actions, foretold the death of his beloved daughter 'Tetsy'[12] and warned of the invasion of the Pretender. Doddridge was impressed by her, and took several of her sayings very much to heart.

In some ways Doddridge epitomises contrasting viewpoints in the eighteenth century; on the one hand he held to a Calvinist view of the world in which a supernatural agency was constantly at work, while on the other we see his deep and growing interest in scientific subjects. The high incidence of sickness and death is a constant undercurrent in Doddridge's correspondence and diary, and in September 1739 he wrote: '. . . it pleased God to afflict me with a violent fever, which assaulted me in such a manner that had he not been pleased to put a stop to its fury, it must quickly have ended in my death.'[13] To Doddridge there was no doubt that it was the direct work of God; and in this he shared the almost universal belief of his times in God's supernatural agency. Cattle disease in the County in October 1747, allied to the moral state of the nation, he considered as cause for serious humbling before God. In the previous September he had written to Mercy:

> The Distemper among the Cattle prevails more & more. Of 240 Cows at Walgrave six miles from hence 210 are dead. In the Neighbourhood of Daventry a much worse Calamity is broke out. A pestitential kind of Distemper among the Children which occasions a Swelling of the Throat in which they die in three Days & some whole Families are swept away with this Besom of Destruction. What will the End of these Things be. Many Pastures are utterly desolate. Tis said Butter will be a shilling [5p] or 18d [7½p] per pound & hardly any Milk is on any Terms to be had in several Towns.[14]

On 28 July 1738 a fierce fire broke out in Wellingborough which resulted in the gutting of over two hundred houses and numerous other buildings; so intense was the heat that molten lead cascaded down from the church roof. Damage was calculated at about £26,000; Northampton in common with other local towns sent financial help for the relief of the sufferers.[15] On the following 9 November a day of fasting and prayer was observed in Wellingborough at which Doddridge was asked to preach. Taking his text from Amos iv verse 2 on the overthrow of Sodom and Gomorrah, Doddridge addressed the inhabitants of Wellingborough in unequivocal terms; they were 'brands pluckt out of the Burning' which had been kindled by the judgement of God. Such judgement was also to be seen at work in 'Drought, Blasting, and Mildew, from the Palmer–worm [hairy caterpillar], and the Pestilence'. Yet it was those who withstood the trials of faith who ultimately found salvation in the City of God 'where no flames shall be felt'.

The Day of Judgement was seen by many to be imminent through earthquakes and other unusual phenomena. In February and March 1750 tremors shook London causing widespread alarm. Writing to Doddridge after the second shock Henry Baker spoke of 'a most extraordinary light' which had 'appeared in the sky towards the south east, between six and seven in the evening, and surprised the whole town with the apprehension of a great fire'; a strange diffused light continued throughout 'the whole night after'. Baker commented 'One cannot, I think, let such uncommon phaenomena pass unheeded: if these terrors of the Almighty will not excite reflection, surely nothing will.'[16]

On 20 August 1749 Doddridge had preached a sermon entitled *The Guilt and Doom of Capernaum* to a large audience at the Salters' Hall in London. Although the sermon showed Doddridge's concern at the 'Lethargick State of so many Souls' he was too busy with his *Family Expositor* to prepare the sermon for the press. The violent events of the following February and March however, left Doddridge with a feeling of horror; he felt duty-bound to publish his earlier sermon, believing the earthquakes to be a warning of impending judgement:

> You have now, Sirs, very lately had repeated and surprising Demonstrations of the Almighty Power of that Infinite and adorable Being, whom, in the midst of your various Hurries and Amusements, you are so ready to forget. His Hand hath once and again within these five Weeks lifted up your mighty City from its Basis, and shook its Million of Inhabitants in all their Dwellings. The Palaces of the Great, yea even of the Greatest, have not been exempted; that the Princes of the Land might be wise, and its Judges and Lawgivers might receive Instruction. . . . The second Shock was it seems more dreadful than the first; and may not the third be yet more dreadful than the second? So that this last may seem as a merciful Signal to prepare—for what may with the most terrible Propriety be called an untimely Grave indeed; a Grave that shall receive the Living with the Dead. . . . Let me then beseech those that have neglected Religion, to think more attentively of it; and those that trifle in it, more seriously to lay it to Heart.[17]

Thomas Sherlock, the Bishop of London, wrote to Doddridge congratulating him on his 'very excellent and seasonable sermon'.[18] On 30 September another tremor affected parts of Northamptonshire; Creaton, Cottesbrooke, Kelmarsh, Maidwell, Weston and other villages between Northampton and Market Harborough felt its full force. Steeple bells clattered, houses shook and in Northampton a chimney stack toppled into College Lane. Doddridge, in response to Baker's request, submitted a detailed report for the perusal of the Royal Society.[19]

On 11 November 1743 the Northampton Philosophical Society was formed, consisting of professional gentlemen who met to discuss scientific matters and undertake experiments. Amongst the members was Edward Cave, founder of the *Gentleman's Magazine*, Dr Johnson's publisher, and proprietor of the Northampton Cotton Mills, which were situated beside the Nene. With him were William Shipley, who in later life founded the Society of Arts in London, and Thomas Yeoman,[20] who was the manager of the Cotton Mills and later a Fellow of the Royal Society. Doddridge was an active member from the Philosophical Society's inception, and in 1744 read two papers on *The Doctrine of Pendulums* and *The Laws of the Communication of Motion as well in elastic as in non-elastic Bodies*.

Doddridge was in close association with the Royal Society and three papers by him, one on the earthquake of 1750, are in the published *Transactions*. In 1737 he had described a dangerous experiment by a Mr Oliver who had allowed a viper to bite his finger in order to prove the efficacy of his experimental antidote: 'He applied his specific immediately,' wrote Doddridge, 'and though he was exceedingly ill all night, his hand and arm being violently inflamed, and his whole body somewhat convulsed, yet he is this morning perfectly recovered.'[21] Ten years later we find Doddridge corresponding with Henry Baker on electrical experiments across the Thames at Westminster.[22] In 1750 he wrote to Baker on the question of lockjaw, recalling the death some years earlier of one of his students, William Worcester, who had been pierced in the foot by a piece of bone whilst playing football. At other times he corresponded on subjects ranging from the dissection of a locust, to reports of people claiming to have second sight. Fascinated by unusual occurrences, he wrote in July 1744 of visiting the exact spot in Ipswich where an old woman mysteriously burned to ashes, apparently by spontaneous combustion. Four years later he sent a detailed report to Henry Baker of a monstrous lamb (Siamese twins) born at Newport Pagnell which had been brought to him for inspection.[23]

The ambivalence between his belief in divine activity through the natural world and his search for a more rational explanation, can best be seen in the question of inoculation against smallpox. Doddridge well knew the horrors of this scourge; he attempted to change the prevalent belief that inoculation was meddling in divine affairs, and would be punished by the visitation of yet more disease. In 1750, when smallpox was raging in local villages, he published from the original manuscript of the late David Some written in 1725; *The Case of Receiving the Small-pox by Inoculation, Impartially considered, and especially in a Religious View*. Doddridge, always anxious to alleviate suffering, affixed to the title the bold text, 'I will ask you one Thing, Is it lawful . . . to save Life, or to destroy it?' (see Appendix V).

Northampton was served by two physicians in the early 1740s, but

# THE
# CASE

Of Receiving the

# SMALL-POX

BY

# INOCULATION,

Impartially confidered, and efpecially
in a Religious View.

Written in the Year M.DCC.XXV.

By the late

Rev<sup>d</sup>. Mr. DAVID SOME,

of *Harborough*:

And now publifhed from the Original Manufcript,

*By* P. DODDRIDGE, *D.D.*

*I will afk you one Thing, Is it lawful to fave Life, or to
deftroy it ?* Luke vi. 9.

LONDON:
*Printed for* James Buckland, *in* Pater-nofter Row; *and*
James Waugh, *in* Lombard-Street. M.DCC.L.

36. Doddridge attempted to change public attitudes towards inoculation against
smallpox by publishing the late David Some's paper on the subject.

in March 1743 Dr (later Sir) James Stonhouse arrived in the town from Coventry.[24] Possessed of an ample fortune he settled in Northampton and, as Doddridge recorded, 'has determined to fix here, and wait an opportunity of doing something as a physician when either of those already settled in the town may drop, for till then he has but very little expectation'.[25] Stonhouse was aged twenty-seven and had lived a reckless life, often finding himself in trouble over rash statements; he had already published a pamphlet against Christianity. The death of his young wife left him in the depths of despair, but it was Doddridge's *Rise and Progress*, together with the friendship and advice of Doddridge himself and their mutual friend, the Revd James Hervey of Weston Favell, that induced a change of heart in Stonhouse. Obeying the instructions laid down in the will of a former patient, Stonhouse went to her funeral at Castle Hill Church; there, standing inconspicuously at the back, he listened to Doddridge preaching—the words sank deep into his heart. He eventually recanted his anti-Christian views, becoming a clergyman in the Church of England.

Stonhouse and Doddridge became firm friends, and together set on foot the foundation of the present Northampton General Hospital. Earlier in 1731 John Rushworth, a Northampton physician, had highlighted in a pamphlet the desperate need for every county to have its own infirmary; apart from London and Edinburgh none existed. Very slowly infirmaries in the provinces began to be opened, the first at Winchester in 1736, followed in the next year by one at Bristol.[26] Christian leaders within both the established church and Dissent were active in such initiatives. Doddridge and Stonhouse formed a determined partnership, but the impetus for the Northampton scheme undoubtedly derived from Doddridge's immense energy.

The first task was to involve men of means and public influence. The Duke of Montagu, Lord Lieutenant of Northamptonshire, agreed to be 'Grand Visitor' and the Earl of Northampton 'The Perpetual President'. With the support of Joseph Jekyll of Dallington, Ambrose Isted of Ecton and the Earl of Halifax, the whole scheme was proposed at the summer assizes in July 1743; it was warmly received by the grand jury. In a published *Plan for the more immediate Execution of the Proposals for Establishing a County Hospital at Northampton* the writer urged:

> Let no trifling Objection, no slight Misrepresentations, or Party Feuds . . . deter us from that fundamental Principle of Morality, THE DOING AS WE WOULD BE DONE BY. Let nothing discourage our

Compaſſion to the SICK recommended and urged,

IN A

# SERMON

PREACHED AT

## NORTHAMPTON,

SEPTEMBER 4, 1743.

In Favour of a Deſign then opening to erect a COUNTY INFIRMARY there for the Relief of the Poor *Sick* and *Lame.*

---

*Publiſhed at the Requeſt of ſeveral who heard it.*

## By P. DODDRIDGE, *D. D.*

*Homines ad Deum nullâ Re propius accedunt, quam* Salutem *Hominibus dando.* Cic. pro Lig. *ad fin.*

---

## LONDON:

Printed for M. FENNER, at the *Turk's Head* in *Gracechurch-ſtreet*; and W. DICEY, at *Northampton.* M DCC XLIII.

[ Price Six-pence. ]

---

37. Doddridge's eloquent preaching greatly contributed to the founding of the County Infirmary in Northampton in 1743.

charitable Brethren: He that observeth the Wind shall not sow, and he that regardeth the Clouds shall not reap. . . .'[27]

The style and sentiments are unmistakably Doddridge's, as are the practical details of providing a suitable house and gardens for the hospital, the employment of competent physicians and 'A prudent Man to dispense the Medicines &c with a Motherly Woman to reside constantly in it'. Other details such as the provision of 'Fire, Candles and Soap' were all carefully arranged.

On 4 September Doddridge preached a sermon at Castle Hill advocating the foundation of the hospital. The sermon was subsequently printed and widely circulated. William Dicey, editor of the *Northampton Mercury* supported the scheme, and frequently printed the latest news of 'this Glorious Undertaking'. Thus public opinion was roused. On 20 September the scheme was accepted at a large meeting of 'Nobility, Gentry and Clergy' at the *George* inn. Subscriptions poured in for the £750 needed to open the proposed eighty-bed infirmary in a hastily adapted house situated in George Row. The opening had been scheduled for the following Lady Day, and Doddridge became worried that the subscriptions might prove inadequate; by December 1743 six hundred pounds had been collected. In January 1744 he wrote of his disappointments: 'The Clergy are strangely backward on the Occasion & I fear my Sermon has rather alienated that [than] conciliated their Regard. For among some men even Charity grows odious when recommended by a Dissenter.'[28]

With characteristic modesty Doddridge took an inconspicuous part in the formal opening of the infirmary on 29 March 1744, when civic dignitaries went in procession to All Saints Church to hear the rector of Hinton, Dr Richard Grey, preach the inaugural sermon. In the following June Doddridge spoke of 'the obligation which our town and county owes to him [i.e. Stonhouse] as the founder of our Infirmary'.[29] Once begun, the work of the hospital was constantly supported by Doddridge who annually gave five guineas from his stipend. He was chairman of the 'Weekly Committee' on various occasions, constantly visited the hospital, drew up reports, rectified irregularities and misunderstandings, and encouraged financial support from other Dissenting churches in the County. The Bishops of Worcester and Oxford wrote to Doddridge congratulating him on his work. He in turn was delighted to see them establishing similar institutions in their own cathedral cities modelled on the Northampton venture.

Doddridge was respected in Northampton not only for his involvement in public life, but for his unwavering moral principles. In December 1742 he attended a banquet at which Sir John Robinson had used 'dreadful expletives'. Doddridge promptly left as a personal protest; the following day Sir John received a firm yet not unpleasant letter upbraiding him on his unbecoming use of 'the venerable name of the ever blessed God in so light a manner'. The Earl of Halifax, impressed, exclaimed: 'Ah, there goes a Christian and a gentleman.'

Like all Dissenters, Doddridge was an ardent supporter of the Hanoverian monarchy. He was wise enough to realise that the contemporary generation of young Dissenters, not having experienced the persecutions of their forefathers, might be growing slack in their vigilance towards the enemies of their liberty. In comparison with the polished and cultured image of the Stuarts, the Hanoverians seemed rather dull and mundane; consequently many people did not care who reigned. But leading Dissenters were again active in the 1730s, warning their followers against a Stuart return to power and the re-establishment of Catholicism. In Northampton Doddridge lectured on the subject, and in 1736 preached a sermon which was later printed entitled *The Absurdity and Iniquity of Persecution for Conscience-sake.* It was prefaced by David Some who wrote: 'The emissaries of the Roman See are so far from giving up their Cause in this Kingdom as lost, that the most distant Prospects of Success produce new and vigorous Efforts to promote it.'[30] Doddridge was intent on showing how unjustifiable persecution was on religious, moral and practical grounds, yet he well knew that political intrigues were undermining the security of the nation. In 1727, upon the death of George I, Doddridge had preached eloquently in favour of the Hanoverian succession. Consequently he became a target of Jacobite hostility.[31] In 1740 he spoke out again in a sermon, *Necessity of a General Reformation . . . to . . . Success in War,* which showed his disquiet over the moral and religious state of contemporary society.

Whilst the undercurrent of political instability eddied in the background Doddridge continued with his many duties. His warmth and kindness resulted in many real and lasting friendships, and one in particular during this period was remarkable. Most of his closest friends were Dissenting ministers, but a bond of deep affection was forged between Doddridge and a Scottish cavalry officer, Colonel James Gardiner. A one-time atheist and loose-liver, Gardiner had had an amazing conversion when *en route* to an assignation with a married woman. Coming into contact with each other Doddridge and Gardiner commenced 'an enduring intimacy' which only ended with the latter's untimely death.

Writing to his wife in June 1741 Doddridge spoke of his hopes that the Colonel would stay with his troop as long as possible in Northampton, and that they would not keep missing meeting each other 'like buckets in a well'. Doddridge had welcomed Gardiner to communion at Castle Hill and was even prepared to alter the date of the Lord's Supper, 'for it is something very much like Heaven to me to meet that excellent Christian at the Lords Table'.[32] Whenever he could, the Colonel would visit Doddridge's home:

> With his Hessian boots, and their tremendous spurs, sustaining the grandeur of his scarlet coat and powdered queue, there was something to youthful imagination very awful in the tall and stately hussar; and that awe was nowise abated when they looked on his high forehead, with overhung grey eyes, and weather-beaten cheeks, and when they marked his fine and dauntless air.[33]

In June 1743 the Colonel spent several days with the Doddridge family, during which the conversation turned on the political uncertainties of the times. Doddridge expressed his worries 'with the sad state of things as to religion and morals', and that he was surprised that an invasion from France in favour of the Pretender had not been mounted earlier. In 1745 Charles Edward Stuart the Young Pretender left Brittany and landed at Eriskay in the Hebrides on 23 July. By 19 August he had raised his standard at Glenfinnan, claiming the throne of England on behalf of his father. Perth and Edinburgh were quickly taken. Doddridge was keenly excited by the news; Mary Wills had foretold the invasion six years previously, predicting a great and dangerous threat to the English throne which would have to be settled by the sword. Colonel Gardiner took a sad leave of the Doddridge family and proceeded northwards with his regiment under General Cope. On 21 September the loyalist troops engaged the enemy in a fierce battle at Prestonpans, less than a mile from Gardiner's home at Bankton. Cope seems to have been incompetent as a general, and not willing to listen to Gardiner's advice as to the best terrain on which to fight. 'Taken almost by surprise in the early hours of the morning, the royal troops had behaved disgracefully. Gardiner's dragoons fled at the first onset, and their unfortunate commander received two gunshot wounds in the body and a sword-cut on the head, of which he died in the Manse of Tranent the following day.'[34]

Doddridge was deeply distressed when the news reached him. Writing to Isaac Watts he confessed: 'Never was my Heart more painfully wounded that [than] by the Death of dear Colonel Gardiner.'[35] Realising the full import of the news from Prestonpans, Doddridge knew that unless the Pretender's southward march was halted, London and the throne lay at the mercy of the Scots. A few days before the battle of Prestonpans, Doddridge wrote to the Earl of Halifax suggesting that measures should be taken to defend the country. Halifax replied on 19 September agreeing with Doddridge's sense of urgency, even though 'this rebellion is not yet considered in so serious a light as to render any extraordinary offers of this nature acceptable to those in power'. Nevertheless Halifax promised to 'spur up those, who have the care of the whole, to the same spirit that animates myself and you'.[36]

The following week Doddridge dined with Halifax upon his return to Horton, and the two men discussed the possibility of raising a volunteer force in and about Northampton. Within days a public meeting was held at the *George* inn at which Halifax spoke of the need to defend the County. Already the whole tone of public debate on the misguided rebels had begun to change from ridicule to panic. The newspapers represented the Young Pretender's forces as wild savages ready to destroy all and everything in their path. Doddridge sent out a printed circular by special messengers to all Dissenting ministers in the locality urging their support. Fourteen or sixteen of the chief members in his own congregation supported him. In a short time Halifax and Doddridge raised a force of eight hundred and fourteen men; the Duke of Bedford recruited a similar force, and the Duke of Montagu brought in a troop of two hundred and seventy-three cavalry.

Northampton became a focal point of military activity. 'Soldiers were exercised daily; and every hour troops and rations and ammunition and other war material were hurried through the town for the North.'[37] On 9 October Field Marshal Wade, Commander in Chief of the loyalist forces in the north, reached the town, stayed the night at the *George*, and hurried on early the next day. Two days later the Mayor, John Gibson, issued a public proclamation inviting 'all the Inhabitants able to bear Arms to enter into Associations for the Defence of his Majesty's Person and Government and the Preservation of our happy Constitution in Church and State'. The bonfires on 5 November now had added significance for the town; the day had been 'usher'd in with Ringing of Bells', civic leaders had attended a special service at All Saints, whence the Mayor and corporation proceeded to the Guildhall to drink loyal toasts to the King. In the evening outside Doddridge's academy an effigy of the Young Pretender was burned on a huge bonfire. On 11 November 1745 the *Northampton Mercury* recorded that 'the Doctor's House was finely illuminated, the Candles, by their Position, forming these Words, KING GEORGE, NO PRETENDER; there were also Sky Rockets, and other Fireworks'. A massive public demonstration concluded the evening.

Doddridge's energy knew no bounds. On 13 October he wrote to Samuel Clark that he had sent Halifax another 'twenty-four brave soldiers', adding 'we join in a weekly Contribution for supporting them when they are to march out; but I am in great hopes the rebels will quickly disperse without a battle, else I fear it will be a very obstinate one. We have had renewed Days of Fasting & Prayer'.[38] By mid November the regiment was ready and left the town on the 22nd/23rd of the month. One of Doddridge's students, Lord Kilkerran's son John,[39] carried the standard in the Earl of Halifax's contingent.

All became bustle and panic in Northampton with news that the insurgents had reached Derbyshire, and were intending to march on Northampton. Many fled from the town and others buried their valuables. By early December the Duke of Cumberland was planning to give battle in the open countryside on Harlestone Heath. Meanwhile Doddridge urged the Secretary of State to make good use of 'the zeal of thousands of able-bodied men in different stations, who would gladly learn discipline and serve on occasion near home, if properly authorised, under gentlemen of approved attachment to the Government'.[40] It was an urgent call for a locally based defence force covering the entire country.

Prince Charles Edward Stuart's plans had relied largely on the English Jacobites rising in his support; but having reached as far south as Derby without receiving any substantial support, some five thousand Highlanders stood alone. News from Northampton of the preparations being made for battle, as well as reports of the armies loyal to the English throne gathering to oppose them, proved decisive.[41] The Scots turned back; from that moment their cause was lost and at the battle of Culloden on 16 April 1746 received its death blow.

On 9 February Doddridge preached at Castle Hill after hearing of the precipitate flight of the rebels from Stirling. *Deliverance out of the Hands of our Enemies* was the substance of two sermons in which Doddridge urged his hearers to be thankful: 'Far be it from any of us to resemble the nine lepers, who though they had been so loud in their cries for mercy under their affliction as to be heard afar off, yet having received their cure returned not to give glory to God.'[42]

Throughout the turbulent months of the rebellion Doddridge had remained the man of compassion. Upon hearing of Colonel Gardiner's death he wrote several letters to his widow Lady Frances and her daughter

Fanny, offering spiritual comfort and guidance. Doddridge, whilst willing to defend the liberties of Englishmen, was nevertheless shocked by the barbarities of Culloden; on the first anniversary of the battle he published at his own expense *A Friendly Letter to the Private Soldiers in a Regiment of Foot, one of those engaged in the Important and Glorious Battle of Culloden,* an evangelical tract that attacked the usual vices of soldiers. Doddridge was instrumental through the Earl of Halifax in saving a deserter's life, and on 19 August 1746 was present in London at the executions of two of the rebel leaders—the Lords Kilmarnock and Balmerino; it was an event which saddened him considerably, particularly as Kilmarnock had declared himself a Presbyterian.

Writing of the importance of Doddridge's perception of the grave danger to the English constitution, Stanford notes that 'we claim for him the honour of being the first Englishman in a private station who took action, and roused his countrymen to the like, in defending the threatened throne and liberties of our land'.[43]

The same readiness to take decisive action, though in this case in theological matters, had been shown four years earlier in 1742 when Doddridge refuted a cleverly disguised attack entitled *Christianity not founded on argument.* The pamphlet, written anonymously by the deist Henry Dodwell, was cunningly deceptive in that its apparent intention of supporting Christianity was a mere facade; its underlying motive was to prove that no rational basis could exist to support faith. A number of Christians were deceived by the book but not Doddridge, who published an *Answer* in the form of three separate letters. Writing to his wife who was in Bath, Doddridge commented on the 'most artful Attempt, in the Person of a Methodist but [made] indeed by a very sagacious Deist to subvert Christianity; and it wounds as a two edged sword, tending most dangerously to spread mad enthusiasm among some, and utter irreligion among others'.[44] To his ministerial colleague Samuel Wood he wrote: 'I am engaged in a controversy with one whom I take to be one of the most Dangerous Writers I have met with.'[45] Doddridge was shrewd enough to see the possible consequences upon 'the foundation of natural religion, as well as of revealed'.[46]

Doddridge was more than a match for the clever dialectic of Dodwell, and took him to task point by point, concluding perceptively that in his view the author of the pamphlet was 'a kind of humorous sceptic, who intended chiefly to amuse the world'.[47] Yet Doddridge took note of Dodwell's criticisms of Christians who embraced their religion before carefully considering what they were accepting. Such comments rein-

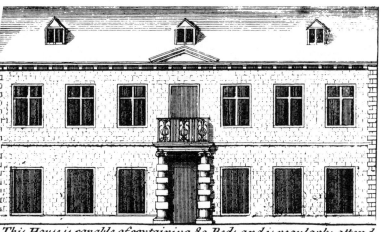

*The public* **INFIRMARY** *for reception of Sick and Lame.* **Poor** *supported by voluntary Subscriptions & Benefactions*

*This House is capable of containing 80 Beds, and is regularly attended by Physicians & Surgeons. The number of out-patients is unlimited, who are supply'd with medicines & advice gratis upon every* **Saturday**, *between the hours of eleven & one; at which time a committee of Governors together with the Physicians and Surgeons punctually meet. So commendable a spirit appear'd in the Nobility and Gentry of the County on proposing this* **Infirmary**, *in 1743, that it was resolv'd on & establish'd in less than two months.* Gent. Mag. 1743. p. 506. 650

38. The County Infirmary, Northampton, from Noble and Butlin's plan of the town (1747). Doddridge and Dr James Stonhouse were co-founders of this important enterprise.

39. The former County Infirmary in George Row in 1979. The facade of the building remains substantially unaltered from Doddridge's time. Other parts of the building to the rear are occupied by the Town and County Club.

42. A jewel cabinet, covered in seventeenth century stump work embroidery, representing scenes from the Book of Esther. It was inherited by Doddridge and was in his house in Sheep Street, Northampton, when he died.

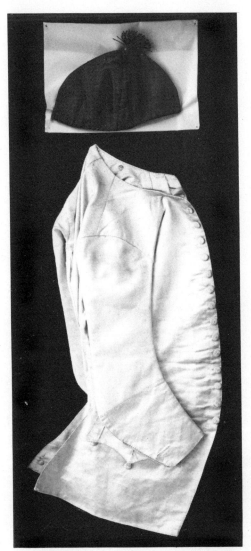

40. Doddridge's skull cap. Also the coat he was wearing on the day of his death.

43. A small brass candle lantern said to have been used by Mercy Doddridge to light her way to chapel after her husband's death. The lantern can be folded flat.

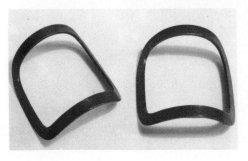

41. A pair of Doddridge's shoe buckles.

forced Doddridge's passionate belief that not only Dissenting ministers but their congregations too, should be well educated in the essentials of their faith. Truth, Doddridge asserted, had no need of any authority save that of itself. Doddridge's reply to Dodwell's attack showed him as an incisive and formidable Christian apologist; Christians in both the Church of England and Dissent were quick to congratulate him.

Doddridge maintained a large circle of friends and acquaintances. His vast correspondence kept him extremely busy and although occasionally he would ask one of his students to write out a letter dictated by himself, he had no regular amanuensis. On one occasion he had tried hard for a fortnight to catch up with his replies to letters, but still had one hundred and six left to answer. Some of his correspondents merely wrote in order to get a courteous reply from 'Doctor Doddridge', but most had matters of importance to discuss, or news to impart. Virtually all show a remarkable degree of respect and affection for him.

Although Northampton was the centre for his varied activities, Doddridge's influence spread far and wide. Not only did he correspond with educationalists and ministers in America, he was also in touch with Presbyterian ministers in Rotterdam and Amsterdam. Three students in the academy came from Holland,[48] and Doddridge corresponded with their parents and their churches. At the request of David Longueville, the English Presbyterian minister in Amsterdam, Doddridge wrote two *Addresses to Dutch Protestants* at a time of political turmoil (1747–8); these were translated into Dutch by Longueville, and subsequently into French by Pierre Courtonne of the Walloon Church in Amsterdam. Through such translations Doddridge gained a high reputation abroad.

Doddridge was in close touch with bishops and clergy of the established church; indeed he was invited by the Archbishop of Canterbury to Lambeth Palace on three separate occasions to discuss a number of matters, especially ideas for bringing about greater 'comprehension' between Anglicans and Dissenters. Requests for Doddridge's advice on literary and theological matters were frequent. In 1748 he edited the works of Archbishop Leighton of Glasgow, and abridged the second volume of Bishop Warburton's *Divine Legation*. In 1741 he gave advice to the Revd John Jones, an Anglican clergyman, before the publication of his *Serious and Friendly Address*. The future Lord Lyttelton requested his views of his *Monody* (1747) and two years later Gilbert West submitted to him his *Odes of Pindar*. The Scottish poet Robert Blair sent him via Dr Watts his poem *The Grave;* the Professor of History at Glasgow (William Anderson) sent him an essay for his comments, and the Revd

John Bonar his *Observations* on the life of Judas Iscariot. Doddridge's literary abilities were also in demand; in 1743 Charles Erskine appealed to Doddridge to write an account of how Old Testament prophecies had been fulfilled in the New; 'valuable consequences' would follow such a work, Erskine stated, 'if undertaken by a hand so fit for it'.[49]

During his summer vacations Doddridge travelled extensively, fitting in visits to friends, conducting preaching engagements and ordinations of students as well as general sight-seeing. He enjoyed this 'beating the hoof from place to place'. Writing from Stratford-upon-Avon on 12 July 1743, he tells his wife how he had been soaked to the skin 'almost from my Shoulders to my Toes' but had dried himself out at an inn at Southam where 'I supped like the King in Bed on Poached Eggs, & [afterwards] got a large Draught of Sack Whey'. We glimpse the difficulties of travel in the eighteenth century even in the summer: 'The Roads are not only very slippery but in some Places deep & we had 35 Gates between this & the last Market Town most of them very heavy & made fast with Latches.'[50]

Despite these difficulties Doddridge frequently visited London, East Anglia and the West Country. Each journey turned into a miniature royal progress; everywhere he travelled he was warmly welcomed and treated with almost embarrassing respect. Writing to Mercy from Taunton on 17 June 1742 he spoke of one such occasion: 'We had, I suppose, near two thousand persons present; of whom forty were ministers. I was treated by them with a deference of which I was quite unworthy; and forced by them to submit to honours which I should rather have bestowed on the least of my brethren, and bless God, I went through my work with cheerfulness, though I had no sleep the night before.'[51]

Few English Christians in the eighteenth century considered it necessary that other races should be brought within the pale of the faith. 'Protestantism,' writes Payne, 'had been slow to undertake missionary enterprises, or even to admit missionary obligations. Many of its earliest leaders believed that the end of the world was imminent. Their task, they felt, was to restore and preserve the purity of the faith in a final age of corruption and apostacy.'[52] Nevertheless, small but far from insignificant missionary undertakings had been initiated in the seventeenth century; Roger Williams and John Eliot pioneered the viewpoint that North American Indians were fellow human beings in need of redemption, not savages to be mercilessly butchered. In 1649 the Society for the Propagation of the Gospel in New England was formed and half a century later the *S.P.C.K.*[53] and *S.P.G.*[54] espoused the cause of slaves and indigenous inhabitants of the developing colonies. It is hardly surprising that Doddridge, with his ardent evangelistic concerns, should be interested in such enterprises.

In September 1737 he met Benjamin Ingham who had just returned from two years' missionary work in Georgia with John and Charles Wesley. Doddridge marvelled at Ingham's account of their work among the Indians. Ingham did not return to America but joined the Moravian Brethren, a newly emergent and forceful evangelising body. Doddridge kept up correspondence with Ingham, who sent him reports of the Moravian success in America and Greenland. Doddridge requested full details, and in 1741 became a corresponding member of their 'Society for the Furtherance of the Gospel'. After writing to one of their leaders, Count Nicholas von Zinzendorf, Doddridge met 'that blessed herald of our Redeemer' in St Albans. Many of Doddridge's friends were sceptical of Moravian theological notions and practices; Doddridge, too, eventually became disenchanted with the Moravians and gradually 'dropped that intimacy of correspondence which I once had with them'.[55] Moravian inroads into the Castle Hill congregation in later years worried Doddridge, yet in spite of this his interests in missionary enterprises remained un-diminished.

Disappointed by the Moravians, Doddridge was nevertheless greatly encouraged by other contemporary enterprises taking place in America. Appropriately enough, at Northampton in New England a remarkable religious revival was becoming apparent through the work of Jonathan Edwards. Doddridge read Edwards' *Faithful Narrative of Surprising Conversions* with its introduction by Dr Watts and Dr Guyse, on its publication in 1737. Doddridge also followed with interest the labours of another pious and devoted missionary, David Brainerd, who in three intense years (1744–7) wore himself out by his work with the American Indians. Doddridge greatly valued Brainerd's *Journal* which the latter had published in 1746, and his *Life* which Edwards had published together with his *Diary*, in 1749. In the previous year Doddridge wrote a dedica-tion to an abridged version of Brainerd's *Journal*, paying tribute to such a 'faithful and zealous servant of Christ'.

Such influences nourished Doddridge's deep desire to extend the gospel to all. On 30 June 1741 whilst making an extensive visit through East Anglia he took the opportunity of challenging his ministerial col-leagues with ten proposals for revival. It was a hot day and the service lasted between four and five hours, yet Doddridge held his listeners enraptured. It was, he said, 'one of the most delightful Days of my whole Life. . . . We held a Kind of Council afterwards concerning the

Methods to be taken for the Revival of Religion & I hope I have set them on Work to some good Purpose'.[56] In the following month, returning home from Brentwood, he lamented the signs of disunity and lack of purpose in the ministers there: 'I long to begin a Reformation in Northamptonshire, that I may with the better Grace attempt to propagate it elsewhere.'[57]

Within a month the proposals were communicated to the ministers of Northamptonshire, and in the following October Doddridge preached a memorable sermon at Kettering entitled *The Evil and Danger of Neglecting the Souls of Men*. Added to the ten propositions for religious revival was an eleventh: 'Whether something might not be done, in most of our Congregations, towards assisting in the propagation of Christianity Abroad, and spreading it in some of the darker Parts of our own Land?' For ever practical, Doddridge added notes on how he was attempting to involve his own congregation in missionary enterprise. Doddridge's plans involved regular prayer, Bible study, the sharing of news 'relating to the progress of the gospel' and the raising of money to finance the establishment of schools, the printing of bibles and tracts, and the sending of missionaries abroad. He admitted that 'the Effects of it in one Congregation can be but very small: But if it were generally to be followed, who can tell what a Harvest such a little Grain might at length produce?'[58]

It is evident that Doddridge's initiative for home and overseas missions met with little immediate practical response; he certainly lacked the time and energy extensively to pursue the matter himself. Yet his efforts were far from wasted, because it is no coincidence that within half a century Northamptonshire became the cradle of modern missions. Thirty-two years after Doddridge's death William Carey was baptised in the River Nene, having used Doddridge's former vestry for the occasion.[59] In 1791 Carey published his famous *Enquiry into the Obligations of Christians to use means for the Conversion of the Heathens*, and in the following year the Baptist Missionary Society was formed in Kettering on lines closely resembling those proposed by Doddridge.

Carey by single-minded determination brought Protestant missionary endeavour to global dimensions, yet it was men like Doddridge who prepared the soil and first sowed the 'little grain' of future enterprises.

# The Final Journey

Doddridge never enjoyed robust health and was frail in appearance. 'In stature,' writes Kippis, 'he was somewhat above the middle size, with a stoop in his shoulders, and he was very thin and slender.'[1] Aware of his vulnerability his family and friends often chided him for working so hard; in March 1738 the Revd John Barker wrote:

> . . . you are always catching fresh colds, and exposing yourself to all sorts of winds. Is yours a fit body to go out of a hot immediately into a cold bath? What comfort will it be to Mrs Doddridge and your friends, to be told, in your funeral sermon, that you died, or rather killed yourself, at such an age, with colds and labour.[2]

Although Doddridge appreciated such attentive concern, he nevertheless continued his busy life 'just like a Hair [hare] running with the Dogs running at her Heels'.[3] Inevitably the combination of physical frailty and hard work began to take a severe toll. On 16 December 1750 he had contracted a heavy cold when journeying to St Albans to take the funeral of his friend and father-figure, Samuel Clark.[4] It was an illness that remained with him for the rest of the winter; it eased during the spring of 1751, but the symptoms returned in the summer.[5] Writing from Sudbury to the Revd Samuel Wood on 20 June 1751 Doddridge admitted his low state of health:

> . . . the frequent returns of my cough alarm my friends, and those in town say I am grown many years older since they saw me last. I leave the event with God; but for my own part apprehend no immediate danger. . . .[6]

Doddridge was prepared for death at any time, and on each birthday expressed his thankfulness for yet another year of life. By the early part of 1751 he was clearly on the verge of a complete breakdown. At the last Lord's Supper over which he presided at Castle Hill on 2 June he alluded

Notes and references for this chapter begin on page 170

to his own approaching death. On the previous day he had written in his diary about an alarming state of mind and body experienced whilst alone in his vestry: 'my spirits were much out of order', he wrote; he had tried to recover his senses by sleeping 'but it availed little, and even while I was recording these memorandums of my own stupidity, I grew still more stupid, and felt depressed with a heaviness and a wandering of thought I scarcely ever experienced before'.[7]

For several months the congregation at Castle Hill had watched these developments with uneasiness and alarm. Doddridge had ceased to preach, and came only occasionally to the services. Meetings were held three times a week to pray for his recovery and for the welfare of his wife and children. Plans were made for Samuel Clark (junior) to take over the administration of the academy.

On 16 July, accompanied by his wife Mercy, Doddridge left Northampton for Bewdley in Worcestershire where he preached at the ordination of the Revd John Adams on the 18th. It was Doddridge's last sermon. Many remarked upon his pale countenance and trembling voice. From Bewdley they travelled to Shrewsbury to stay for four weeks with Job Orton, who had left Northampton in 1741.[8] Here Doddridge received a host of letters showing with what concern friends all over the country viewed his declining health. Nathaniel Neal wrote: 'You may be sure that we are all greatly affected with the danger that threatens a life so universally desirable, and to us so peculiarly endeared.'[9] Thomas Yeoman sent his 'sorrow of heart' from Northampton where he had been assisting the people at Castle Hill in prayer for Doddridge: 'you may depend upon an interest in the prayers of all your dear friends here . . .'.[10] John Barker pleaded 'Stay—Doddridge—O stay & strengthen our hands whose shadows grow long. Fifty is but the height of Vigour usefulness & honour. Do'nt take leave abruptly'.[11]

By August Doddridge's health had reached a critical point; his hoarse voice, incessant coughing, extreme weariness, pallid complexion and feverishness were the undeniable symptoms of consumption. Doddridge's physicians placed their fading hopes for him in the hot wells. On 12 August he wrote to his daughter Polly: 'Tho I am greatly better within these six Days, my Cough & Hoarseness is such that it is judged advisable by my Friends here that we should try Bristol, which has, sometimes, been wonderfully serviceable in such cases.'[12]

Upon reaching Bristol in August Doddridge was much comforted by the affection and care with which he was treated. Friends and strangers alike did their utmost to assist him. The Bishop of Worcester, Dr Maddox, called and offered the use of his 'chariot' to take Doddridge to the wells. Members of the Dissenting church in Bristol visited him, as did a clergyman of the established church who initially gave Doddridge hospitality under his own roof until lodgings closer to the wells were found. Several friends from Castle Hill travelled to Bristol to visit him.

The waters proved as ineffective as the asses' milk and tarwater which Doddridge took to relieve his distress. His health declined daily, and as a last course his physicians advised a warmer and drier climate for the winter. Lisbon, enjoying contemporary popularity as a health resort, seemed an ideal place. Doddridge hesitated, worried that the expense would decrease what little money he had to leave to Mercy and the children. He had not reckoned on the generosity of his many friends; an Anglican clergyman quickly organised a subscription; the Countess of Huntingdon rode over from Bath with Doddridge's friend Dr Oliver and subscribed £100, the Coward Trustees donated £30, and other friends including the Castle Hill congregation made the sum up to £300. A sea passage from Falmouth was speedily arranged; Bishop Warburton and Ralph Allen[13] ensured that Doddridge had the exclusive use of the captain's cabin whilst on board the packet (the captain not sailing on that occasion).

Doddridge left Bristol on 17 September pausing for a few days as the guest of Lady Huntingdon at her home in Bath. Upon finding him weeping in his room she was told:

> I am weeping, madam, but they are tears of comfort and joy. I can give up my country, my relations, and friends into the hand of God; and as to myself, I can as well go to heaven from Lisbon as from my own study at Northampton.[14]

Doddridge journeyed on, spending one night at the home of his former student the Revd Risdon Darracott, now a popular minister.

The Doddridges finally reached Falmouth on 27 September. Their journey had been marred by heavy rain; in spite of using a large well-sprung coach to ease the jolts of the stony roads, Doddridge was exhausted. He stayed with Dr Turner until the day of embarkation arrived; Turner recommended that Doddridge put himself under the care of Dr Cantley, who had a practice in Lisbon. For a day or so Doddridge felt a little better but on the night prior to departure his symptoms returned with renewed violence. Emanuel Austin, who spent the evening with him, reported: '. . . the doctor was at that time in so emaciated a condition, that he was obliged to shift from one side to another every minute.'[15]

Much alarmed by his condition Mercy urged him either to return to Northampton or postpone sailing. But her husband had made up his mind: 'The die is cast, and I choose to go,' he replied laconically. They set sail on Monday 30 September after saying farewell to a number of their friends, knowing that the thoughts of thousands went with them. Nathaniel Neal summed up the universal feeling: 'You go with a full gale of prayer, and I trust we shall stand ready on the shore to receive you back with shouts of praise.'[16]

Doddridge's departure from England had a symbolism peculiar to itself; as the shores of Cornwall receded toward the horizon it seemed as if all his earthly labours and concerns were slipping into the distance of memory. As the ship passed into the breezy expansive ocean Doddridge's spirits and vitality partly returned, although Mercy and their servant suffered acute sea-sickness. Doddridge was able to stay in his chair on deck for several hours a day or sit in his cabin. Becalmed in the Bay of Biscay for a time, the heat became so unbearable to him that he had great difficulty in breathing, and developed intense sweating and feelings of faintness; at last a welcome breeze developed, allowing the ship to continue on its journey, thus giving him much needed relief.

Most of his time spent on board was preoccupied with ecstatic spiritual meditations which brought a rapturous look to his face: 'Such transporting views of the heavenly world is my Father now indulging me with, no words can express,'[17] he told Mercy. Doddridge enjoyed this state of spiritual joy and inner peace as the ship rose and dipped in the Atlantic swell. Behind him receded the frustrations of the latter years of his ministry: his worries about the numerical decline of Castle Hill and the loss of members to the Moravians; the deaths of two of his dearest friends and supporters, Isaac Watts and Samuel Clark; the increasing demands for his advice and leadership as the foremost figure within the Dissenting movement; and the mounting correspondence, hitherto a delight, which had grown into a time and energy-consuming monster. Now such cares were put into their proper perspective as the boat moved southwards along the Portuguese coast.

Before his departure from Falmouth, Doddridge had received many expressions of esteem and affection. He replied with cheerfulness: 'If I survive my Voyage, a line shall tell you how I bear it. If not, all will be well. . . .'[18] In the previous February Benjamin Forfitt[19] had wished Doddridge a long and useful life, and had commented: '. . . when the solemn hour comes, may you enter the port of bliss, like a gallant ship laden with the spoils of victory.'[20] Forfitt's words were prophetic; the

44. The cover from one of the last letters received by Doddridge before leaving Falmouth for Lisbon. Dated 21 September 1751 it was written by William Jackson of Cannon Street, London, directed to 'Mr Persalls at Taunton; Sommersetshire' and endorsed 'with care & speed'. Doddridge had already left Taunton, hence the urgent request by Richard Pearsall, minister at Taunton, to the postmaster at Falmouth to ensure that the 'weak Gentleman going abroad in the pacquet boat for his helth' should receive it before departure. Nuttall letter 1795 (Doddridge MS 60, Northamptonshire Studies Collection, Central Library, Northampton).

Lisbon packet had entered the Tagus and was preparing to tie up in the harbour. It was Sunday 13 October 1751.

The Doddridges were welcomed to the home of David King, a wealthy merchant whose mother was a member at Castle Hill. Mercy found some relatives of her's nearby, and together with the help of Dr Cantley (who refused all fees) and the Revd Williamson, Chaplain to the British Factory, they were well cared for in every respect. On the 21 October upon the advice of Dr Cantley, the Doddridges moved to a country house several miles outside Lisbon. Unfortunately their advisers in England had not taken into consideration the annual rainy season which usually set in at the end of October. Quite suddenly the weather changed;

the air became damp and rain fell in torrents. Mercy wrote of their difficulties:

> . . . I was taken so violently ill in the night on Wednesday with a disorder which I found generally attends persons on their first coming into that climate, as not to be able to stir out of my room for three days. On the Thursday the dear deceased was seized with the same disorder—and we was both too ill to be able to move our quarters. But on the Monday, as we were both better, we went to our lodgings though I was then so weak as hardly able without help to walk across my room. Our lodgings were about three miles out of Lisbon and though he was conveyed to them in a sedan chair and carried very slow, yet he was so extremely fatigued that he wanted to have gone to bed as soon as we got in. But not-with-standing the repeated charges which had been given, and the promises of the person of the House that the rooms and beds should be throughly aired, when I came to examine his bed I found it so damp that I was forced to have large fires made and every part of the bedding aired, so that he could not be got to bed for more than three hours—this you will allow was a distressing accident to him and to me in my present weak state.—As to my own bed which was in the same room I had taken no other care of that but of having it aired with a pan of coals—and which when I got into was so damp that I felt it wrap around me like a wet sheet.—But through great weakness and excessive fatigue I dropped asleep, and what is very surprising I caught no cold, but was so far strengthened as to be able to render him the few little services he further needed. . . .[21]

Forced to stay indoors Doddridge's health rapidly deteriorated; severe diarrhoea exhausted his last reserves of strength. Through the night of Thursday 24 October 'his mind continued in the same vigour, calmness and joy, which it had felt and expressed during his whole illness'.[22] Attended by his wife Doddridge expressed his sorrow of causing her grief yet added: 'So sure am I that God will be with you and comfort you, that I think my death will be a greater blessing to you, than ever my life hath been.'[23]

During the following day he lay in a gentle doze, and after a bout of restlessness he fetched several deep sighs and died on 26 October at approximately three o'clock in the morning. The post mortem examination, which Doddridge had requested, showed his lungs to be badly ulcerated. He was buried in the cemetery attached to the British Factory in Lisbon, where his grave and tomb may still be seen today.[24]

*The Northampton Mercury* reported the 'melancholy Advice' under its *Plantation News* dated 23 November 1751:

> . . . He had been Minister of the Dissenting Meeting in this Place 22 Years,—and had establish'd an ACADEMY here, which he supported with such Reputation, as brought Students to it from all Parts of the Kingdom.—He was a Man of a fine Genius, rich in the Stores of Learning, and of unexampled Activity and Diligence —His Piety was without Disguise, his Love without Jealousy, his Benevolence without Bounds.—His Candour was so uncommonly extensive and unaffected, as to gain him the general Esteem of the Clergy, and the Particular Friendship of some very eminent Men—In the several Characters of a Friend, a Preacher, a Writer, a Tutor, he had few Superiors: In all united, he had no Equal— His disconsolate Widow (whose chief Dowry is, that she inherits the Spirit of this excellent Man) is returning to England, to asswage the Griefs and form the Minds of her amiable Offspring; and to forward those Writings to the Press, which were designed for the publick View.[25]

# Epilogue

It has been remarked that Doddridge attempted to do too much, and that consequently his considerable talents were spread thinly over too wide an area of activity. It is undoubtedly true that as a preacher Doddridge did not rise to the heights of eloquence as did Whitefield, or as a hymnwriter, rival the polished poetic utterances of Wesley or Watts. Neither can we claim for him the distinction of being a profoundly original thinker, as his system of lectures, for example, was based upon that of Jennings. Doddridge's genius lies in his ability to assimilate and synthesise a vast amount of knowledge and ideas, and equally in his skill at imparting them in an intelligible form to a wide cross-section of eighteenth century society. Writing of the *Family Expositor* Bishop Barrington of Durham summarised it as 'an impartial interpreter and faithful monitor', a description eminently applicable to its author.

Doddridge must be assessed in the light of his overriding purpose and widespread impact. *The Rise and Progress* has been called the best book of the eighteenth century, and the continued interest in it to the present day attests Doddridge's appeal as a writer on theological subjects. Nor can one overestimate his influence upon his contemporaries. Sir James Stonhouse was one of many who made dramatic changes in their lives due to Doddridge's influence; writing thirty-seven years after the latter's death, Stonhouse could still record his deep appreciation of Doddridge's writings which he esteemed as highly as those of Baxter:

> In the sentiments of these men I shall live and die. They are like a good warm surtout to the body. I feel their effects on my soul. . . .[1]

Not only did Doddridge's writings and hymns continue to speak for him long after his death, a generation of ministers kept alive his tolerant

Notes and references for the epilogue on page 172

evangelical spirit. Many able tutors continued to follow the tradition of teaching established by Doddridge at Northampton. His influence upon domestic life was equally profound; in many homes family religion was revitalised. Through the hymns of Watts and Doddridge a new sensibility was developed that 'opened up a range of thought and feeling far beyond the conception of their Protestant forebears'.[2]

Doddridge's incalculable value to Dissent was realised in his own lifetime; John Barker expressed his fears in a letter to his dying friend:

> Who shall instruct our youth—fill our Vacant churches—Animate our associations—and diffuse a spirit of piety, Moderation, Candour & Charity thro' our Villages and Churches— & a spirit of prayer & supplication into our Towns & Cities when thou art removed from Us! especially who shall Unfold the sacred Oracles—teach us the Meaning & use of our Bibles and rescue us from the bondage of systems—party Opinions—empty & useless speculations— & fashionable forms and phrases—and point out to us the simple intelligible consistent Uniform Religion of our Lord & Saviour.[3]

Bishop Jebb also appreciated Doddridge's universal appeal:

> Doddridge was a burning and shining light which, in days of more than ordinary coldness, Divine Providence was pleased to enkindle, in order to impart both warmth and illumination to the professing Christian world.[4]

Some have criticised Doddridge for being over-fond of his fame, somewhat ostentatious in speaking of his many engagements, and too complimentary and accommodating in his correspondence. The first two faults may have crept in, especially in later life, but are only minor blemishes; the third criticism was more marked in his younger days and was more an expression of his passionate loneliness and youthfulness. If Doddridge erred on the side of flattery it was motivated by an amiable nature that attempted to avoid causing offence. Nevertheless, when strong words were needed Doddridge could rise to the occasion. His frankness, lack of dogmatism and ecumenical outlook have much to say to the twentieth century.

Ultimately, Doddridge's attractiveness lies in his personal qualities as a man of flesh and blood. He possessed a warm sense of humour referring on one occasion to Archbishop Thomas Herring as 'the good A.B. of Canterbury'.[5] In mock royal tones he wrote to Mercy from Yardley Hastings in 1749: 'Philip the King To our trusty & well beloved Consort

Greeting . . . this 20th of May in the Nine-teenth year of our Reign.'
requesting that she bring daughter Polly, 'to meet our Royal Person.'⁶
His relationship with Mercy, although occasionally petulant, was always
that of the lover; he rarely departed from his solemn vow to show
tenderness and avoid the pettishness to which, amidst his cares and
labours, he knew he could be liable.

His love for his children was also deep and his agony of soul over the
deaths of five of them intense; lacking any bitterness, it was typical of
Doddridge to turn his own grief into concern for others in similar
circumstances. Not prepared to accept the appalling consequences of
smallpox, he played his part in changing public attitudes: 'oh, when shall
we see the Importance of inoculating Children!'⁷

Few could emulate him in the use of his time, rising early in the
morning and planning carefully every precious moment. He perceived
too the social implications of the Gospel for his times. His extraordinary
energy in helping to initiate the infirmary, his foundation of the charity
school, as well as his determination to defend his town and the constitution of his country during the uprising of 1745, are eloquent testimony
to his social responsibility and courage.

Dr Johnson wrote of Philip Doddridge: 'He was author of one of the
finest epigrams in the English language. . . . The subject is his family
motto, "Dum vivimus, vivamus" which, in its primary signification, is,
to be sure, not very suitable to a Christian divine; but he paraphrased it
thus:

> "Live, while you live, the *epicure* would say,
> And seize the pleasures of the present day.
> Live, while you live, the sacred *preacher* cries,
> And give to GOD each moment as it flies.
> Lord, in my views let both united be;
> I live in *pleasure*, when I live to *thee*." "⁸

The warmth of Doddridge's humanity emanated from his deep
religious faith. His ardent concern for the salvation of the souls of all
people was the motive that gave cohesion to his activities; as tutor,
preacher, pastor, author, philanthropist, husband, father and friend, he
was above all else, Philip Doddridge the Christian.

# Notes and References

## ABBREVIATIONS

NUTTALL = NUTTALL, G.F. *Calendar of the correspondence of Philip Doddridge, D.D.* 1702-1751 (Northamptonshire Record Society and the Royal Commission on Historical Manuscripts, 1979).

HUMPHREYS = HUMPHREYS, J. D. *Correspondence and diary of Philip Doddridge, D.D.* (Colburn and Bentley, 1829-31) 5 vols.

'Church Book' = Manuscript Church Book of Doddridge and Commercial Street United Reformed Church (Castle Hill) Northampton, 1694 onwards.

## CHAPTER 1 (page 13)

1. EVERITT, A. *The Pattern of Rural Dissent: the nineteenth century* (1972) p. 16.

2. Early use of the word 'Independent' was made by Henry Burton in 1641 to describe a form of church organisation which upheld the autonomy of each congregation. In Parliament, those who opposed the imposition of Presbyterianism on the Church of England became known as 'Independents'. There was much confusion in contemporary use of the term, but both Separatists and Congregationalists (who emerged in the 1640s) can legitimately be called 'Independent', even though their views of the established church differed. 'In the 1640s and 1650s the Separatists and Congregationalists formed two distinct but collateral branches of the larger tree of Independency.' WATTS, M. R. *The Dissenters: from the Reformation to the French Revolution* (1978) p. 99.

3. 'The Moravian Brethren.' The Protestant Church of Bohemia and Moravia —the Unitas Fratrum—was an ancient church dating back to the Bohemian Brethren of the mid-fifteenth century. In 1722 remnants of the church, which survived the severe persecution of the early seventeenth century, were allowed to settle on the estates of Count Nicholas von Zinzendorf (1700-60) at Berthelsdorf in Saxony. In 1727 Zinzendorf established his authority over the village community known as Herrnhut. Transformed by Zinzendorf's missionary zeal, which aimed at revitalising personal religion within the existing denominations of the church, the community embarked on an amazing international missionary enterprise to, amongst others, the Virgin Islands (1732), Greenland (1733), North America (1734), Lapland and South America (1735), South Africa (1736), Labrador (1771), to the Australian Aborigines (1850) and to the Tibetan border (c.1856). The Moravian Peter Boehler

greatly assisted the conversion of John Wesley, and Moravian influence was a major factor in the evangelical revival of the eighteenth century.

4. For the purposes of this book the terms 'Dissent' and 'Nonconformity' are used synonymously, but there is a slight difference. The term 'Dissenter' was used, particularly after the return of Charles II, of those who would not conform to the restored episcopal (i.e. governed by bishops) church. Such individualists had been labelled by different names through the centuries: 'Anabaptists' in Tudor England, 'Brownists' or 'Separatists' in the reigns of Elizabeth I and the early Stuarts, and 'Sectaries' during the Civil War and Interregnum. The term Nonconformist was initially used during Elizabeth's reign, to describe Puritans within the Church of England who refused to conform to some of the practices laid down by the Prayer Book of 1559. Only after the Great Ejectment of 1662, when those with scruples against the Prayer Book had to leave the Church of England, did the term Nonconformist come to mean separation. By the second half of the nineteenth century 'Nonconformist' had virtually replaced 'Dissenter', and was in its turn supplanted at the end of the nineteenth and early decades of this century by the title 'Free Churchman'. *See* WATTS, M. R. op. cit. pp. 1–2.

5. The Marprelate Tracts were a series of scurrilous pamphlets that attacked episcopacy (the authority of bishops). The secret printing press was moved from place to place to avoid detection, and was housed at Sir Richard Knightley's home at Fawsley during the autumn of 1589, before being transferred to Coventry. The tracts boasted of the strength of Northamptonshire Puritanism and 'challenged the mayor and constables of Northampton to apprehend those involved in their publication'. SHEILS, W. J. *The Puritans in the Diocese of Peterborough, 1558–1610* (1979) p. 59.

6. Anabaptism, the General Baptists and Quakerism. 'Anabaptist' was a general term used in Tudor England for those who held principles similar to the Lollards. The essential elements of Anabaptism were belief in the Bible as sole authority, and a belief that Christ died for all mankind; the latter idea was a denial of the Calvinist idea that some were born to damnation. Later, the practice of rebaptism was adopted; there is a clear link between the Lollard view that the baptism of children of Christian parents was unnecessary, and the central belief of the General Baptists of the seventeenth century and after, in 'believer's baptism'. Continental Anabaptism, unfortunately, led to some fanaticism and anarchy, which resulted in a century of persecution and suspicion of all who were suspected of Anabaptist sympathies.

Quakerism (the Society of Friends) originated with George Fox (1624–91) whose experience of 'the inner light . . . which lighteth every man' led him to emphasise that human life could attain perfection. Like the Baptists he repudiated the Calvinist notion of predestination (damnation or salvation at birth), but was far more radical in opposing formalism within the church; the only baptism that mattered, Fox declared, was the baptism of the spirit, and all liturgies and sacraments were 'Babylonish and heathenish'. Quaker worship emphasised a readiness to listen to the 'leading of God' through the prophesying of other Friends, and a willingness to worship God in quietness. The Quakers refused to take off their hats before magistrates and to swear any oaths of allegiance to the state. They insisted upon using the familiar 'thee' and 'thou' to all, irrespective of social position. After 1660

...hear unexpectedly met with this blessed Book & as this Treasa-
... Volum and ye Dr Hymns he usd to imploy himself in reading as much
as his strenght wod admitt during our stay thear as I dont recolect he was
ever able to look into a book after we got to our lodgings nor in some
of ye few days we was at ye Kings but his mind injoyed a delightful
calm full of Joy thanksgiving and praise wh he exprest to all us round
him as far as his great weakness wod permit

My time after we first was chiefly imployd
part of my Nights in writing letters, as no time for this in ye day, wch was
in great measure taken up, in seeking after lodgings—which I was not able
to procure tell wednesday evening—and as the Dr was very desireous
we shd gett into the country as soon as possible, we purposd to have
went to ym on the thursday—but I was taken so violently ill in
the Night on wednesday with a disorder which I found generally attends persons on their first coming into that climate
as not to be able to stir out of my room for three days—
on ye thursday the dear deceased was seizd with ye same
disorder—and we were both too Ill to be able to move our seates
but on the monday as we was both better we went to our lodgings thes
was then so weak as hardly able without help to walk across my room
our lodgings were about three miles out of Lisbon and though he was
conveyd to ym in a sedan chaire and carried very slow, yet he was so extream-
ly fatigue that he wanted to have gon to bed as soon as we got in. But
not with standing the repeated charges yt had been given and the promises of ye person of the house that the rooms and beds should be thoroughly
aird when I came to examining his bed I found it so damp that I was
forced to have large fires made and every part of the beding aird
so that he could not be got to bed for more than three hours—as you
will allow was a distressing accident to him, and to me in my present
weak state—as to my own bed which was in ye same room I had taken
no other care, of that but of having aird with a pan of coals—and wh-
when I got into was so damp that I felt it wrap round me like a
wet sheet—but thro great weakness and excessive fatigue I dropt
asleep and what is very surprizing I caught no cold, but was so far
strenghtend as to be able to render him the few little services he far
ther Needed—but what still increasd ys melancholy scene was
my maids being taken ill I think the very Next day and
incapable of doing any thing for us—for several days—as
well as we got to Lisbon but little more than a week before their wet season, as most of the rain they have their generaly fals ye latterend of Oc-
tr & november—and such rains as fell there the two last days and Nights
of his life I never before nor since saw—this sudden change of wether wh
came on soon after we got into our lodgings which out of soury thing we

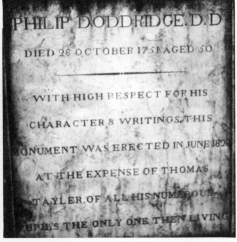

46. The memorial to Philip Doddridge in Lisbon. The original was replaced in 1828 by Thomas Tayler, who claimed to be the only pupil of Doddridge then living.

47. The Lisbon memorial to Philip Doddridge; the inscription.

48. The memorial to Philip Doddridge in Doddridge and Commercial Street United Reformed Church, (Castle Hill), Northampton. The date of his birth is given incorrectly as 26 January 1702, not 26 June 1702. Sculpture by John Hunt, inscription by Gilbert West.

pacificism became a distinctive tenet of Quakerism. Fox's aggressive evangelism and superb organising abilities ensured the rapid growth of the movement. Fox claimed (wrongly) that the name 'Quaker' was first used in 1650 by Justice Bennet of Derby when Fox challenged him, and others, to quake at the word of the Lord. See WATTS, M. R. op. cit. for a full account of the relationships between the sects during this period.

7. For a comprehensive account of the religious transformation of England during the Reformation see WATTS, M. R. op. cit.; KOENIGSBERGER, H. G. and MOSSE, G. L. *Europe in the sixteenth century* (1968); and CHADWICK, O. *The Reformation* (1964).

8. William Laud (1573–1644). After a successful career in the church that brought him the Archbishopric of Canterbury in 1633, Laud attempted to root out Puritanism within the English church. Clergy were labelled as either 'orthodox' or 'Puritan', and the latter felt the full weight of Laud's disciplining hand. High Church doctrines and practices were re-established, such as the doctrine of the real presence, clerical celibacy and confession. Laud's attempts to Anglicise the Scottish church by trying to eliminate Presbyterianism led to rebellion, and were a major cause of the Civil War. Ten weeks after his impeachment for treason by the Long Parliament, Laud was executed as a traitor on Tower Hill (10 January 1645).

9. The term 'High Church' was not a contemporary one; it was first used in 1687 to denote those especially 'stiff for the Church of England' and opposed to Dissent. See CHADWICK, O. op. cit. p. 226.

10. The Solemn League and Covenant was established in 1643 by the English Parliamentarians, and by Scots who pledged themselves to eliminate episcopal power, and to establish Presbyterianism in both England and Scotland. All incumbents of the Church of England were required to obey the Covenant and use *The Directory for the Publique Worship of God*, but these instructions were widely disobeyed, as Parliament never succeeded in effectively imposing religious uniformity on the entire country.

11. MILTON, J. *On the New Forcers of Conscience under the Long Parliament.*

12. WATTS, M. R. op. cit. p. 153.

13. Ibid. p. 221.

14. The Fifth Monarchists were radical political activists who believed in the imminent establishment upon earth of the kingdom of Christ and his saints. Taking their apocalyptic expectations from Daniel 2:44 they considered that this fifth monarchy would succeed the Assyrian, Persian, Macedonian and Roman Empires. All anti-Christian forms including the established church were to be destroyed. The beheading of Charles I in 1649 was one step towards their millennium. When Cromwell was elected Lord Protector in 1653 their hopes were dashed, and the Fifth Monarchists turned against him. Agitation led to rebellion in 1657, and in January 1661 London witnessed scenes of violence which lasted for three days; it was eventually suppressed by the intervention of the military and the London 'train bands' (trained civilians used in times of emergency).

15. The Clarendon Code was named after Edward Hyde, Earl of Clarendon and Lord Chancellor. Hyde was a bitter opponent of Dissent, but was not the sole person responsible for the persecuting legislation. See also Appendix VIII.

16. William Penn (1644–1718), son of Admiral William Penn, became a

zealous Quaker and was frequently imprisoned for his beliefs. While in the Tower of London he wrote his most popular works *No Cross, No Crown* and *Innocency with her Open Face*. In 1682 he established a home for his fellow Quakers in the territory named after his father, Pennsylvania. After meeting with the Indians, he founded the city of Philadelphia. Upon his return to England he campaigned for religious toleration; owing to his exertions thousands of Dissenters, including one thousand two hundred Quakers, were released from prison in 1686. Penn also attempted to mitigate the evils of slavery.

17. WATTS, M. R. op. cit. p. 239.

18. Ibid. p. 225.

19. Ibid. p. 226.

20. MACAULAY, T. B. *History of England* (1863–4 edition) vol. 1, p. 90.

21. SKEATS, H. S. and MIALL, C. S. *History of the Free Churches of England* (1891) p. 61.

22. In all 2029 clergy, lecturers and fellows of colleges were ejected from their posts between 1660 and 1662. See WATTS, M. R. op. cit p. 219.

23. CATER, F. IVES. *Northamptonshire Nonconformity 250 years ago* (1912) p. 6.

Richard Baxter (1615–91). In 1638 Baxter was ordained a deacon by the Bishop of Worcester, being already master of Dudley grammar school. The Civil War had a traumatic effect upon him, and from 1642 to 1644 he ministered to the garrison and inhabitants at Coventry. After the battle of Naseby (1645) Baxter became an army chaplain for the Parliamentarians. In 1650 he published his best known work *The Saints' Everlasting Rest*. In 1662 the *Act of Uniformity* drove him out of the church, and he spent the rest of his life in writing and preaching. In 1685 he was brought on a charge of sedition before Judge Jeffreys, who treated him harshly; he was imprisoned for eighteen months, in default of paying a 500 mark fine.

24. CATER, F. IVES. op. cit. p. 7.

25. For graphic accounts of Nonconformist sufferings see FLETCHER, J. *Independency in England* (1847-9) vol. 4; and WATTS, M. R. op. cit.

26. WATTS, M. R. op. cit. p. 248.

27. Of the Thirty-Nine Articles of Religion only three were completely waived for Dissenters; the thirty-fourth, which gave latitude within the church to vary its traditions and ceremonies; the thirty-fifth, which set out twenty-one homilies to be read in churches; and the thirty-sixth, which concerned the consecration of bishops and ministers. See also Appendix VIII, *Toleration Act*.

28. Isaac Watts (1674–1748) was born in Southampton, the eldest of nine children. His father was a clothier and was frequently imprisoned for his religious beliefs. Isaac became tutor in Hebrew and divinity to Sir John Hartopp at Stoke Newington. Later he became assistant, then pastor, of the Mark Lane Independent Church in that town. Intense study led to frequent illnesses. From 1712 he lived permanently under the care of Sir Thomas and Lady Abney, whilst endeavouring to maintain his pastoral responsibilities. He was also one of the Coward Trustees. Watts was one of the most popular writers of his day; his educational catechisms and scripture histories became standard works and were used by Doddridge. His philosophical and popular divinity works had a wide circulation. His poetical fame rests upon his hymns, of which he wrote some six hundred. *When I survey the*

*wondrous cross* and *Our God, our help in ages past* are notable examples. His *Divine Songs* was the first real hymn-book for children. His works were posthumously edited by Doddridge and David Jennings. His essay on Dissenting charity schools (1728) influenced Doddridge. His best work is *The Improvement of the Mind*, the second volume of which was edited by Doddridge and Jennings in 1751.

29. SKEATS, H. S. and MIALL, C. S. op. cit. p. 211.

30. Queen Anne's Bounty. In 1704 at the suggestion of Bishop Burnet, Anne relinquished her rights to certain taxes—'The First Fruits'—which amounted to approximately £17,000 per annum.

31. SKEATS, H. S. and MIALL, C. S. op. cit. pp. 217–8. The 'Old Pretender' was James Francis Edward Stuart (1688–1766), who attempted unsuccessfully to regain the Scottish and English thrones for his ill-fated family. His eldest son Charles Edward Louis Philip Casimir (1720–88), known variously as the 'Young Chevalier', the 'Young Pretender' or 'Bonny Prince Charlie', raised Jacobite hopes in 1745. See also chapter 6, pp. 125–8, this work.

32. The Grammar schools throughout the seventeenth and eighteenth centuries provide a marked contrast to the Dissenters' schools; the former were encumbered by tradition, harsh discipline and lax morality, and were impervious to any form of change. The Dissenting schools passed rapidly from the Grammar school stage to become 'institutions of University standing'. See PRICE, E. J. 'The Dissenting academies' in *Congregational Historical Society Transactions* (1930–2) vol. 11, pp. 38–51.

33. At least six Anglican bishops were educated in Dissenting academies. Thomas Secker (1693–1768) Archbishop of Canterbury, himself the son of a Dissenter, studied at the Attercliffe academy under Timothy Jollie; at Tewkesbury under Samuel Jones; and at London under John Eames FRS, before going to Oxford.

34. MURRAY, A. V. 'Doddridge and Education' in NUTTALL, G. F. *Philip Doddridge* (1951) p. 110.

35. Robert South (1634–1716), Prebendary of Westminster, was hostile to any form of 'comprehension' within the church and looked upon Dissenters as 'rabble'; to unite them within the church would be like letting a thief into the house in order to avoid the trouble and noise of his tapping at the door, he declared. SKEATS, H. S. and MIALL, C. S. op. cit. p. 119.

36. HENRY SACHEVERELL's sermon *Perils of False Brethren both in Church and State* (1709).

37. Between 1685 and 1785 the Dissenting academies produced eight per cent of the 3500 'famous men' of the century. See HANS, N. *New trends in education in the eighteenth century* (1951) p. 18.

38. Charles Morton (1627?–98) achieved extremely high standards in his academy (c.1675–85) mainly because he taught in English. Half a century later Philip Doddridge's example of teaching in English set the norm for other Dissenting academies. In 1685 Morton became Vice-President of Harvard College in New England.

39. The Royal Society originated in 1645 to discuss 'the New and Experimental Philosophy' popularised by Francis Bacon. For a time it met weekly, but the group dispersed owing to the civil strife of the period. In 1660 activities resumed, and on 28 November of that year a meeting was held to discuss the possibility of founding

'a Colledge for the promoting of Physico-Mathematicall Experimentall Learning'. On 15 July 1662 it was incorporated by Royal Charter, and a further Charter on 22 April 1663 extended the society's privileges.

40. Jan Amos Comenius or Komensky (1592–1670), although regarded primarily as an educational reformer, was also a prominent religious leader. He was the last bishop of the Unitas Fratrum (Moravians) in Czechoslovakia, and strove all his life for the unity of the Christian Church.

## CHAPTER 2 (page 27)

1. DODDERIDGE, S. E. and SHADDICK, H. H. G. *The Dodderidges of Devon* (1909). This work gives a detailed account of the family's origins. See also CHARLES WORTHY's *Devonshire Wills* (1896) for background to this extensive family.

2. DODDERIDGE, S. E. and SHADDICK, H. H. G. op. cit. p. 39.

3. The Doddridge crest is a lion's head over a mural crown. See BURKE, B. *General Armory of England, Scotland, Wales and Ireland* (1878) p. 289.

4. STANFORD, C. *Philip Doddridge* (1880) p. 10.

5. Ibid. p. 10.

6. Ibid. p. 11.

7. John Hus, or Huss (1369–1415), Bohemian reformer and Rector of the University of Prague, condemned the spiritual laxity of the clergy and the sins of the papacy. In spite of being forbidden to preach, he continued his bold denunciations and was eventually excommunicated. Although promised a safe conduct to present himself before the Council of Constance, Hus was seized, tried and burned as a heretic. His death led to the fierce and protracted 'Hussite wars'.

8. HUMPHREYS vol. 1, p. 15.

9. This Bible was printed in Strasburg in 1626. Humphreys describes it thus: 'It . . . is handsomely bound in black morocco, deeply indented with gilt ornaments.' The two volumes (bound as one), are preserved in the Northamptonshire Studies Collection at the Central Library, Northampton. See illustration 1, p. 17.

10. Elizabeth Doddridge married the Revd John Nettleton. They lived first at Hampstead where John kept a school, but later moved to Ongar in Essex upon John's appointment as the dissenting minister there. Elizabeth died in 1735 after a long and debilitating illness. Philip did all he could to support them financially.

11. ORTON, J. 'Life of Dr Doddridge' in Doddridge's *Works* (1802-5) vol. 1, p. 16.

12. Such tiles were extremely popular; they were common in north Holland in the seventeenth century and many found their way to England. The Delft pottery started making them in 1661, and continues to this day.

13. STANFORD, C. op. cit. p. 14.

14. Ibid. p. 17.

15. 'The Orphan's Hope' was the fifth of six *Sermons to Young Persons* (1735).

16. Quoted in HARSHA, D. A. *Life of Philip Doddridge* (1864) p. 26.

17. STANFORD, C. op. cit. p. 17.

18. HARSHA, D. A. op. cit. pp. 28-9.

19. Ibid.

20. The Nettletons had three children, all girls. Doddridge refers to his 'three pretty, neat, merry Neices', NUTTALL letter 1253.

21. Edmund Calamy, DD (1671–1732), is regarded as an historian of Non-conformity mainly through his biographical accounts of early Nonconformist ministers, especially Richard Baxter. Both his father and grandfather were ejected ministers. Calamy was publicly ordained in London in 1694 with six other young men; it was an act of considerable daring as no London Dissenter had been so ordained since the *Act of Uniformity*. He was assistant to Dr Daniel Williams at the Hand Abbey Meeting in Bishopsgate, and later became minister of the Princes Street congregation in London. An upholder of the doctrine of the Trinity and the principles of Dissent, Calamy was also an extensive traveller and preacher. He was one of the original trustees of Dr Williams's Library in London, and preached the first sermon to a gathering of ministers there in 1731.

22. HARSHA, D. A. op. cit. p. 31.

23. Together with Dr Watts and Dr Guyse, Doddridge encouraged the University of Glasgow to confer an honorary Doctorate of Divinity on Clark in 1744. Doddridge paid the £1.6.6 [£1.32½] for the diploma.

24. HARSHA, D. A. op. cit. p. 32.

25. 'Kibworth' comprises two villages, Kibworth Beauchamp and Kibworth Harcourt—the academy was in the latter.

26. NUTTALL letter 234; HUMPHREYS vol. 2, p. 190.

27. NUTTALL letter 6; HUMPHREYS vol. 1, pp. 34–5.

28. NUTTALL letter 6; HUMPHREYS vol. 1, pp. 35–6.

29. NUTTALL letter 1; HUMPHREYS vol. 1, p. 33.

30. HUMPHREYS vol. 1, p. 97.

31. Ibid. vol. 1, p. 98.

32. NUTTALL letter 20; HUMPHREYS vol. 1, p. 105.

33. NUTTALL letter 69; HUMPHREYS vol. 1, p. 251.

34. NUTTALL letter 72; HUMPHREYS vol. 1, pp. 261–2, to Elizabeth Nettleton.

35. NUTTALL letter 22; HUMPHREYS vol. 1, pp. 114–5, to Mr Whittingham.

36. NUTTALL letter 52; HUMPHREYS vol. 1, p. 212.

37. It is significant that his favourite female correspondents during this period of his life were termed 'aunt' or 'mamma', thus partly substituting for parents lost in his childhood. Hannah and Elizabeth Clark were sisters of Dr Samuel Clark, and like Mrs Farrington and Rebecca Roberts, were a generation older than Doddridge. '. . . my own daily experience teaches me that there is nothing in the world more entertaining than the intimate conversation of an agreeable woman. . . .' NUTTALL letter 84; HUMPHREYS vol. 1, p. 288.

38. NUTTALL letter 85; HUMPHREYS vol. 1, pp. 287–8.

39. NUTTALL letter 106; HUMPHREYS vol. 1, p. 341.

40. NUTTALL letter 42; HUMPHREYS vol. 1, pp. 176–7.

41. NUTTALL letter 87; HUMPHREYS vol. 1, p. 292, to John Nettleton.

42. NUTTALL letter 274; HUMPHREYS vol. 2, p. 329, to Elizabeth Nettleton.

43. NUTTALL letter 31; HUMPHREYS vol. 1, pp. 140–1. The text was: 'If any man love not the Lord Jesus Christ, let him be Anathema maran-atha.' Syriac 'maran-atha' means 'the Lord cometh'. The words which happen to come together in 1 Cor. 16 v. 22 are wrongly interpreted as an intensified curse. The regular preacher on this

occasion, John Burnom of Nuneaton, was indisposed with 'convulsions'. NUTTALL letter 31; HUMPHREYS vol. 1, p. 139.

44. NUTTALL letter 48; HUMPHREYS vol. 1, p. 189. This would be a dark blue Genevan gown.

45. Ibid.

46. NUTTALL letter 53; HUMPHREYS vol. 1, p. 197.

47. Approximately two hundred and fifty persons were members or adherents of the church at Kibworth.

48. NUTTALL letter 71; HUMPHREYS vol. 1, p. 255, to Hannah Clark.

49. HARSHA, D. A. op. cit. pp. 52–3.

50. Ibid. p. 55.

51. John Tillotson (1630–94) had strong Presbyterian leanings. He submitted to the *Act of Uniformity* in 1662, and with reluctance in 1691 became Archbishop of Canterbury. He was considered one of the best preachers of the century.

John Howe (1630–1705), Puritan divine, was ejected in 1662 from his living at Torrington. His greatest work is *The Good Man the Living Temple of God* (1676–1702).

Richard Baxter (1615–91), see chapter 1, note 23, this work.

52. NUTTALL letters 53, 108; HUMPHREYS vol. 1, pp. 198–9.

53. Even before the Restoration, Presbyterians and Congregationalists were co-operating in an attempt to bring the two parties together. The Common Fund (which pooled financial resources) was one manifestation of their mutual aims, as was a weekly lecture established in 1672 at Pinner's Hall in the City of London. In 1691 the 'Happy Union' was established between the two denominations 'in and about London' and for a time all went well. Controversy grew, however, over doctrinal issues and was exacerbated by the activities of Richard Davis of Rothwell. The Presbyterian lecturers at Pinner's Hall left to establish a rival meeting at Salters' Hall in 1694. In the following year the Congregationalists left the Common Fund. In the provinces the distinction between the two denominations was more blurred than in London. It was not until 1972 that they became organically integrated into the United Reformed Church.

The Salters' Hall controversy of 1719 resulted in a division between those who subscribed to a formal declaration of the Trinity and those who, whilst believing in the Trinity, held that the only perfect rule of faith was the Bible (the Non-Subscribers). Doddridge was an ardent supporter of non-subscription. See WATTS, M. R. op. cit. pp. 375–6.

54. NUTTALL letter 108; HUMPHREYS vol. 1, p. 335.

55. NUTTALL letter 91; HUMPHREYS vol. 1, p. 304, to Anthony Massey.

56. NUTTALL letter 70; HUMPHREYS vol. 1, p. 254.

57. KIPPIS, A. 'Life of the author' in *The Family Expositor* (1811 edition) vol. 1, pp. xix–xx.

58. Son of Dr Benyon, tutor at Shrewsbury academy.

59. HUMPHREYS vol 2, p. 476.

60. Ibid. pp. 478–9. Doddridge was none too happy at Watts' suggestion that the tutor should be a single man.

61. Ibid. p. 483.

62. STANFORD, C. op. cit. p. 36.

## CHAPTER 3 (page 46)

1. The north gate of Northampton stood close to the present Regent Square.

2. SHEILS, W. J. *The Puritans in the Diocese of Peterborough, 1558–1610* (1979) p. 26.

3. The earliest reference to a 'prophesying' or 'exercise' in Northampton is 1570. The aims of the reformers were to improve standards of education among the clergy, and develop pastoral care. 'Idolatrous' practices in churches were suppressed. The clergy who subscribed their names to a list of those believing in 'Christ's true religion' took their turns in speaking for forty-five minutes on a text of scripture, which was then discussed by two other members for fifteen minutes each. Moral as well as intellectual criticism could be given and the Saturday meeting usually concluded with a confession of faith. See SHEILS, W. J. op. cit. p. 24 et seq.

4. COLLINSON, P. *The Elizabethan Puritan movement* (1971) p. 51.

5. Ibid. p. 142.

6. Sir Richard Knightley (1533–1615) exerted his influence in parliament for Puritan reforms, and was one of the local gentry responsible for bringing Percival Wiburn to Northampton. In spite of Knightley's opposition to the government's ecclesiastical policy, he gave outstanding service to Northamptonshire: Sheriff of the County three times, MP for the County (twice) and Northampton (twice), a JP, Deputy-Lieutenant of the County (once) and a member of the musters' and other commissions. He was fined for his part in the Marprelate Tracts' scandal, and removed from two of his offices for a short time.

7. Richard Davis, the Congregational minister at Rothwell, caused much offence by his fervent evangelism and outspokenness, his use of lay preachers, his appeal to emotionalism, and his inroads into other ministers' territories. Even at his ordination, ministers who had been invited to attend were not allowed to take part in the actual ordination as Davis, being a strict Congregationalist, believed that only the officers of the church should perform the ceremony. Several members of the Rothwell Church lived in Northampton and some friction was caused between them and members of College Lane Church. One person, a Mrs Hardin, was actually forbidden by Rothwell Church to take communion at Castle Hill until it was ascertained that it was 'a church rightly constituted, and that they own this as a true Church of Christ'. 'Rothwell Church Book', in TAYLOR, J. 'Bicentenary volume' (1896) p. 88. The cordial relationships between Castle Hill and the Rothwell Church during Doddridge's ministry can best be seen in the appointment of Samuel Hayworth, a member at Rothwell but living in Northampton, to the eldership of the Castle Hill church in 1741.

8. *A Plain and Just Account of a Most Horrid and Dismal Plague begun at . . . Rowell* (1692). See WATTS, M. R. op. cit. p. 295, who gives some evidence of the pamphlet's authorship.

9. Jeremiah Lewis and his church were undoubtedly Puritan; the pewter church plate bears the inscription 'Gilles' without any word for Saint (Giles).

10. TAYLOR, J. 'Bicentenary volume' (1896) p. 85.

11. The *Declaration of Indulgence* issued in 1672 suspended the penal laws against Dissenters and Roman Catholics. The *Indulgence* only lasted until March 1673.

12. John Harding was the son of John Harding, Rector of Brinkworth, Wilts

(1642 until ejected in 1662) and described as 'a most violent presbyterian'. The younger John Harding was Vicar of Ambrosden, Oxon (1655–62) and Melksham, Wilts (1658–62). Like his father, he was ejected in 1662. Both father and son are buried at St Peter's, Northampton.

LONGDEN, H. I. *Northamptonshire and Rutland Clergy since 1500* (1938–52) vol. 6, pp. 139–41.

13. GODFREY, B. S. *Castle Hill Meeting* (1947) pp. 10–11.

14. CATER, F. I. *Northamptonshire Nonconformity 250 Years Ago* (1912) p. 32.

15. Numbers of those who died in the great fire differ in various accounts. There were relatively few deaths considering the intensity and scale of the fire. *The State of Northampton from the beginning of the Fire,* by 'A COUNTRY MINISTER' (1675) p. 23, records: 'Eight Persons Burnt: Besides two Women and a young Youth Killed by the fall of a stack of Chimneys since.'

16. COX, J. C. and SERJEANTSON, R. M. *A history of the Church of the Holy Sepulchre, Northampton* (1897) p. 186.

17. *The State of Northampton from the beginning of the Fire,* by 'A COUNTRY MINISTER' (1675) p. 14.

18. MARLOW, N. *The diary of Thomas Isham of Lamport* (1971) pp. 318–19.

19. Fire Court Register 20 December 1677 and 5 March 1678, Northampton-shire Record Office (MS FF83–9). The *Swan* was situated on the site of the present Debenham's (formerly Adnitt's) department store. The curious 'jitty' linking the Drapery with College Street was established as a right of way in the mid-sixteenth century, on payment of rent from the *Swan* of twopence every Sunday to each of thirteen poor people.

TAYLOR, J. op. cit. p. 9.

20. 'Church Book' p. 10.

21. Harding and Blower were contemporaries at Magdalen College, and during the later years of the Protectorate worked in fairly close proximity to each other in Oxfordshire.

22. TAYLOR, J. op. cit. pp. 7–8.

23. The Baptists hold a distinctive view of baptism which may only be administered to 'believers'; the faith of the believer makes baptism effective and not the act itself, and thus adult baptism is practised, not the baptism of infants (paedo-baptism). Originally the Baptists practised affusion (pouring on) but from the 1640s total immersion has been the practice.

24. Second entry in 'Church Book'.

25. ARNOLD, T. and COOPER, J. J. *The history of the Church of Doddridge* (1895) p. 46.

26. Thomas Shepard settled at Bocking-cum-Braintree in Essex in 1700 where he pursued a very successful ministry until his death in 1739. His writings are of considerable merit, and some are included in the Northamptonshire Studies Collection (Taylor Collection) in the Central Library, Northampton.

27. The measurements of the chapel were 39ft 4ins (12m) north to south, and 52ft 6ins (16m) east to west. The pulpit was situated against the north wall and was reached by ten steps. The vestry was situated at the intersection of the west and north walls. In 1852 the two wooden pillars were removed when the building was re-roofed. In 1862 the church was doubled in size with major extensions on the

north side. In 1890 the vestibule on the south side was added, and three years later when Quart Pot Lane was renamed Doddridge Street, the old boundary wall was rebuilt; the iron palisade and gates from the front of All Saints Church were donated by Canon Hull and were re-erected at Castle Hill, thus improving the approach to the chapel.

28. 'Post est occasio calva' derives from Cato's 'opportunity has locks before, but behind is bald'; one should grasp opportunity before it is too late.

29. GASCOIGNE, T. 'Castle Hill Meeting and Dr Philip Doddridge' in TAYLOR, J. op. cit. p. 10.

30. Dated 1698 in 'Church Book'.

31. GASCOIGNE, T. op. cit. p. 13.

32. *Northampton Mercury* (1729) vol. 9, p. 183.

33. The original letter is preserved at Castle Hill, cf. HUMPHREYS vol. 2, pp. 493–4, where extensive alterations to the text have been made.

34. NUTTALL letter 323; HUMPHREYS vol. 2, p. 497.

35. NUTTALL letter 322; HUMPHREYS vol. 2, p. 495.

36. NUTTALL letter 326; HUMPHREYS vol. 2, p. 507.

37. HUMPHREYS vol. 3, pp. 3–4.

38. NUTTALL letter 331.

39. NUTTALL letter 333; HUMPHREYS vol. 2, pp. 516–7.

40. NUTTALL letter 334; HUMPHREYS vol. 2, p. 518.

41 HUMPHREYS vol. 3, p. 4.

42. After his infatuation with Kitty Freeman, Doddridge became attracted to Jenny Jennings. On 29 May 1730 he assured her of his love and sought to minimise their age difference (Jenny was then fifteen and Doddridge twenty-seven) by quoting a case of an extremely successful marriage where the partners were sixteen and thirty-two respectively. NUTTALL letter 339; HUMPHREYS vol. 3, p. 20.

43. HUMPHREYS vol. 3, p. 24.

44. The ordination of an Independent minister involved not only the solemn laying upon him of his new tasks, but also an exhortation ('charge') to church members to take their share of responsibilities. The 'charge' was given in a sermon by an ordained minister. The practice continues to the present day.

45. The original certificate is fastened to Doddridge's copy of the first volume of his *Family Expositor* now preserved at Dr Williams's Library, London. No explanation is available for David Some's absence, although there is no suggestion that he was still critical of Doddridge's sudden removal. Indeed, the two ministers remained on the best of terms, Doddridge sadly lamenting 'my most honoured and beloved friend' upon Some's death in June 1737. W. Hunt who signed the ordination certificate was the Revd William Hunt who succeeded his father, the Revd John Hunt (former minister of Castle Hill), in the pastorate of Newport Pagnell.

46. HUMPHREYS vol. 5, p. 273.

47. HUMPHREYS vol. 5, pp. 277–8.

48. HUMPHREYS vol. 3, p. 27.

49. The full implementation of the penal code against Dissenters was virtually impossible in England due to the lack of a centralised administration. Many Anglicans refused to persecute Dissenters, and in such towns as Yarmouth and

Coventry, Dissenters were strongly represented on the corporations, and were able to resist persecution. It is therefore not surprising to find Mercy's uncle, a Dissenter, as Mayor of Coventry. See WATTS, M. R. op. cit. pp. 244–9.

50. NUTTALL letter 340; HUMPHREYS vol. 3, p. 28, 6 August 1730.

51. NUTTALL letter 340; HUMPHREYS vol. 3, pp. 30–1.

52. NUTTALL letter 353; HUMPHREYS vol. 3, p. 61.

53. NUTTALL letter 839; HUMPHREYS vol. 4, p. 172.

54. NUTTALL letter 364, HUMPHREYS vol. 3, pp. 89–90.

55. NUTTALL letter 792; HUMPHREYS vol. 4, pp. 117–8.

56. NUTTALL letter 655; HUMPHREYS vol. 3, p. 527.

57. NUTTALL letter 485; HUMPHREYS vol. 3, p. 302, 3 February 1733.

58. NUTTALL letter 1741.

59. For examples of Doddridge's shopping for Mercy see NUTTALL letters 433, 997, 1081, 1256, 1638, 1640. See also Appendix VII.

60. A fragment of the skirt from this beautiful dress is preserved in Castle Hill vestry, also a pair of Mrs Doddridge's shoes. See illustrations 23 and 24, p. 92.

61. NUTTALL letter 1383.

62. NUTTALL letter 562; HUMPHREYS vol. 3, p. 400, 14 September 1739.

63. NUTTALL letter 846; HUMPHREYS vol. 4, pp. 186–7. Doddridge continued by informing his wife that he had taken to wearing 'a skin of bear' to keep out the cold; it was a humorous reference to a recently purchased woollen great-coat.

64. NUTTALL letter 759; HUMPHREYS vol. 4, p. 98, 25 June 1742.

65. NUTTALL letter 768; HUMPHREYS vol. 4, p. 102, 16–18 July 1742.

66. NUTTALL letter 778; HUMPHREYS vol. 4, pp. 106–7.

67. NUTTALL letter 450; HUMPHREYS vol. 3, p. 220.

68. HUMPHREYS vol. 5, p. 362.

69. Tetsy was buried beneath the communion table at Castle Hill. In Charles Reed's transcript from Doddridge's own writing, Anna Cecilia's birth is given as 3 July 1737 although it has often been quoted as 6 July. (Doddridge MS 191, Northamptonshire Studies Collection, Central Library, Northampton).

70. In addition to his family responsibilities Doddridge accepted the guardian-ship of twelve-year-old Sarah Ekins who had been orphaned in 1745. Sarah was due to come into a fortune of £12,000 upon reaching twenty-one. She was sent to a boarding school in Worcester run by Ann Linton; Doddridge's daughters Polly and Mercy, together with the daughters of Sir Arthur Heslerig, Molly and Dolly, attended the same school. The Heslerigs had been near-neighbours of the Doddridge's in Marefair, and their house still stands (1980) almost opposite the site of the former Doddridge home. See also chapter 5, note 1, this work.

71. NUTTALL letter 621; HUMPHREYS vol. 3, p. 485.

72. Evidently Joseph Collier was a wealthy man and seems to have been the tenant of Delapré for a time in 1740. The County Poll Books for 1730 and 1748 show that the property was owned by Bartholomew Tate. On 14 April 1740 the *Northampton Mercury* carried the following advertisement: 'To be Lett, furnished or unfurnish'd, and entered upon immediately, a Good Genteel House, call'd Delapree, near Northampton, with all conveniences for a large family. . . .' On 11 December 1740 Doddridge mentioned to his wife that the Colliers were planning to leave Delapré. He had visited Mrs Collier in early August at the start of the

smallpox epidemic, and it is clear that the Colliers urged the Doddridges to accept their hospitality. Mrs Collier sent her carriage to bring Mercy Doddridge to Delapré upon her return to Northampton in September 1740.

Joseph Collier had two daughters, Sally and Becky, who afterwards became members of the Church of England (NUTTALL letter 995). It is not clear which profession Joseph Collier followed. His name appears as a subscriber to the *Family Expositor*, and he was a member of the Northamptonshire Book Society of which Doddridge was a leading figure (see NUTTALL, p. 374). Collier was an early member of the Northampton Philosophical Society and joined at the same time as Doddridge (by 13 December 1743). Amongst others, Collier is reported to have lent apparatus to illustrate the society's lectures. *Gentleman's Magazine* (1746) vol. 26, p. 475.

73. NUTTALL letter 636, 30 August 1740.

See Appendix V for further details of the 1739-40 smallpox epidemic in Northampton.

74. One tenth of Doddridge's regular income from his academy and the church, and one eighth of any 'extraordinary' income from the publication of his books, were used for charitable purposes.

75. NUTTALL letter 764 (Doddridge MS 13, Northamptonshire Studies Collection, Central Library, Northampton). Some spelling has been amended.

76. STANFORD, C. op. cit. pp. 58–9.

77. NUTTALL letter 1512; HUMPHREYS vol. 5, p. 139. William Roffey (d. 1785) was a wealthy distiller who lived in Southwark.

78. NUTTALL letter 1515; HUMPHREYS vol. 5, pp. 142–4.

## CHAPTER 4 (page 72)

1. STANFORD, C. *Philip Doddridge* (1880) p. 127.

2. HUMPHREYS vol. 5, pp. 339–40.

3. ORTON, J. 'Life of Dr Doddridge' in Doddridge's *Works* (1802–5) vol. 1, pp. 48–59.

4. Ibid. p. 51.

5. Ibid. p. 49.

6. Ibid. p. 50, footnote; also KIPPIS, A. 'Life of the author' in *The Family Expositor* (1811 edition) p. xxvii.

7. ORTON, J. op. cit. p. 51.

8. STOUGHTON, J. *Philip Doddridge* (1851) p. 80.

9. STANFORD, C. op. cit. p. 129.

10. NUTTALL letter 150; HUMPHREYS vol. 1, p. 439.

11. ROUTLEY, E. 'The Hymns of Philip Doddridge' in NUTTALL, G. F. *Philip Doddridge* (1951) p. 71.

12. WATTS, M. R. *The Dissenters: from the Reformation to the French Revolution* (1978) pp. 308–13. Hymn singing in Anglican churches 'did not meet with universal approval until well into the nineteenth century' writes Watts, and adds that only the Quakers have remained completely unaffected by this major contribution of Dissent to English worship.

13. The opinion of the Revd John Ryland, minister of College Street Baptist

Church, See Stanford, C. op. cit. p. 128. Job Orton also remarked that Doddridge was 'a man who had no ear for music'.

14. Hymn 203, Doddridge's *Works* (1802–5) vol. 3, pp. 547–8. In all, 375 of Doddridge's hymns have been published; the first edition by Orton, appeared in 1755 (370 hymns), the second edition in 1759 (374 hymns), and the third and final edition in 1766 (375 hymns).

15. ROUTLEY, E. op. cit. p. 75. Routley gives a full account of Doddridge as a hymn writer.

16. Hymn 369 v. 4, Doddridge's *Works* (1802–5) vol. 3, p. 640.

17. Hymn 4 v. 1, Ibid. vol. 3, p. 435. The wording has been changed in modern hymnals.

18. Hymn 257 v. 4, Ibid. vol. 3, p. 576.

19. Hymn 19 v. 4, Ibid. vol. 3, p. 443.

20. HUMPHREYS vol. 5, p. 324.

21. ORTON, J. op. cit. p. 53.

22. HUMPHREYS vol. 5, pp. 520–1.

23. 'Church Book' p. 74.

24. Ibid. p. 84, 1 January 1747.

25. ORTON, J. op. cit. p. 53.

26. *A plain and serious address to the Master of a Family on the Important Subject of family-religion* (1750) p. 7.

27. Doddridge's *Works* (1802–5) vol. 2, p. 154.

28. 'Church Book.' It was a common habit to dual-date letters and other documents (Old Style and New Style) for the first three months of the year i.e. up to Lady Day (the festival of the Annunciation) on 25 March. The reform of the calendar by Pope Gregory XIII in 1582, restored 1 January as New Year's Day which had formerly been celebrated on 25 March. This reform was not adopted in Great Britain until 1752.

29. ORTON, J. op. cit. p. 55.

30. NUTTALL letter 822; HUMPHREYS vol. 4, p. 157.

31. NUTTALL letter 752; HUMPHREYS vol. 4, pp. 88–9.

32. 'Church Book' p. 60. On 6 March 1741 Doddridge gave details of his four elders to Daniel Wadsworth of Connecticut Colony (NUTTALL letter 663): (1) John Evans, a former Anglican clergyman (2) Samuel Hayworth, a Baptist lay preacher who had settled at Castle Hill (3) Job Orton, 'my Assistant both in the Academy & Congregation', and (4) John Browne 'a very modest humble serious Christian who teaches a Charity School lately Erected amongst the Dissenters in this place. . . .' (See also NUTTALL letters 672, 833.) Doddridge's choice of elders is thus remarkably broad-based.

In the Poll Book of 1768 for Northampton, John Browne is still recorded as 'schoolmaster'; the election map of the same year shows that he lived in the lower part of Bridge Street, opposite the present *Plough Hotel*. It is possible that the charity school met in Browne's house for a time although Doddridge's letter (above) could mean that a building was specially erected for the purpose.

33. A copy of Doddridge's 'Counsels to his Elders' is held at Castle Hill Church. See ARNOLD, T. and COOPER, J. J. *The history of the Church of Doddridge* (1895) pp. 112–14; the original manuscript is misquoted.

34. 'Church Book' p. 64.
35. Ibid. p. 65.
36. HUMPHREYS vol. 5, pp. 537–8.
37. NUTTALL letters 535, 538.
38. NUTTALL letter 662; HUMPHREYS vol. 3, pp. 543–4.
39. NUTTALL letter 1270; HUMPHREYS vol. 4, pp. 551–2, 30 August 1747, to Samuel Clark.
40. NUTTALL letter 645, 1 October 1740.
41. TAYLOR, J. 'Bicentenary volume' (1896) p. 100.
42. WADDINGTON, J. *Congregational history 1700–1800* (1876) p. 284.
43. Doddridge's *Works* (1802–5) vol. 5, p. 188.
44 DODDRIDGE, P. *A course of lectures on the Principal Subjects in Pneumatology, Ethics and Divinity*, ed S. Clark (1763), introduction, pp. 1–3. See also HARRIS, F. J. P. 'Philip Doddridge and Charges of Arianism' in *Congregational Historical Society Transactions* (1969) vol. 20, no. 9, p. 267.
45. THOMAS, R. 'Philip Doddridge and Liberalism in Religion' in NUTTALL, G. F. *Philip Doddridge* (1951) p. 151.
46. NUTTALL letter 416; HUMPHREYS vol. 3, p. 163. See also Appendix III for contemporary theological debate.
47. KIPPIS, A. 'Life of the author' in *The Family Expositor* (1811 edition) vol. 1, p. cx.
48. Doddridge's comment on 'the new fashioned divinity' is a reference to the development of Arianism amongst the Arminian Presbyterians which was eventually to lead to Socinianism and Unitarianism. For detailed treatment see WATTS, M. R. op. cit.; also Appendix III.
49. James Foster (1697–1753), was noted for a long controversy with Dr Henry Stebbing (1687–1763), maintaining that heresy 'when it amounted to no more than intellectual error, was not blameworthy'. Foster held 'heretical opinions (Arianism) of which Doddridge was persistently suspected'. See THOMAS, R. 'Philip Doddridge and Liberalism' in NUTTALL, G. F. *Philip Doddridge* (1951) p. 148.
50. NUTTALL letter 480; HUMPHREYS vol. 3, pp. 293–4, 6 January 1738.
51. George Whitefield (1714–70) was an eloquent and effective open air preacher who regularly delivered up to twenty sermons a week for thirty-four years. Whitefield's fiercely held Calvinistic views led to disputes between himself and his colleague John Wesley who held Arminian views. Whitefield's visit to Northampton was part of a ten-day tour; on 21 May 1739 he was at Hertford and from thence he preached at Bedford, Olney, Northampton, Hitchin and St Albans, before finally returning to Kennington. For further details see the *Gentleman's Magazine* (1739) vol. 9, pp. 162, 238–43. Such tours were typical of Whitefield who visited Scotland fourteen and America seven times. Horse racing on Harlestone Heath was an established sport in the time of Charles I. From 1632 onwards the Northampton Corporation gave an annual prize of a silver-gilt cup. The races on the heath ceased after 1739 when the Duke of Marlborough claimed the land as his. Other races were held in the common fields.
52. NUTTALL letter 922; HUMPHREYS vol. 4, p. 274, 11 October 1743.
53. Revd James Hervey (1714–58) was born at Hardingstone and educated at the free grammar school in Northampton. Initially a somewhat idle student at

Oxford, he became deeply influenced by Methodism, and taught himself Hebrew at the suggestion of John Wesley. After curacies in Hampshire and Devon, Hervey returned to the County in order to become his father's curate at Weston Favell. His father held the livings of Weston Favell and Collingtree, and upon his death in 1752 Hervey became the incumbent at Weston Favell. His writings were extremely popular with contemporaries; his best known works are *Meditations among the tombs* and *Dialogues between Theron and Aspasio*. His appreciation of the wonders of nature was unusual for his times, though his use of language was often inflated. As a man he was gentle, pious and unworldly. Profits from his writings were used for charitable ends, and upon his death his body, by his own request, was covered with the poor's pall. His literary and parochial exertions and delicate constitution led to his early death on Christmas Day 1758. He is buried beneath the centre of the altar in Weston Favell parish church.

54. Thomas Hartley (1709?–84) was the son of a London bookseller and a graduate of Cambridge. He became rector of Winwick in 1744. He was influenced by the evangelism of Hervey and Whitefield, and greatly admired the Countess of Huntingdon. Hartley's interest in Swedenborgianism commenced in 1769; frequent contact with Swedenborg led to Hartley's translation of some of the former's works. Swedenborg took note of Hartley's views when formulating his own distinctive view of the doctrine of the Trinity. For details of Swedenborgianism, see Appendix III.

55. Selina Hastings, Countess of Huntingdon (1707–91) owed her Christian conversion to the Moravians but became a prominent figure in the evangelical revival, appointed evangelical Anglicans as her chaplains (including George Whitefield) and established chapels in Brighton, Bath, London and Tunbridge Wells; her aim was to reach the upper classes with the Gospel. In 1768 she established a college at Trevecca in South Wales for the training of evangelical clergy, but in 1779 her Anglican clergy were forced to resign when it became mandatory for the Countess to register her chapels as Dissenting meeting-houses. In all she built sixty-four chapels. The Countess was an ardent admirer of Doddridge, sharing his deep passion for active Christianity. She supported Whitefield's orphanage in Georgia and corresponded with George Washington, a distant relative, about the needs of the Red Indians. She also advocated progress in education and helped sponsor Dartmouth college and Princeton university in the USA. In 1750 Doddridge dedicated his sermon *Christian Candour and Unanimity* to her.

56. NUTTALL, G. F. 'Doddridge's life and times' in NUTTALL's *Philip Doddridge* (1951) p. 25.

57. *Dictionary of National Biography*, article on Doddridge by A. Gordon.

CHAPTER 5 (page 90)

1. Doddridge's house (no. 34 Marefair) and Pike Lane have disappeared, their former location being where the present Barclaycard offices stand. Pike Lane was a narrow passage parallel to Quart Pot Lane (renamed Doddridge Street in 1893) and served to link Gold Street and St Mary's Street. The name probably derived from the pikes or posts erected at both ends of the lane to exclude cattle and horses.

Part of the Sheep Street academy still remains as a row of shops and offices (nos. 18–24) close to Greyfriars bus station.

2. NUTTALL letter 390; HUMPHREYS vol. 3, pp. 205–6.

3. PEVSNER, N. *Northamptonshire* (Buildings of England Series, 1973) p. 332. The *Victoria County History* refers to the academy as an early eighteenth-century building.

4. George Montagu, Earl of Halifax, succeeded his father in 1739. The family seat was at Horton in Northamptonshire. Halifax was a Privy Councillor, First Commissioner of Trade, Master of the Buckhounds and Lord Lieutenant of the County. He was also Lord Lieutenant of Ireland, First Lord of the Admiralty, Secretary of State, and Lord Privy Seal. In 1741 he married a Miss Dunk and assumed her surname. He died without issue in 1771 when his titles became extinct. Halifax exerted considerable influence in Northampton, and was a powerful patron of Whig interests in the town until his defeat in the election of 1768. He strongly supported Doddridge.

5. NUTTALL letter 390; HUMPHREYS vol. 3, p. 206.

6. STANFORD, C. *Philip Doddridge* (1880) p. 73.

7. In 1738 William Coward (1657?–1725), left £20,000 to be administered by four trustees for the advancement of the Dissenting cause. In 1690 a group of Congregational and Presbyterian ministers in London set up a Common Fund to support impoverished ministers, and congregations struggling to maintain a minister. Differences of opinion led the Congregationalists to set up their own fund in 1695 but the Common Fund continued to support Congregationalists and was only officially termed 'Presbyterian' in 1771. See also chapter 2, note 53.

8. TAYLOR, J. 'Bicentenary volume' (1896) p. 73.

9. Doddridge's assistant tutors in order were: Job Orton, Thomas Brabant, James Robertson and Samuel Clark (son of Dr Samuel Clark). Job Orton (1717–83) was the elder son of Job Orton, a grocer of Shrewsbury. Initially apprenticed to his father he decided to train for the Christian ministry; he entered the Dissenting academy at Warrington in 1733 and transferred to the Northampton academy in August 1734. In 1739 he became Doddridge's assistant tutor, and was licensed as a minister in the same year. Orton left in 1741 to become minister of a combined Independent and Presbyterian congregation in his native town of Shrewsbury. After Doddridge's death he was urged to succeed Doddridge at Castle Hill, Northampton. Orton finally resigned his Shrewsbury pastorate in 1765 due to ill-health, and moved to Kidderminster where he died in 1783. His later years were engaged in literary activities which included his *Memoirs* of Doddridge, the completion of Doddridge's *Family Expositor*, and editing Doddridge's hymns. Like Doddridge, he was extremely well-read and became influential through his wide correspondence. Andrew Kippis considered him to be one of the most striking preachers he had ever heard. In 1773 Orton declined an honorary Doctorate of Divinity offered by New Jersey College; in his later years he signed himself 'Job Orton S.T.P.' (Sanctae Theologiae Professor—'Professor of Theology'). A lifelong bachelor, he was of a serious turn of mind, unpretentious and methodical in his habits, and generous in using his substantial means for charitable purposes. He followed Doddridge's Sabellian views of the Trinity (see Appendix III). Although he had strong Presbyterian leanings, he considered himself 'quite an Independent'. In stature Orton

was tall and rather lean. He is buried near the altar in St Chad's Church, Shrewsbury where his intimate friend Thomas Stedman was vicar.

10. ORTON, J. 'Life of Dr Doddridge' in Doddridge's *Works* (1802–5) vol. 1, p. 60.

11. Ibid. vol. 1, p. 61.

12. Being a 'parlour boarder' had its advantages, as Doddridge pointed out to one parent because it 'gives him [the student] a preference in the Choice of a Chamber which may the better secure his having an agreeable Bedfellow'. NUTTALL letter 1268, to William Farr, 21 August 1747.

13. ORTON, J. op. cit. vol. 1, p. 74.

14. Correspondence between Doddridge and Lord Kilkerran shows that both put considerable pressure upon John to mend his ways. John made it plain that he did not wish to pursue a legal career as his father wished. Complaints against John included extravagence in the choice of clothes, excessive travelling, the purchase of expensive riding equipment, and lack of care with his studies, including illegible handwriting. On 13 September 1744 he presented his accounts to his father amounting to fourteen guineas. It appears that by the end of 1744 John did settle down to work with greater application. See FERGUSSON, J. *John Fergusson 1727-50* (1948) pp. 13–90.

15. NUTTALL letter 946; HUMPHREYS vol. 4, pp. 308–9; see also HUMPHREYS vol. 5, p. 465.

16. NUTTALL letter 931; HUMPHREYS vol. 4, p. 163, 21 November 1743.

17. NUTTALL letter 942.

18. *Dictionary of National Biography*, article on Doddridge by A. Gordon.

19. KIPPIS, A. 'Life of the author' in *The Family Expositor* (1811 edition) vol. 1, p. xxxvi. Kippis comments: 'The doctor, I believe, towards the close of his life was of opinion that he had gone far enough in this matter.'

20. Each student paid one guinea per year in order to purchase books for the library. Students' names were entered in the books as their contribution to the library. Over two thousand volumes were held, many of which Doddridge had purchased himself. A considerable number of them are preserved in Dr Williams's Library, London.

21. KIPPIS, A. op. cit. p. xxxvii.

22. Ibid.

23. Doddridge's *Works* (1802–5) vol. 5, p. 461; and MURRAY, A. V. 'Doddridge and Education' in NUTTALL, G. F. *Philip Doddridge* (1951) p. 105.

24. A lecture by Doddridge was based upon the following method: (1) proposition; (2) demonstration (arguments in support of the proposition); (3) axiom (making assumptions); (4) scholium (further explanations, often giving objections but providing answers to those objections); and (5) corollary (formulating conclusions). In practice Doddridge varied the format slightly to suit his purposes, and used definitions, solutions, arguments and lemmas (leading thoughts or themes); nevertheless, the plan of each lecture was precisely structured.

25. NUTTALL letter 1166; HUMPHREYS vol. 4, p. 493.

26. ISAAC PITMAN in *Phonetic Journal* 3 April 1886 et seq. Gives details of Doddridge's influences on shorthand. See also Appendix IV for further details of Jeremiah Rich's system of shorthand.

27. William Wykes, J.P. and Tory M.P. for Northampton (1710–22). In later years he was granted a monopoly by the Northampton Corporation to provide piped water for the town.

28. NUTTALL letter 450; HUMPHREYS vol. 3, p. 220, 1 January 1737.

29. The curate at Kingsthorpe has been called 'the Revd Mr Wills' through the centuries, but has now been identified by Mr P. I. King (from the Northampton Archdeaconry Call Books) as the Revd James Wells; see NUTTALL letter 375. The Rector of Kingsthorpe was Richard Reynolds who also held the livings of St Peter's, Northampton, and Upton, to which he had been presented by Queen Anne in 1706. Reynolds held these combined livings together with other preferments until his death in 1744. He was Prebendary of Peterborough from 1704, Dean of Peterborough from 1718, Bishop of Bangor from 1721, and Bishop of Lincoln from 1723. Reynolds had been Archdeacon of Northampton from 1701, but this office passed to his brother-in-law Richard Cumberland in 1707. See SERJEANTSON, R. M. *A history of the Church of St Peter, Northampton* (1904) p. 99, and LONGDEN, H. I. *Northamptonshire and Rutland clergy from 1500* (1938-52) vol. 3, p. 317 and vol. II, p. 177.

30. NUTTALL letter 378; HUMPHREYS vol. 3, p. 85.

31. TAYLOR, J. op. cit. p. 21.

32. NUTTALL letter 393; HUMPHREYS vol. 3, p. 128, to John Barker, 25 November 1733.

33. NUTTALL letter 419; HUMPHREYS vol. 3, p. 167, to Mercy Doddridge, 29 June 1734.

34. NUTTALL letter 390; HUMPHREYS vol. 3, pp. 207–8, to John Barker, August 1733.

35. ORTON, J. op. cit. p. 56.

36. Ibid. p. 57.

37. Doddridge was in touch with Welsh charity schools.

38. STOUGHTON, J. *Philip Doddridge* (1851) p. 119.

39. Ibid. p. 120.

40. Published posthumously in 1807.

41. Doddridge's *Works* (1802-5) vol. 5, p. 461.

42. NUTTALL p. xxxv.

43. NUTTALL letter 932; HUMPHREYS vol. 4, p. 298, to Samuel Clark.

44. *The Rise and Progress of Religion in the Soul* (1745).

45. NUTTALL letter 1562; HUMPHREYS vol. 4, p. 373, to Anton Heinrich Walbaum, 20 December 1749.

46. This assessment of the unreformed Stonhouse is by Doddridge. Stonhouse's outspokenness caused trouble in later years and there were attempts to remove him from the Northampton Infirmary.

47. NUTTALL letter 443; HUMPHREYS vol. 3, p. 219, 24 March 1736.

48. NUTTALL letter 527; HUMPHREYS vol. 3, p. 349. Doddridge notes in the same letter his 'purpose to wait on her [i.e. the Princess] some time or another & to accept the Honour of kissing her Hand; but I chuse rather to present my Book by the clerk of the closet [Francis Ayscough] than in Person lest it should look like courting a Present'.

49. NUTTALL letter 1630; HUMPHREYS vol. 5, p. 172, to Benjamin Fawcett.

50. EVERITT, A. *The pattern of Rural Dissent: the nineteenth century* (1972) p. 17.

51. Ibid. Everitt notes that only a small percentage of subscribers came from London, the majority being fairly evenly divided between large provincial towns, small rural market towns, and wholly agrarian parishes. Such was Doddridge's widespread influence.

52. NUTTALL letter 1448; HUMPHREYS vol. 5, p. 107, 9 February 1749.

53. EVERITT, A. op. cit. p. 65.

54. Doddridge's *Works* (1802–5) vol. 2, p. 49.

55. Ibid. vol. 2, p. 11.

56. Ibid. vol. 2, p. 79.

57. NUTTALL letter 926; HUMPHREYS vol. 4, p. 282, 4 November 1743.

58. Doddridge was able to show his surprised host certain writings deposited by Oliver Cromwell in the University library, and long since forgotten. NUTTALL letter 680; HUMPHREYS vol. 4, p. 30.

### CHAPTER 6 (page 114)

1. CLARK, P. and SLACK, P. *English towns in transition, 1500–1700* (1976) p. 100. The authors seem to underestimate the amount of rebuilding in stone, rather than brick, after the fire.

2. See EVERITT, A. *Perspectives in English Urban History* (1973) for an interesting account of Northampton inn life during this period.

3. For insight into Northampton life see the files of the *Northampton Mercury* (founded in 1720) held in the Northamptonshire Studies Collection, Central Library, Northampton.

4. In February 1742 Doddridge advised Jane Holden on the distribution of £20,000 to charity which had been bequeathed by her husband; much went to the support of Dissenting ministers, their widows and children (NUTTALL letter 731). In January 1748 Doddridge refers to his distribution of money from the charity established by Sir Joseph Jekyll of Dallington (1663–1738). NUTTALL letter 1304; HUMPHREYS vol. 5, p. 36.

5. ORTON, J. 'Life of Dr Doddridge' in Doddridge's *Works* (1802–5) vol. 1, p. 127.

6. Ibid. pp. 124–5.

7. NUTTALL letter 1633; HUMPHREYS vol. 5, p. 174. Humphreys has considerably altered the text of the letter.

8. TAYLOR, J. 'Bicentenary volume' (1896) p. 26.

9. NUTTALL letter 664; HUMPHREYS vol. 3, p. 545, 14–15 March 1741.

10. NUTTALL letter 667; HUMPHREYS vol. 3, p. 560.

11. *Northampton Mercury* vol. 26, pp. 195–203.

12. See chapter 3, pp. 68–9 this work.

13. HUMPHREYS vol. 5, p. 409.

14. NUTTALL letter 1185, 31 August/2 September 1746.

15. Northampton sent £315, Kettering £105 and Oundle £42.

16. NUTTALL letter 1581; HUMPHREYS vol. 5, p. 151, 15 February 1750.

17. *The Guilt and Doom of Capernaum, seriously recommended to the consideration of the Inhabitants of London.* Preface, pp. v-vii.

18. NUTTALL letter 1591; HUMPHREYS vol. 5, p. 153.

19. Writing to Mercy on 28 July 1750 Doddridge reported, 'Since the Earthquakes the King has forbid playing [cards] at Court on Sunday Nights. NUTTALL letter 1636; and p. 376 for details of Doddridge's report to the Royal Society on the earthquake.

20. Thomas Yeoman F.R.S. (1704?-81) was one of the leading civil engineers of his day. His varied interests included the design and construction of agricultural machinery and scientific instruments, the operation of the Northampton Cotton Mills, the construction of turnpikes, architecture, and land surveying. He installed a weighbridge at Northampton and fixed ventilators in the infirmary (1748) and the gaol (1749).

The Northampton Philosophical Society met in Yeoman's house in Gold Street, and he was president several times. From 13 December 1743 he conducted, with other members, experiments with electricity. In September 1746 the *Gentleman's Magazine* reported: 'Mr Yeoman having elctrify'd a man, while a vein was open in his arm, the blood flow'd then much faster, and slower on ceasing to electrify.' Yeoman may have been one of the occasional lecturers employed by Doddridge at the academy. See MUSSON, A. E. and ROBINSON, E. *Science and technology in the Industrial Revolution* (1969) p. 383; the authors devote an interesting chapter to the career of Yeoman, but incorrectly credit Doddridge with an F.R.S.

Yeoman was a member of College Lane Baptist Church and took part in the prayers at Castle Hill in 1751 for Doddridge's recovery (NUTTALL letter 1771). On 29 September 1747 Doddridge, writing to his daughter Polly, remarked that Yeoman 'who buried his former wife since you left us has now got another, Mr Remington's Sister, in whom I hope he is very happy'. (NUTTALL letter 1278.) Yeoman's first wife seems to have died of smallpox.

21. NUTTALL letter 469; HUMPHREYS vol. 3, p. 273, to Samuel Clark, 8 September 1737.

22. NUTTALL letter 1292; HUMPHREYS vol. 5, pp. 24-30 from Henry Baker.

23. NUTTALL letters 1595, 1416, 1339, 1273; HUMPHREYS vol. 4, p. 557.

24. NUTTALL letter 859, 22 February 1743. Sir Thomas Samwell persuaded Stonhouse to come to Northampton as a possible replacement for either Dr Freeman or Dr Kimberley.

25. A fourth physician, the poet Mark Akenside (1721-70), arrived in Northampton in 1744 but did not stay long.

26. The earliest hospital was St Bartholomew's in London, founded in 1123 by Rahere. Its objectives were to assist the poor, orphans, outcasts, and the sick. Similar institutions continued to be founded up to the Reformation, but only St Bartholomew's and St Thomas's (founded 1213) survived into the eighteenth century. Both hospitals were refounded in the sixteenth century, as were St Mary's Bethlem and the Bridewell. Christ's Hospital, founded in 1553, thus brought the number of royal or chartered hospitals to five; all were situated in London. Outside the capital there was Bellott's Mineral Water Hospital in Bath (founded 1610) and the Greenwich Hospital for wounded and disabled seamen. Although sadly deficient for the vast needs of the population, these institutions had to suffice until the voluntary

hospital movement of the eighteenth century. Voluntary hospitals antedating the Northampton Infirmary are: Westminster (1720), Guy's (1724), Edinburgh (1729), St George's (1733), Winchester (1736), Bristol Royal Infirmary (1737), London (1740), York County (1740), Royal Devon and Exeter (1741), Aberdeen Royal Infirmary (1742) and Bath General (1742). Unlike the chartered hospitals, the voluntary hospitals were dependent upon subscriptions and gifts rather than endowments, administration was in the hands of the subscribers, medical and surgical staff held honorary positions, and patients were not required to pay any fees. In comparison with today's standards hygiene and medical care were rudimentary, but the voluntary hospitals provided a service for a section of the population which had previously been neglected.

WOODWARD, J. *To do the sick no harm* (1974).

27. Northamptonshire Record Office, ref. IL 2561; see also *Names of first subscribers to the Infirmary*, ref. IL 2826; and *Progress of the Infirmary*, ref. IL 133.

28. NUTTALL letter 946; HUMPHREYS vol. 4, p. 307.

29. When the infirmary opened in March 1744, thirty beds were in use; the first report in the following October noted that 103 in-patients and 79 out-patients had been treated.

30. Doddridge's *Works* (1802–5) vol. 3, p. 117.

31. The Earl of Halifax considered that the Mayor of Northampton showed his prejudice against Dissenters by not handing out even-handed justice to the culprits. See NUTTALL letter 397, where Halifax complains of the 'poor artifices as the mayor has lately practised'. It was an age when Dissenting meeting houses could still be broken up by hostile mobs.

32. NUTTALL letter 756; HUMPHREYS vol. 4, p. 37, to Mercy Doddridge, 18 June 1742.

33. See STOUGHTON, J. *Philip Doddridge* (1851) pp. 155–6, who quotes from the *North British Review*, p. 28.

34. FERGUSSON, J. *John Fergusson 1727–1750* (1948) p. 93. James Gardiner (1688–1745), served as a cadet from an early age, then became an ensign at fourteen in a Scots regiment fighting the Dutch. From 1702 he served under Marlborough and distinguished himself by his conduct at the battle of Ramillies in 1706. Rapid promotion followed, and for a time he was Lt Colonel of the Inniskilling Dragoons. According to Doddridge, Gardiner was converted after reading WATSON's *The Christian Soldier*, but according to Alexander Carlyle, GURNALL's *Christian Armour* led to his sudden conversion. On 19 April 1743 Gardiner succeeded General Humphrey Bland as Colonel of the 13th Hussars. Doddridge wrote a biography, *Some Remarkable Passages in the Life of . . . Col. James Gardiner*, in which he eulogised Gardiner and the manner of his conversion to Christianity. Some critics were quick to condemn the book and Doddridge's assessment of Gardiner's character. See *A Letter to the Revd P. Doddridge D.D. concerning his Life of Col. Gardiner* (1749) in which the anonymous author upbraids Doddridge for his inaccuracies, yet addresses himself to 'the Reverend Doctor Patrick Doddridge'. Doddridge certainly relied too much on the imagination of Gardiner's servant, and his picture of Gardiner holding out heroically to the end at Prestonpans is unsubstantiated. See FERGUSSON, J. op. cit. p. 93.

35. NUTTALL letter 1101.

36. NUTTALL letter 1094; HUMPHREYS vol. 4, p. 430.

37. TAYLOR, J. (ed) op. cit. p. 33.

38. NUTTALL letter 1099; HUMPHREYS vol. 4, p. 443.

39. John Fergusson enraged his father, Lord Kilkerran, by accepting Lord Halifax's offer of an ensign's commission. Relationships between Doddridge and Lord Kilkerran became ruffled until the latter accepted his son's decision. John became the 'darling' of his regiment and marched away from Northampton accompanied by the tears of the Doddridge girls who kissed his dog Punch '20 times a day as your representative' whilst he was away (NUTTALL letter 1108). John wrote to Doddridge regarding the course of the struggle; on 19 January 1746 he wrote from Carlisle: 'All the way as we went we met with visible marks of the distress and confusion of the rebels, such as graves of men and the roads strew'd with dead horses' (NUTTALL letter 1120). In the previous June, John had begun to spit blood; this was the first sign of consumption. He died near Edinburgh on 25 July 1750, and was buried two days later on his twenty-third birthday. FERGUSSON, J. op. cit. p. 197.

40. STANFORD, C. *Philip Doddridge* (1880) p. 144.

41. Panic throughout England was intense; 30,000 men were held at Finchley to guard London. However, even the Jacobites failed to rise in support of Charles; Manchester, deemed a strong Jacobite stronghold, provided only limited support— a gift of £2,000, some illuminations, and an insignificant number of recruits.

42. Doddridge's *Works* (1802–5) vol. 3, p. 147.

43. STANFORD, C. op. cit. p. 150.

44. NUTTALL letter 789; HUMPHREYS vol. 4, p. 110, 29 September 1742.

45. NUTTALL letter 799; HUMPHREYS vol. 4, p. 129, 6 November 1742.

46. Doddridge's *Works* (1802–5) vol. 1, p. 472.

47. Ibid. vol. 1, p. 589.

48. Doddridge's Dutch students were Pieter de Hondt, son of a bookseller at the Hague; Pierre Rocquette, son of a wine merchant in Rotterdam; and Hendrik Beman, son of a Rotterdam bookseller.

49. NUTTALL letter 894; HUMPHREYS vol. 4, p. 246, 28 April 1743.

50. NUTTALL letter 904; HUMPHREYS vol. 4, p. 260. Sack (or wine) whey formed part of DR CHEYNE's 'A Method to Cure a Cold' *Gentleman's Magazine* (1736) vol. 6, p. 619. 'Lye much a-bed; drink plentifully of small, warm Sack-Whey [boiling water poured over skimmed milk and white wine, with a lump of sugar, plus balm or a slice of lemon added to the Whey], with a few Drops of Spirit of Hart's Horn [sal volatile or smelling salts]; Posset-Drink [similar to sack-whey but including bread, milk, nutmeg and, sometimes, eggs]; Water Gruel [strained water from boiled oatmeal, with salt and butter added], or any other warm, small Liquors … go cautiously and well cloathed into the Air afterwards.' A formula ideally suited to one of Doddridge's weak disposition, and which would no doubt be largely ignored by him.

51. NUTTALL letter 755; HUMPHREYS vol. 4, p. 92.

52. PAYNE, E. A. 'Doddridge and the missionary enterprise' in NUTTALL, G. F. *Philip Doddridge* (1951) p. 80.

53. The Society for Promoting Christian Knowledge. See BULLOCK, F. W. B. *Voluntary religious societies 1520–1799* (1963) pp. 231–4.

54. The Society for the Propagation of the Gospel in Foreign Parts. See Bullock as in 53.

55. Benjamin Ingham finally left the Moravians, and the Archbishop of Canterbury, like Doddridge, cooled in his earlier support of Moravian activities. See NUTTALL letter 1398, to Risdon Darracott, September-October 1748.

56. NUTTALL letter 686; HUMPHREYS vol. 4, p. 38, to Mercy Doddridge, 2 July 1751.

57. NUTTALL letter 690; HUMPHREYS vol. 4, p. 48, to Mercy Doddridge, 10–11 July 1741.

58. For detailed treatment of Doddridge's missionary interests see PAYNE, E. A. 'Doddridge and the missionary enterprise' in NUTTALL, G. F. *Philip Doddridge* (1951) pp. 79–101.

In the Castle Hill 'Church Book' is the following entry in Doddridge's handwriting:

'Received of the Collection made at the 1st meeting of the Society for the Propagation of the Gospel March 26 1742 £3.16.10. Recd since from Several Hands 2s.6d. 2s.6d. 2s.'

(2s.6d. = 12½p and £3.16.10 = £3.84) It is interesting to note that a similarly small sum of £13.2s.6d. (£13.12½) launched William Carey's Baptist Missionary Society in Kettering on 2 October 1792, the beginning of the modern missionary movement.

59. Relations between College Street Baptist Church and Castle Hill Church were extremely cordial; the vestry was frequently used by the former church so that candidates for adult (believers') baptism could be prepared and then walk the two hundred yards to the Nene, which flowed close to the remains of the castle walls. The spot where William Carey was baptised on 15 October 1783 is now beneath the railway station, the Nene having been redirected when the railway was built. On Sunday 19 November 1978 the Revd R. Baker, former minister of College Street Baptist Church, rededicated the old vestry following intensive restoration work by members of the Castle Hill Church.

CHAPTER 7 (page 135)

1. KIPPIS, A. 'Life of the author' in *The Family Expositor* (1811 edition) vol. 1, p. xc.

2. NUTTALL letter 499; HUMPHREYS vol. 3, p. 315.

3. NUTTALL letter 542; HUMPHREYS vol. 3, p. 369, to Samuel Clark, 16 April 1739.

4. Dr Clark died on 4 December 1750, aged 65. Doddridge preached his funeral sermon at St Albans on 16 December.

5. KIPPIS, A. op. cit. p. lxxi.

6. NUTTALL letter 1747; HUMPHREYS vol. 5, p. 205.

7. HUMPHREYS vol. 5, p. 527.

8. Job Orton's removal from Northampton deeply disappointed Doddridge; he had hoped that Orton would eventually take over his place in the academy as well as the ministry of Castle Hill. Nevertheless they remained devoted friends

(see 'Church Book' p. 65). Orton became minister to a united Independent and Presbyterian congregation in Shrewsbury where he remained until 1765. See also chapter 5, note 9.

9. NUTTALL letter 1770; HUMPHREYS vol 5, pp. 210–11, 6 August 1751.

10. NUTTALL letter 1771; HUMPHREYS vol. 5, p. 212.

11. NUTTALL letter 1769; HUMPHREYS vol 5, p. 208, 5 August 1751.

12. NUTTALL letter 1772; HUMPHREYS vol. 5, p. 214, 12 August 1751.

13. William Warburton (1698–1779), Bishop of Gloucester, had a high regard for Doddridge. Together with Alexander Pope, Warburton visited Ralph Allen at his residence at Prior Park in 1741. Allen, like Doddridge, took the initiative in 1745 and raised a hundred-strong corps of volunteers at his own expense to defend Bath. As Deputy Postmaster for Bath, Allen devised a system of mail distribution for England and Wales and thereby became a wealthy man.

14. STANFORD, C. *Philip Doddridge* (1880) p. 190, quoting from Augustus Toplady's *Works* vol. 4, pp. 141–2.

15. *The New Christian's Magazine* pp. 535–6—a fragment at Castle Hill, date unknown.

16. NUTTALL letter 1796; HUMPHREYS vol. 5, p. 227, 21 September 1751.

17. To capture the dreamlike state of Doddridge's mind during and after the voyage see NUTTALL letter 1801: 'The most undisturbed Serenity continues in my Mind . . . I hope I have done my Duty, and the Lord do, as seemeth good in his Sight.' There was a mystical element in Doddridge's religious experience; see NUTTALL letter 867; HUMPHREYS vol. 4, p. 211; and *A Remarkable Dream of the late Dr Doddridge of Northampton* a printed sheet costing one penny 'Printed for the Benefit of Matthew Bruce a Blind Young Man' (London, date unknown), Castle Hill archives.

18. NUTTALL 1799; ORTON, J. 'Life of Dr Doddridge' in Doddridge's *Works* (1802–5) vol. 1, p. 344; and HUMPHREYS vol. 5, p. 233, possibly to Samuel Clark (junior), 28 September 1751.

19. NUTTALL letter 1703; HUMPHREYS vol. 5, p. 193, 23 February 1751.

20. NUTTALL letter 1703; HUMPHREYS vol. 5, p. 193, 23 February 1751. In this letter Benjamin Forfitt emphasised that due to Doddridge's influence, especially his earthquake sermon, he decided to found The Charitable Society for Promoting Religious Knowledge among the Poor. It was interdenominational and the first of its kind in England. Its first donation of Bibles was given to Doddridge on 6 September 1750; see RIPPON, J. *Discourse on the . . . Society for Promoting Religious Knowledge among the Poor* (1803). The society continued to operate until c.1920 when its work was merged with that of the Scripture Gift Mission; see BULLOCK, F. W. B. *Voluntary religious societies* (1963) p. 237. See also NUTTALL letters 1543, 1606, 1703, 1714.

21. Doddridge MS 190, Northamptonshire Studies Collection, Central Library, Northampton.

22. ORTON, J. op. cit. vol. 1, p. 199.

23. Ibid.

24. Doddridge had always expressed a wish to be buried at Castle Hill next to his beloved 'Tetsy', but he had become indifferent to the matter during his final illness. The difficulties and expense of transferring his body to England precluded any attempt to do so.

25. The *Northampton Mercury* vol. 32, p. 139. Mercy faced the ordeal of returning to England to clear her husband's affairs with great composure. She was treated with much kindness and generosity by her friends, especially the members of Castle Hill and the academy. She continued to live in Northampton for some years, but eventually moved to Tewkesbury with her two unmarried daughters, Mary and Anna Cecilia. She died in 1790 aged eighty-two.

Upon Doddridge's death the academy moved to Daventry under the tutorship of Dr Caleb Ashworth. One of the students at the Daventry academy (1752–5) was the Unitarian Joseph Priestley, who later taught languages at the Warrington academy and held several successive pastorates. He was deeply interested in history and scientific experimentation; he discovered ammonia and sulphur dioxide, was co-discoverer of oxygen, and invented soda water as an intended remedy for scurvy. Priestley was one of the most notable products of the Dissenting academies. The Daventry academy returned to Northampton (1789) under the tutorship of the Revd John Horsey, the minister of Castle Hill. Ten years later the Coward Trustees, who controlled the academy, moved it to Wymondley in Hertfordshire. In 1833 it moved to London (Courtauld House), becoming known as Coward College. Merging with other academies in 1850, Coward College became New College, London, which discontinued as a school of divinity in the University of London in 1977. Books and manuscripts from all these institutions are preserved in Dr Williams's Library, Gordon Square, London. See NUTTALL, G. F. *New College, London and its library: two lectures* (1977).

The church at Castle Hill underwent considerable expansion during the ministry of the Revd Thomas Arnold (1860–82); in 1862 the church was renamed 'Doddridge Chapel'. In St James one of the church's branch Sunday schools met in a former smithy; the work flourished so much that the building of a new church named 'Doddridge Memorial Church' commenced in 1895 to mark the bicentenary of the founding of Castle Hill, and to bear witness to the continuing inspiration of Philip Doddridge. The first service in the new church was held on 11 November 1896.

## EPILOGUE (page 142)

1. STEDMAN, T. (ed.) *Letters from . . . Job Orton and . . . Sir James Stonhouse . . . to . . . T. Stedman* (2nd edition, 1805) vol. 2, p. 233, letter 31. A 'surtout' is a man's overcoat.

2. EVERITT, A. *The pattern of Rural Dissent: the nineteenth century* (1972) p. 67.

3. NUTTALL letter 1769; HUMPHREYS vol. 5, p. 208, 5 August 1751.

4. ALLIBONE, A. S. *A critical dictionary of English literature and British and American authors* (1878) vol. 1, p. 510.

5. NUTTALL letter 1649; HUMPHREYS vol. 5, p. 178.

6. NUTTALL letter 1477.

7. NUTTALL letter 1679.

8. KIPPIS, A. 'Life of the author' in *The Family Expositor* (1811 edition) vol. 1, p. xxvi; and *Boswell's Life of Johnson*, ed. G. B. Hill and L. F. Powell (Clarendon Press, 1934–50) vol. 5, p. 271.

APPENDIX I

# Chronology of the Life of
# Philip Doddridge

1702 (26 June) Born at an unknown location in London.
1711 (12 April) Death of his mother.
1712 Enters the Revd Daniel Mayo's grammar school, Kingston-on-Thames.
1714 (1 August) Death of Queen Anne and accession of George I.
1715 Death of his father.
 Death of Uncle Philip.
 Doddridge placed under the guardianship of Downes.
 Doddridge removed to Mr Nathaniel Wood's school at St Albans.
 The 'Fifteen' Jacobite rebellion in favour of the Old Pretender.
1718 (1 January) Joins Dr Samuel Clark's church, St Albans.
 Bankruptcy of Downes.
 Doddridge leaves school to stay with his sister, Elizabeth Nettleton, at
 Hampstead.
 Duchess of Bedford offers Doddridge preferment in the Church of England.
 Dr Calamy advises Doddridge not to become a minister.
 Doddridge is helped by Dr Clark to train for the ministry.
1719 (October) Enters the Revd John Jennings' academy at Kibworth.
1722 Moves with the academy to Hinckley.
 (30 July) Preaches his first sermon.
1723 Qualifies as a Christian minister.
 (8 July) Death of John Jennings.
 Acceptance of the Kibworth pastorate and removal to Stretton in order to
 take up pastoral duties.
1724 Refuses to subscribe to religious formulae.
 (4 November) Remarks that he is 'in all the more important points a Calvinist'.
1725 (9 April) Death of David Some, junior.
 (30 September) Moves to Market Harborough in united pastorate with the
 Revd David Some, senior.
1727 Accession of George II.
 Doddridge expresses loyalty to Hanoverians.
1729 (July) Commences duties as principal of the academy at Market Harborough.
 (28 September) Doddridge receives an invitation to the pastorate of Castle
 Hill, Northampton.
 (6 December) Doddridge accepts the Northampton pastorate.
 (24 December) Moves to Northampton.
 John and Charles Wesley found the Methodist Society at Oxford.

1730 (13 January) Doddridge commences organising the Northampton academy at his house in Marefair.

Doddridge is seriously ill.

(19 March) Ordination at Castle Hill meeting, Northampton.

(summer) Finally relinquishes his suit for Miss Jenny Jennings, and falls in love with Miss Mercy Maris.

(October) Mercy accepts his proposal of marriage.

(22 December) Married.

1731 (8 October) Daughter Elizabeth ('Tetsy') born.

1732 (August/September) Doddridge's preaching in a Kingsthorpe barn the subject of criticism.

1733 (7 May) Daughter Mary ('Polly') born.

1733–4

(November) Conflicts with diocesan authorities over his right to teach without episcopal licence.

(December) Doddridge's house is stoned by an anti-Dissenting mob.

1734 (early April) Death of his only sister Elizabeth Nettleton at Ongar.

(26 August) Daughter Mercy born.

1735 (6 August) Son Philip born.

1736 (27 May) Receives honorary Doctorate of Divinity from the University of Aberdeen.

(1 October) Death of daughter Elizabeth aged almost five.

1736 (21 October) Riot at Brixworth.

1737 (27 May) Death of David Some senior.

(3 July) Daughter Anna Cecilia ('Caelia') born.

(10 September) Meets Benjamin Ingham.

1738 Commences charity school for twenty poor boys.

(28 July) The great fire at Wellingborough.

(9 November) Doddridge's sermon there.

(December) Denies James Foster the Castle Hill pulpit.

1739 (30 April) Son Samuel born.

(23 May) George Whitefield visits Northampton.

1740 Removes from Marefair to Sheep Street.

(15 March) Death of son Samuel.

Smallpox epidemic in Northampton.

(before October) Saves Newport Pagnell chapel from bankruptcy.

1741 (3 April) The execution of Bryan Connell for murder, in spite of Doddridge's attempts to prove him innocent.

(7 September) Doddridge meets Count Zinzendorf.

Activities promoting overseas missions.

(30 June) Meeting of ministers at Denton, Norfolk.

(October) Doddridge's pastoral responsibilities shared by four elders.

Doddridge and the elders admonish church members who cause scandal.

1742 Mercy, seriously ill, travels to Bath for a cure.

(June/July) Doddridge visits the West Country and the former estates of his family at Mount Radford.

1742 (September) Takes Mercy to Bath following a miscarriage and serious illness.
(8 December) Rebukes Sir John Robinson for swearing.
Controversy over Henry Dodwell's writings, and Doddridge's spirited defence of Christianity.

1743 (Late February/early March) Arrival of James Stonhouse in Northampton.
(March) Attempts to prevent execution of two convicted murderers.
Promotion of the Northampton Infirmary.
(October) Visit of George Whitefield to Castle Hill, resulting in fierce controversy.
(11 November) Foundation of Northampton Philosophical Society.

1744 (25 March) Official opening of the Northampton Infirmary.
Doddridge reads two scientific papers to the Northampton Philosophical Society.

1745 (19 August) The 'Forty-five' Jacobite rebellion. The Young Pretender's standard raised at Glenfinnan.
(5 September) Visit of John Wesley to the academy.
(21 September) Death of Colonel James Gardiner at the battle of Prestonpans.
(Autumn) Doddridge active in forming a local militia in case Northampton is attacked by the Young Pretender's forces.

1746 (16 April) The battle of Culloden.
(22 April) Twin daughters Sarah and Jane born.
(24 April) Deaths of Sarah and Jane.
(19 August) Doddridge present at execution of rebel leaders in London.

1748 Doddridge worries about the numerical decline of the Castle Hill congregation.
(5 November) Son William born.
(11 November) Death of William.
(25 November) Death of Isaac Watts.

1750 (Feb/March) Earthquakes shake London.
(30 September) Earthquake affects Northampton.
Advocacy of inoculation against smallpox.

1750 (16 December) Doddridge catches a severe chill whilst attending Samuel Clark's funeral at St Albans.

1751 (14 July) Preaches for the last time at Castle Hill.
(16 July) Leaves Northampton for Bewdley, Worcestershire.
(18 July) Preaches for the last time at Bewdley.
(August) Travels to Bath and Bristol.
(17 September) Leaves Bristol for Falmouth.
(27 September) Arrives in Falmouth.
(30 September) Leaves Falmouth for Lisbon.
(13 October) Arrives at Lisbon.
(26 October at 3 a.m.) Death near Lisbon.

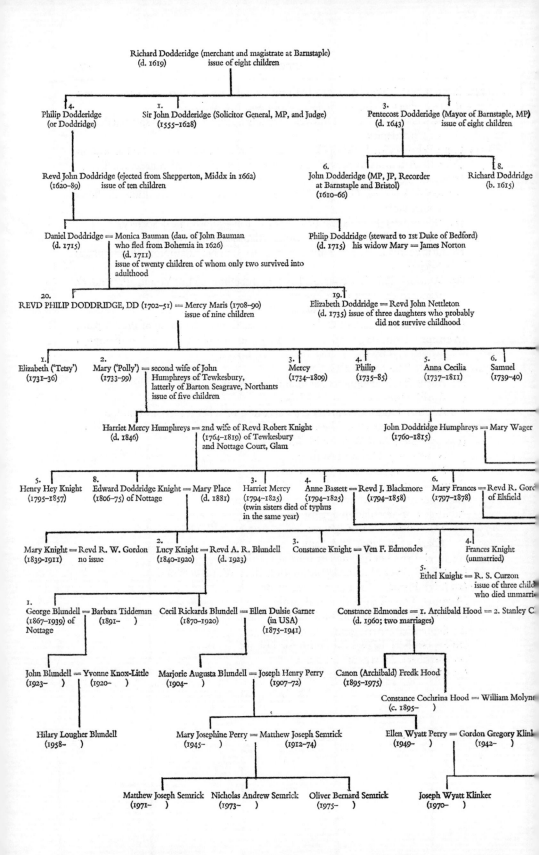

Richard Dodderidge (merchant and magistrate at Barnstaple)
(d. 1619)    issue of eight children

4.
Philip Dodderidge
(or Doddridge)

1.
Sir John Dodderidge (Solicitor General, MP, and Judge)
(1555–1628)

3.
Pentecost Dodderidge (Mayor of Barnstaple, MP)
(d. 1643)    issue of eight children

Revd John Doddridge (ejected from Shepperton, Middx in 1662)
(1620–89)    issue of ten children

6.
John Dodderidge (MP, JP, Recorder
at Barnstaple and Bristol)
(1610–66)

8.
Richard Doddridge
(b. 1615)

Daniel Doddridge == Monica Bauman (dau. of John Bauman
(d. 1715)           who fled from Bohemia in 1626)
                    (d. 1711)
                    issue of twenty children of whom only two survived into
                    adulthood

Philip Doddridge (steward to 1st Duke of Bedford)
(d. 1715)    his widow Mary == James Norton

20.
REVD PHILIP DODDRIDGE, DD (1702–51) == Mercy Maris (1708–90)
                                       issue of nine children

19.
Elizabeth Doddridge == Revd John Nettleton
(d. 1735) issue of three daughters who probably
          did not survive childhood

1.
Elizabeth ('Tetsy')
(1731–36)

2.
Mary ('Polly')
(1733–99) == second wife of John
            Humphreys of Tewkesbury,
            latterly of Barton Seagrave, Northants
            issue of five children

3.
Mercy
(1734–1809)

4.
Philip
(1735–85)

5.
Anna Cecilia
(1737–1811)

6.
Samuel
(1739–40)

Harriet Mercy Humphreys == 2nd wife of Revd Robert Knight
(d. 1846)                  (1764–1819) of Tewkesbury
                           and Nottage Court, Glam

John Doddridge Humphreys == Mary Wager
(1760–1815)

5.
Henry Hey Knight
(1795–1857)

8.
Edward Doddridge Knight == Mary Place
(1806–75) of Nottage       (d. 1881)

3.
Harriet Mercy
(1794–1825)
(twin sisters died of typhus
in the same year)

4.
Anne Bassett == Revd J. Blackmore
(1794–1825)    (1794–1858)

6.
Mary Frances == Revd R. Gord
(1797–1878)    of Elsfield

Mary Knight == Revd R. W. Gordon
(1839–1911)   no issue

2.
Lucy Knight == Revd A. R. Blundell
(1840–1920)   (d. 1923)

3.
Constance Knight == Ven F. Edmondes

4.
Frances Knight
(unmarried)

5.
Ethel Knight == R. S. Curzon
               issue of three child
               who died unmarrie

1.
George Blundell == Barbara Tiddeman
(1867–1939) of     (1891–    )
Nottage

Cecil Rickards Blundell == Ellen Dulsie Garner
(1870–1920)               (in USA)
                          (1875–1941)

Constance Edmondes == 1. Archibald Hood == 2. Stanley C.
(d. 1960; two marriages)

John Blundell == Yvonne Knox-Little
(1923–    )     (1920–    )

Marjorie Augusta Blundell == Joseph Henry Perry
(1904–    )                  (1907–72)

Canon (Archibald) Fredk Hood
(1895–1975)

Constance Cochrina Hood == William Molyn
(c. 1895–    )

Hilary Lougher Blundell
(1958–    )

Mary Josephine Perry == Matthew Joseph Semrick
(1945–    )             (1912–74)

Ellen Wyatt Perry == Gordon Gregory Klink
(1949–    )          (1942–    )

Matthew Joseph Semrick
(1971–    )

Nicholas Andrew Semrick
(1973–    )

Oliver Bernard Semrick
(1975–    )

Joseph Wyatt Klinker
(1970–    )

# Genealogy of the Doddridge Family

(Numbers indicate sequence of birth within a family, or order of marriages)

7/8
Sarah and Jane (twins)
(22–24 April 1746)

9.
William
(5–11 November 1748)

Doddridge refers in his letters to 'cousin' John Doddridge (d. 1723) and to an aunt, Kimburrow Chandler, and her son 'cousin Philip' (1685–1739/40). These seem to have been his only living relatives, other than his sister, after 1715.

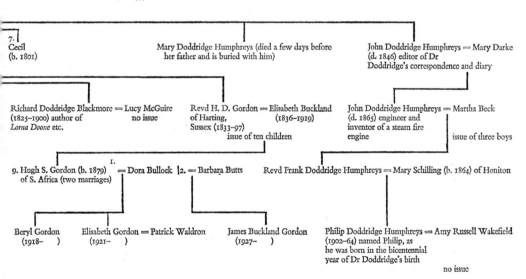

Revd Philip Humphreys (Rector of Portland, Jamaica)
(d. 1835)

7.
Cecil
(b. 1801)

Mary Doddridge Humphreys (died a few days before her father and is buried with him)

John Doddridge Humphreys == Mary Darke
(d. 1846) editor of Dr
Doddridge's correspondence and diary

Richard Doddridge Blackmore == Lucy McGuire
(1825–1900) author of          no issue
*Lorna Doone* etc.

Revd H. D. Gordon == Elisabeth Buckland
of Harting,                (1836–1919)
Sussex (1833–97)
issue of ten children

John Doddridge Humphreys == Martha Beck
(d. 1865) engineer and
inventor of a steam fire
engine                          issue of three boys

9. Hugh S. Gordon (b. 1879)  I. == Dora Bullock  |2. == Barbara Butts
of S. Africa (two marriages)

Revd Frank Doddridge Humphreys == Mary Schilling (b. 1864) of Honiton

Beryl Gordon
(1918–    )

Elisabeth Gordon == Patrick Waldron
(1921–    )

James Buckland Gordon
(1927–    )

Philip Doddridge Humphreys == Amy Russell Wakefield
(1902–64) named Philip, as
he was born in the bicentennial
year of Dr Doddridge's birth
                                    no issue

Marjorie Elaine Klinker
(1976–    )

# APPENDIX III

# Philip Doddridge and Contemporary
# Theological Debate

(a) **Calvinism:** Doddridge did not indulge in abstruse theological speculation, and refused to subscribe to any form of words that sought to confine theological truths. Nevertheless, as he himself commented, he was 'in all the most important points, a Calvinist'.[1]

Calvinism was a complex doctrine, which originated with Swiss reformer John Calvin (1509–64) and was set forth in his *Institutes of the Christian Religion* (1536) and further elaborated by the Council of Dort in 1618. Calvinist theology largely directed the course of the Reformation in Europe and came to dominate the theology of the Church of England in the sixteenth century, providing the motivation for Puritanism.

Calvinism emphasised the importance of the Bible as the authority for Christian faith and practice, and the only source of man's understanding of the nature of God, His will for mankind and His works. Calvin believed in the total depravity of man, and the absolute sovereignty of God who is constantly active in sustaining and determining the operation of the universe. He taught that some were predestined from birth eventually to find salvation. These could not be 'lost' (i.e. damned), but it also followed that those who were not predestined were condemned to eternal damnation from birth.

With the belief in the ultimate sovereignty of God, Calvin thought that man should seek to serve Him in all his activities, eschewing his own pleasure or glory. Man's depravity and irresponsibility could so easily pollute the goodness of Creation. Therefore, the whole of man's life was to be aimed at demonstrating God's glory; all man's activities in seeking personal perfection, his social life or evangelistical concerns were all subservient to this ultimate aim.

(b) **Arminianism:** the theological system named after a Dutch theologian Jacobus Arminius (1560–1609) attempted to soften the strict Calvinistic doctrines of pre-destination. Arminius declared his belief that salvation was not just for 'the elect' but for all who believe in Christ and persevere in their faith, simply because Christ died for all mankind. Arminius also asserted that man needed the Holy Spirit to help him do good and, contrary to Calvin's idea that God's grace is irresistible, Arminius stated that some would ignore it. Furthermore, argued Arminius, Christians could actually lose their faith, so how could their lives be predestined?

(c) **Deism** asserted that the universe was created by God but had been left to its own devices to operate by natural laws. This was contrary to the Calvinist belief in the constant activity of God in His universe.

(d) **Arianism** was an ancient heresy dating from the fourth century AD, when Arius of Alexandria denied the eternity of Christ the son of God, as the Logos (the Word of God made flesh). If God 'begat' Jesus, then Jesus must have had a beginning and was, therefore, not co-eternal with the Father. The heresy involved much complicated argument and was condemned at the Council of Nicaea in AD 325.

(e) **Sabellianism:** Doddridge was charged with Arian tendencies but in fact his theological position tended in an opposite direction towards Sabellianism. In the third century AD Sabellius, perplexed by the problem of accepting the deity of Christ yet maintaining the unity of the Godhead, concluded that the Son and Holy Spirit are revelations or physical manifestations of God the Father and were, therefore, not co-ordinate personalities.

(f) **Socianism:** Sabellianism tended to be accompanied by the Socinian doctrine of Jesus as the revelation of God, but solely as a man. Socinianism derived from Laelius and Faustus Socinus (a sixteenth century Italian and his nephew) and was to develop into Unitarianism. Doddridge avoided the Socinian trap by holding the doctrine 'of the pre-existence of Christ's human soul, which has ever been inseparably united to the Godhead....' In the estimation of Doddridge, this scheme guarded on the one hand against the error of reducing Christ to a mere creature, and on the other against that of conceiving him as another God, either inferior or co-ordinate with the Father'.[2]

(g) **Swedenborgianism** originated with Emanuel Swedenborg (1668–1772) a Swedish scientist, theologian and philosopher. Swedenborg's mystical experiences led him to publish his views on spirits and angels, his denial of the Trinity, and his conception of God as an invisible spaceless and timeless being, who became manifest in the person of Christ. Swedenborg asserted that the churches had lost the original meaning of the word of God, and that a new messianic age would begin in 1757. Swedenborg's influence has been considerable, especially upon psychic research and on the Romantic Movement.

Doddridge found it difficult to express himself accurately in strictly theological terms. Only in his lectures do we find the relatively few references he made to such controversial subjects as the nature of the Trinity and the person of Christ. Doddridge's busy timetable left him little time to indulge in such speculation.

1. NUTTALL, G. F. *Calendar of the correspondence of Philip Doddridge* (1979) letter 150; HUMPHREYS, J. D. *Correspondence and diary of Philip Doddridge* (1829-31) vol. 1, p. 437.
2. GORDON, A. 'Philip Doddridge and the Catholicity of the Old Dissent' in *Addresses, Biographical and Historical* (1922) p. 916.

# APPENDIX IV

## Doddridge's use of Shorthand

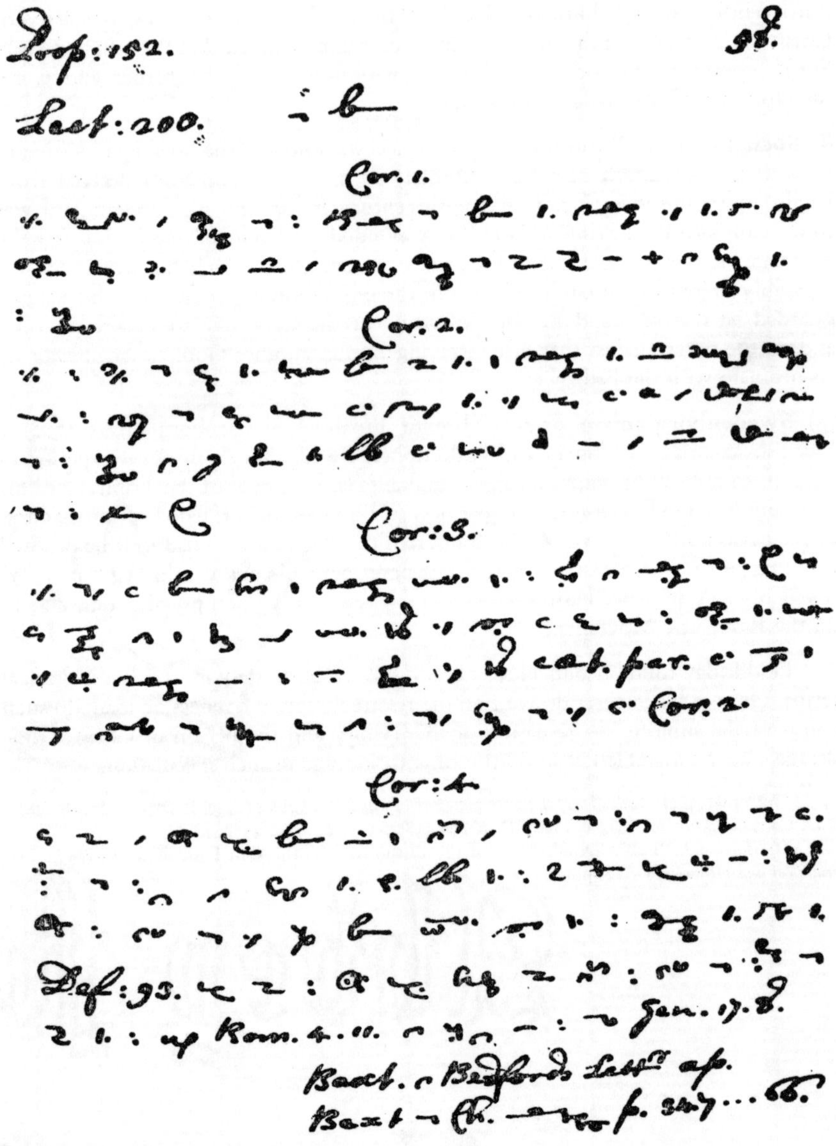


49. Shorthand illustration.

Doddridge expected all his students to master shorthand and used it himself in his correspondence, in preparing sermons, and in the taking of notes. The system derived from Jeremiah Rich who died c.1660. Rich was taught shorthand by his uncle William Cartright, and in his first publication *Semigraphy, or Short and Swift Writing* . . . (1642) acknowledged his indebtedness to his uncle for devising the system. In later publications Rich seems to have claimed for himself the sole authorship of the system, which included over three hundred symbolical and arbitrary signs. The first edition of *The Pen's Dexterity* . . . appeared in 1659, and enjoyed wide popularity. John Locke was an admirer of the system, and many of Doddridge's ministerial colleagues, particularly Isaac Watts, used shorthand in their correspondence and work.

Shorthand notes taken by an unknown student of Doddridge's two hundredth lecture on Divinity. The lecture is entitled 'Of Christian Baptism'; Doddridge begins with a definition, follows with the proposition that 'The law of Christ requires that all who believe the gospel should be baptised' and continues with a demonstration of the use of baptism in scripture. The lesson concludes with seven corollaries the first four of which are illustrated:

Translation:

Cor. 1. It is evidently a prostitution of the ordinance of baptism, to administer it to any adult person, who does not make a creditable profession of his faith in Christ and subjection to the gospel.

Cor. 2. It is the duty of those by whom baptism is to be administered, to make diligent inquiry into the character of those whom they admit to it; whether they have a competent knowledge of the gospel, and give reasons to believe they will behave in a manner becoming members of the christian church.

Cor. 3. It is fit that baptism should be administered only by the teachers and ministers of the church, where their assistance can be had; not only because it appears that these were the persons by whom it was administered in the New Testament, but because (cæt. par.) [other things being equal] they must be most capable of judging who are the fit subjects of it. Vid. Cor. 2.

Cor. 4. There is a sense in which baptism may be called a seal of the covenant of grace; for though the benefits of the covenant are secured to every believer by the death of Christ, which was the great foundation of it, yet baptism plainly appears by the proposition to answer to Definition 93, which is the sense in which circumcision is called the seal of the righteousness of faith by the apostle, Rom. iv. ii and God's covenant in the flesh, Gen. xvii. 8.

> Baxt[er] & Bedford's Lett[er] ap[ropos]
> Baxt[er] of Ch[urch] Membership p. 347 . . . 66.

Source: A volume of lectures (manuscript) in Doddridge and Commercial Street United Reformed Church (Castle Hill) Northampton.

# APPENDIX V

# Smallpox in Northampton

---

Alexander Phillips, parish clerk of All Saints, published the annual bill of mortality for the year ending 21 December 1740. Phillips noted that 'the Small-Pox has been very much in this Town this Year, and more mortal by far than in any one Year in the memory of Man'. In the town eight hundred and ninety-nine people had had smallpox of whom one hundred and thirty-two had died; the worst hit parish was All Saints with five hundred and sixty-eight cases of the disease, with eighty-five deaths. Anxious to refute false rumours which were adversely influencing the town's trade Phillips added 'I also have the Pleasure to assure the Publick, that on the 20th of this Instant December, when I finish'd the above Account, no more than nine Persons lay ill of the Small-Pox in this Town'.

August 1740 was a particularly worrying time for the Doddridge family. Mercy Doddridge was sent out of the danger to 'Reverend Mr Godwin's in Artillery Court near Moore Fields London' and parted from her husband on 1 August at St Albans. Doddridge returned to Northampton on the 4th, and was cheered by the news that daughter Mercy was recovering from a mild attack of smallpox. The Doddridge's companion, Elizabeth Rappitt, also became very ill as did students in the academy and members of the church. On 13 August Doddridge feared that Caelia 'is going to drop' and within five days she had lost her sight due to the disease. Philly and Polly also became ill but less severely than Caelia. The children were nursed at the home of Sarah Dunkley whose next door neighbour lost two children during the epidemic. By 25 August Caelia's life hung in the balance, and on the next morning (Sunday) a messenger from the physician came to tell Doddridge that there was little hope. A Moravian visitor, James Hutton, went to Caelia and prayed for her; 'from that hour' wrote Doddridge, 'the Child began to mend . . . and I think she will be spared'.[1] By the end of the month Caelia was out of danger. On 15 August Doddridge had written to his wife, 'the Dear little Lamb . . . is exceeding patient, and has behaved for a long time, in a manner so very engaging that I have been obliged to be very much upon my guard, or I should have grown over fond of her.'[2]

Smallpox frequently recurred in the town and in 1746–7 another epidemic claimed many lives. In 1750 Doddridge wrote: 'The smallpox is just broke out, with a very unusual Violence in some neighbouring Villages, in which several of my Friends reside, I am told, that in one of them between forty and fifty Persons, most of them young, fell within very little more than a Week; and the Terror with which it fills these Parts of the Country is exceeding great.' Doddridge explained that he had decided to publish a paper written by the late David Some, junior on the subject of inoculation against the disease:

# To the RIGHT WORSHIPFUL the
# M A Y O R,
## *The* Aldermen, Bailiffs, Burgeſſes,
### And the Reſt of the Worthy INHABITANTS of the Town of *NORTHAMPTON*;
#### *This* Yearly Bill of Mortality

*Is preſented by their moſt Obedient and Humble Servant,*

## ‑ ALEXANDER PHILLIPS.

The Yearly Bill of Mortality within the Pariſh of *All-Saints* in the Town of *Northampton*, from the Twenty-Firſt Day of *December*, 1739, to the Twenty-Firſt Day of *December*, 1740.

## DISEASES.

| | | | | | |
|---|---|---|---|---|---|
| Abortive and Stilborn | 6 | Convulſion | 21 | Rheumatiſm | 1 |
| Aged | 15 | Dropſy | 2 | Small-pox | 67 |
| Apoplexy | 2 | Fevers | 7 | Stone | 1 |
| Childbed | 2 | Lethargy | 1 | Stoppage in the Stomach | 3 |
| Conſumption | 23 | Palſy | 3 | Teeth | 3 |

## CHRISTENED.

Males 44. Females 55. Total 99.
Including Males 5, Females 6, who were not Baptized according to the Rites of the *Eſtabliſh'd Church.*

Increaſed in the Births this Year 12.

## BURIED.

Males 84. Females 73. Total 157.
Including thoſe Buried at the *Quaker's* Burying-Ground 8. The Meeting on the *Green* 5. The Meeting in *College-Lane* 2.

Increaſed in the Burials this Year 48.

### Whereof have dy'd,

| | | | | | |
|---|---|---|---|---|---|
| Under Two Years old | 51 | Twenty and Thirty | 13 | Sixty and Seventy | 10 |
| Between Two and Five | 21 | Thirty and Forty | 5 | Seventy and Eighty | 6 |
| Five and Ten | 15 | Forty and Fifty | 7 | Eighty and Ninety | 6 |
| Ten and Twenty | 10 | Fifty and Sixty | 12 | Ninety and a Hundred | 1 |

N. B. *As the Small-Pox has been very much in this Town this Year, and more mortal by far than in any one Year in the Memory of Man; and becauſe various falſe Reports have been ſpread in the Country, to the great Prejudice of the Trading Part of the ſaid Town; I have taken the Pains to go through the ſeveral Pariſhes thereof, and, upon a ſtrict and impartial Enquiry, do find that in the Pariſh of* All-Saints *568 Perſons have had the ſaid Diſtemper, whereof 85 have died;* St. Sepulchre's *165, 27 died;* St. Giles's *106, 9 died; and* St. Peter's *60, 11 died: In all 899, whereof 132 have died. In which Numbers are included thoſe that were buried in the ſaid Town and elſewhere.*
A. PHILLIPS.

We having read and examined the above Account, do believe it to be true:

*Aaron Locock,* Vicar of *All-Saints,*
*John Gibſon,*
*Thomas Greenough,* } Churchwardens.

*John Clark,* Vicar of *St. Sepulchre's,*
*Robert Morris,*
*Law Spencer,* } Churchwardens.

*Edward Wadkin,* Vicar of *St. Giles's,*
*Richard Sanders,*
*Samuel Judkins,* } Churchwardens.

*John Payne,* Curate of *St. Peter's,*
*Samuel Maud,*
*Joſeph Sturges,* } Churchwardens.

*I alſo have the Pleaſure to aſſure the Publick, that on the 20th of this Inſtant December, when I finiſh'd the above Account, no more than nine Perſons lay ill of the Small-Pox in this Town.*
A. P.

50. The Bill of Mortality for the Parish of All Saints, Northampton, 1740, with reference to other parishes in Northampton.

I have long been firmly persuaded in my own mind of the Lawfulness and Expediency of Inoculation as tending greatly to the Preservation of human life. I have never known a single Instance, in which a Child has miscarried by it. I have seen, or been most credibly informed of a Multitude of Instances, in which grown Persons have passed through it safely and very comfortably, who must, humanly speaking, have run the greatest imaginable Risque if they had met the Distemper in the natural way.[3]

Peter Razzell[4] estimates that approximately fifteen per cent of infants died from smallpox before inoculation was introduced. This is certainly supported by the mortality bills for Northampton.

1. NUTTALL, G. F. *Calendar of the correspondence of Philip Doddridge* (1979) letter 634.
2. Ibid. letter 625; HUMPHREYS, J. D. *Correspondence and diary of Philip Doddridge* (1829-31) vol. 3, p. 490.
3. SOME, DAVID. *The case of receiving the Small-pox by Inoculation* (1750).
4. RAZZELL, PETER. *The conquest of smallpox* (1977).

# Philip Doddridge's Itinerary
# 8 June–13 August 1742

Below is a typical example of one of Doddridge's summer excursions.

| | |
|---|---|
| 8 June | Leaves Northampton and reaches Banbury at '4 in the afternoon'. |
| 9 June | Spends the night at the *Bull*, Burford. |
| 10 June | Reaches Bath via Cirencester. |
| 14 June | At Taunton. Visits Poundisford Park, 3 miles south of Taunton. |
| 16 June | Preaches at the ordination of Benjamin Fawcett at Taunton: 2000 present. |
| 17 June | Sets out for Wellington to visit Risdon Darracott who is 'fat & flourishing vastly the better for Matrimony'. |
| 19 June | Reaches Exeter where he is received by 'a whole Synod of Ministers'. Visits Mount Radford, former home of the Doddridges. |
| 22 June | Preaches at Lympstone. |
| 24 June | Preaches at Tiverton. |
| 25 June | Sets out for Barnstaple via South Molton. |
| 29 June | From Barnstaple he writes, 'My Horse is quite well & performs to admiration'. |
| 2–4 July | At Plymouth, where he goes 'dancing in a little Boat on the Swelling Sea & afterwards feeding a Tame Bear with Bisket'. He writes to Mercy, 'I am now at the greatest Distance from you in Person that I ever was or I hope ever shall be'. |
| 5 July | Reaches Dartmouth. |
| 6/7 July | Exeter. |
| 8/9 July | Axminster and Blandford. |
| 10 July | Lymington. 'I have rid 150 Miles in 5 Days' and have been 'six several Times wet to the Skin during my Travels thro that delightful Countrey of Devonshire without getting any Cold'. |
| 12 July | Newport, Isle of Wight. 'I have rid 420 miles & have about 320 more before me.' |
| 18 July | Reaches Portsmouth after visits to Wilton, Salisbury, Romsey, Southampton and Fareham. |
| 21 July | At Lewes for the ordination of Ebenezer Johnson. |
| 27 July | Reaches London. |

3 August　At Brentwood.

5 August　Returns to London.

8 August　Preaches at Little St Helen's, Bishopsgate Street 'to a vastly crowded Auditory'.

9 August　Writes to Mercy from London that 'It is but about 108 Hours to our Meeting' as he hopes to be home on the 13th. He admits, 'when I am not engaged in some Publick Service I seem to be a poor Fragment of my self.'

10 August　Mercy writes to Doddridge at St Ives, Huntingdonshire (where they had earlier hoped to meet) that her heart 'burns and throbs with Love & Impattiency . . . for our happy Joyfull Meeting'. On the following day she has a miscarriage, and upon Doddridge's return to Northampton he finds her dangerously ill.

See letters 750–82 in Nuttall, G. F. *Calendar of the correspondence of Philip Doddridge* (1979).

# APPENDIX VII

# Shopping for Mercy Doddridge

When Philip and Mercy Doddridge were apart, they wrote frequently to each other expressing their love, giving news of friends and recording items of domestic business. On Thursday 2 August 1750, during a visit by Doddridge to London, Mercy sat down at seven o'clock in the morning to send her husband a shopping list: '. . . I am to dine to day on an haunch of venison . . . but the want of my dear's presence will much spoil its relish, fat and fine as I hear it is. By this time the box and my sad scrawl is I suppose come to hand, the contents will a little surprise you. I shall therefore beg leave to explain them: the China plate comes to beg my good dear to get me a pair of side dishes as near as possible to match it, and if he pleases six blue and white coffee cups & a neat set of blue & white China for my best viz. 8 cups & saucers & two basins as I have not one whole set left of my coloured China: my ring to be set and what of the rings I have sent you think proper, to be charged away to pay the expense of it & mending my chain. When you go to Mr Bliss's I should be obliged to you to choose me two pair of handsome brass screw candlesticks: we are in great want of spoons. I think a dozen of silver ones will be too great an expense, & when to it is added half a dozen of tea spoons which I must have or my best spoons will be quite spoiled; be so good therefore to consult with Mr Bliss or Mrs Waugh whether they could not procure for me at second hand half a dozen of large spoons & half a dozen of tea spoons. I believe we must add to them half a dozen of French plate as I think we can't do with less than a dozen of large ones. I intend to collect together all the old silver lace & odd things I have to charge away to pay part of the expense, & as to the rest I believe my poor blue purse must answer it. . . . The cannister you will please to send to be filled with breakfast tea price 8/6d either at Mrs Arbuthnot's or Mrs Cromwell's as you judge best. I think the tea Mrs Cromwell sent to me to taste of the same price, was equally good. I am really concerned to give my dear love so much trouble with my trifling affairs but I know his goodness will excuse it, & will I hope indulge me in the request I am going to make . . . that he will not expend one penny upon me either by way of dress or ornament as he sees so much money must be laid out for things that are quite necessary—not that the ring and chain are in that number—do with them just as you please. I am quite indifferent whether they return done or undone. Adieu my dearest best friend, be assured my hourly prayers & best wishes ever attend you from your most obliged & ever affectionate

M. DODDRIDGE.'

Nuttall, G. F. *Calendar of the correspondence of Philip Doddridge* (1979) letter 1640. The spelling and punctuation of this letter (Doddridge MS 50 in Northamptonshire Studies Collection, Central Library, Northampton) have been amended.

# Major Legislation affecting Dissenters, 1661-1714

1661 **The Corporation Act** (13 Car. 2, St. 2, c. 1) required all magistrates, officers and members of civic corporations to take the oaths of Allegiance and Supremacy declaring that 'it is not lawfull upon any pretence whatsoever to take Arms against the King'. They were required to declare that the oath 'commonly called The Solemn League and Covenant ... was in it selfe an unlawfull Oath and imposed upon the Subjects of this Realm against the knowne Laws and Liberties of the Kingdome'. Failure to take the oaths would result in removal from office. In addition no one would be placed in office unless within the preceding year he had taken the sacrament of the Lord's Supper according to the rites of the Church of England.

1662 **The Act of Uniformity** (14 Car. 2, c. 4) ruled that *The Book of Common Prayer* be used 'by all and every Minister or Curate in every Church, Chappell or other place of Publique Worshipp within this Realme of England'. Every incumbent within the Church of England was required before the Feast of St Bartholomew (24 August) to read both the morning and evening prayer as set out in the Prayer Book, and declare his 'unfaigned assent and consent to al and every thing contained and prescribed' within it. Failure to comply would lead to deprivation of office. Similarly all deans, canons and prebendaries of cathedrals or collegiate churches, masters, fellows, tutors or chaplains of colleges or hospitals, professors and readers in the universities, anyone in holy orders and all schoolmasters and private tutors were required to take the oaths of Allegiance and Supremacy. All schoolmasters and tutors were required to obtain a licence to teach from their respective archbishop, bishop or ordinary of the diocese at the cost of twelve pence; the penalty for non-compliance in the first instance was three months' imprisonment. Governors and heads of colleges were required publicly to read morning prayer and service once every three months upon pain of suspension from office.

1664 **The First Conventicle Act** (16 Car. 2, c. 4) Making no distinction between a preacher or a member of the congregation, the act laid down the penalties for being present at an illegal conventicle: first offence, imprisonment for three months; second, six months, and third offence transportation for seven years unless fines of £5, £10 and £100 respectively were paid.

1665 **The Five Mile Act** (17 Car. 2, c. 2) acknowledged that many had not complied with the *Act of Uniformity* and had 'taken upon them [selves] to preach in unlawfull Assemblyes Conventicles or Meetings ... thereby takeing an oportunity to distill the poysonous Principles of Schisme and Rebellion into the hearts of His Majestyes Subjects'. All preachers of unlawful assemblies were forbidden 'unlesse onely in passeing upon the Road come or be within Five miles of any Citty or Towne Corporate or Burrough that sends Burgesses to the Parlyament'. Punishment would be a fine of £40, a third of which would be paid to the King, a third to the poor of the parish where the offence was committed, and a third to the informer.

1670 **The Second Conventicle Act** (22 Car. 2, c. 1) attempted 'more speedy Remedies against the growing and dangerous practices of Seditious Sectaries and other disloyall Persons who under pretence of tender Consciences have or may at their Meetings contrive Insurrections (as late experience hath shewen). . . .' Any person over sixteen found taking part in an assembly of more than five persons, apart from those in a family, whether it be in a house or field could be fined five shillings (25p) for a first offence and ten shillings for subsequent offences. Fines could be levied by seizure of goods and the members of the conventicle were made responsible for the £20 fine exacted on any preacher or teacher who escaped. Penalties incurred by a married woman were to be levied on her husband, and those who allowed their property to be used for meetings could be fined £20. The act gave local magistrates and justices of the peace wide powers to use whatever means they considered necessary 'to suppresse and dissolve . . . such unlawfull Meetings, and take into their Custody such . . . as they shall thinke fitt. . . .' Failure to report such meetings would result in a fine of £5 for minor officials such as churchwardens and constables, and £100 for justices of the peace and magistrates.

1673 **The First Test Act** (25 Car. 2, c. 2) set out to prevent 'dangers which may happen from Popish Recusants and quieting the minds of his Majestyes good Subjects' and required all officers holding civil or military posts to swear oaths of Supremacy and Allegiance and also to receive the Sacrament of the Lord's Supper according to the rites of the Church of England, especially denying the doctrine of Transubstantiation. Those who refused to comply were adjudged 'uncapeable and disabled in Law to all intents and purposes whatsoever to have occupy or enjoy . . . Offices . . . or Imployments'. Other disabilities were the loss of the right to be a guardian of a child, to be an executor or administrator of any person, or to be able to sue or prosecute in a court of law, receive a legacy or deed of gift, or occupy any official position. Offenders could be also fined £500. Although mainly aimed at Roman Catholics, conscientious Dissenters were affected in so far as they could not comply with the requirement of receiving the Lord's Supper according to the rites of the Church of England.

1689 **The Toleration Act** (1 Will. & Mar. c. 18) hoped that 'some ease to scrupulous Consciences in the Exercise of Religion may be an effectual means to unite their Majestyes [i.e. William and Mary's] Protestant Subjects in Interest and Affection'. Whilst all people were still required to go to church on Sunday, and the laws remained unchanged regarding Roman Catholics, Dissenters were able to attend their chapels and were freed from the threat of prosecution in ecclesiastical courts for their nonconformity. Dissenters were required to take the oaths of allegiance and supremacy, and preachers and teachers were required to assent to the Thirty-Nine Articles of religion (excluding nos 34, 35 and 36, and part of the 20th on the church's right of arbitration in controversies of faith). Provisos in the act ensured that all Dissenting places of worship had to be licenced through the Bishop, Archdeacon or Justice of the Peace; all Dissenting assemblies for worship had to be held with doors unbolted; and any Dissenter unwilling to swear the oaths could make and subscribe a Declaration of Fidelity which promised loyalty to the Crown, abhorred the Popish encouragement of murdering excommunicated princes, and finally professed faith in the Trinity and in the divine inspiration of both Old and New Testaments.

1711 **The Occasional Conformity Act** (10 Anne, c. 6) sought further to secure both the Protestant succession to the throne and the Church of England. All civic, military or other office holders who, 'are obliged to receive the Sacrament of the Lord's Supper according to the Rites and Usage of the Church of England . . . knowingly or willingly resort to or be present at any Conventicle Assembly or Meeting . . . for the Exercise of Religion in other Manner than according to the Liturgy and Practice of the Church of England . . . shall forfeit Forty Pounds . . .' as well as the offices held. Conformity would likewise restore offices and employment. This act was mostly repealed in 1718 (5 Geo. 1, c. 6 *An Act to Ease Officers of Corporations*) but mayors and other officers were disabled from holding such positions if they attended Dissenting chapels wearing the insignia of their office.

1714 **The Schism Act** (13 Anne, c. 7) declared that all unauthorised persons keeping any public or private school or seminary and instructing any youth as tutor or schoolmaster should be imprisoned for three months. Authorisation meant the granting of a licence to teach by the archbishop, bishop or ordinary of the diocese; this was dependent upon whether the laws relating to the Lord's Supper and the declaration against transubstantiation were satisfactorily made. Subsequent attendance at 'any Meeting . . . where Her Majesty . . . and the Elector of Brunswick . . . shall not there be prayed for in express words according to the Liturgy of the Church of England' would be sufficient grounds for revoking the licence. The instruction of any catechism other than that of the Church of England was forbidden. It was also declared 'lawful to and for the Bishop of the Diocese or other proper Ordinary to cite any Person or Persons whatsoever keeping School or Seminary or teaching without Licence as aforesaid and to proceed against and punish such Person or Persons by Ecclesiastical Censure'. Following the death of Queen Anne (1 August 1714) the act was not enforced, and was eventually repealed in 1719.

---

Constitutions Orders & Rules relating to the Academy at Northampton agreed upon by the Tutors & the several Members of it in December 1743 & then Established as the future Conditions of Admission into the Academy or Continuance in it.

## Sect I.   Of Academical Exercises

1. In the first year Translations are to be made from Latin into English & vice versa as appointed by the Tutors to be shewed them at the Day & Hour appointed, & in the last three months of this year Orations are to be exhibited in Latin & English alternately every Thursday which is also to be the Time of the following Exercises.

2. In the first half of the Second Year these Orations are to be continued & in the latter Part of the Year each is in his Turn to exhibit a Philosophical Thesis or Dissertation.

3. In the third year Ethical Theses or Dissertations are to be exhibited weekly as above, & toward the End of this Year & during the Fourth Theological.

4. The Revolution of these is to be so adjusted that every Student may compose at least six Orations, Theses or Dissertations before the Conclusion of his fourth year, & if the numbers of Students should be such that more Theses be exhibited than can be disputed on weekly with the allowance of one vacant Thursday in the Month Disputations are to be held on the Remainder at any Time in the Morning in the presence of the Assistant Tutor on Days when the Principal Tutor is obliged to be absent.

5. All the Subjects to be disputed upon are to be given out with the Names of the Respondent & Opponent affixed to the particular Questions at least as soon as the Academy meets after the long Vacation & that at Christmas, & where it can be done with certainty before it breaks up at those Vacations.

6. The Absence of the Tutor is not to occasion the Omission of any of these Exercises & if the person to exhibit them be disabled by Illness or otherwise unavoidably prevented the next in Order is to take his Place & the Turns to be exchanged; in order to provide for which each Exercise is to be delivered into the Tutor's Hand on the Day he shall appoint at what he judges a proper Distance of Time between that of Assignment & Exhibition.

7. Exercises are to be first written in a paper Book, then reviewed & corrected by one of the Tutors, after that fairly transcribed & after they have been exhibited in the Manner which shall be appointed a fair Copy of them with the Authors' Names annexed shall be delivered to the Tutor.

8. Two sermons on given Subjects are to be composed by every Theological Student in his eighth half year to be read over by him in the Class & having been there corrected to be preached in the Family if the student does not

propose preaching in publick before he leave the Academy & besides these at least six schemes of other Sermons on given Texts are to be exhibited in the Class during the fourth year by each Student.

9. If any Student continue a fifth year he is to compose at least one Sermon & exhibit two Schemes every Quarter whether he do or do not preach in Publick. Besides which he is this fifth year to exhibit & defend two large Theological Theses; or if he stay but a part of the 5th year a proportionable Part of these Exercises is to be performed.

10. Four Classics viz One Greek & one Latin poet, One Greek & one Latin prose writer as appointed by the Tutor are to be read by each Student in his Study & Observations are to be written upon them to be kept in a distinct Book & communicated to the Tutor whenever he shall think fit.

11. Each Student of the upper Class may be allowed to propose a difficult Scripture to the principal Tutor every Thursday Morning to be discussed & examined by him the next Thursday Morning. But it will be expected that the person proposing them write some Memorandums of the Solution to be afterwards subjected to Review.

12. From the Entrance on the 2[n]d to the end of the 8th half year each Theological Pupil will be expected to write either at Meeting or afterward in a proper Book notes of all the Sermons he hears to be examined by the Tutor when he shall require & the neglect of this shall be deemed the Omission of a Stated Exercise & as such shall expose to yt[it] a proper Fine.

13. On the four Thursdays immediately preceding the Long Vacation (or in Case of an unavoidable Hinderance then on the next Lecture Day following that on which there has been an Omission) the whole Academy is to meet at Ten in the Morning & all the Forenoon is to be spent in the Examination of Students in the several Studies of the preceding year. And on the two first of these Days Disputations shall be held by the two upper Classes in the presence of the Juniors that they may learn by Example the Method of Disputation & this is the only Exercise of this Kind at which the Junior Classes may be present.

14. In case of a Total Neglect of preparing an appointed Exercise sixpence is to be forfeited to the Box & two pence if a rough Dra[ft of] it be not ready for the first Examination a Fortnight after it is assigned, at which Time it is to be brought to the Tutor without being particularly called for; nor is Forgetfulness to be allowed as any Excuse when the Order has been registered in the Library Book.

Vid. addenda.

## Sect II.   Of Attendance on Family Prayer & Lecture at appointed Times

1. Every Student boarding in the House is to be present at the Calling over the Names in the great parlour at 10 Minutes after six in the Morning or to forfeit a penny.

2. Family prayer is to begin in the Morning at eight a Clock & in the Evening at Seven, unless publick Notice be given of any Occasional Change in the Hour, & every one absenting himself from either so as not to answer to his Name is to forfeit two pence. And if any one who has answered to his Name goes

out without sufficient Reason before the Service is concluded he is to forfeit as if he had been totally absent.

3. Every Student is to be ready for Lecture in the proper Room appointed for his Class within five minutes of the Hour fixed for the Beginning of the said Lecture or to forfeit two pence & if the Lecture be intirely neglected & no Reason can be assigned which the Tutor (who is always to be judge of such Reasons) shall think sufficient he is to be publickly reproved at the next meeting of the whole Society, & if the Neglect be repeated within a Month he is to have some extraordinary Exercise appointed as the Tutor shall think fit.

4. Each Pupil after he hath entered on the Second Half Year of his Course shall take his Turn at Family Prayer in the Evening [on] Fryday Nights not excepted & each Student in the Senior Class shall take his Turn in Praying before Repetition on Lord's Day Evening while it is kept up at Home. And if that coincide with his stated Turn or happen the Day before or after it, he shall be excused in the ordinary Course of the Family for that Time.

5. If any Stranger pray in the Family or any other Person whose Turn it is not, it shall not excuse the Person whose Turn it was unless the person officiating shall expressly declare that he intended it in that View. Nor shall a Change of Turns be admitted without the Tutor's express Leave.

6. If the Person whose Turn it is to go to prayer in the Evening absent himself & have not procured another to officiate for him he shall forfeit 6d[2½p] or take his Turn twice together & if any person who had expressly undertaken to supply the place of that other fail to attend he shall incur this penalty & the other to whom he stood engaged shall only forfeit as for ordinary absences.

## Sect III.   Of the Hours Place & Order of Meals

1. The Time of Breakfast is to be from the End of Family Prayer in the Morning till five Minutes before Ten.

2. It is to be eaten either in the Hall or the great Parlour a Blessing having first been asked by the Senior Pupil present at each Table if the Assistant Tutor be not at one of them.

3. They that chuse Tea in the Morning may either breakfast with the Tutor in his Parlour or at the other Tea Board in the great Parlour, Each in that Case providing his own Tea & Sugar in a just proportion as the Company shall agree.

4. Dinner is to be set on the Table precisely at Two, when every Student is to be in the Hall before the Blessing is asked & not to leave the Room till thanks be returned.

5. Supper is to be eaten in the Hall between the Conclusion of Evening Prayer at 8½ & nine o'clock after which the Table is to be cleared, & if it happen to be cleared before any Student, not having supped before, may Command his Supper there till that Time.

6. Neither Breakfast Dinner nor Supper is to carried into any Room besides that appointed for the Family Meal except in Case of Sickness & no Commons are to be delivered out at other Times.

7. As making Toasts & Butter & Toasting Cheese has been found to be more

expensive than can conveniently be afforded on the usual Terms here that Custom is to be disused except by the Parlour Boarders.

8. No Food is to be dressed in the Kitchen but by the Direction or permission of the Mistress of the Family.

9. That the Servants may not be hindred in their Business none of the Students are on the penalty of forfeiting an half penny each Time to be in the Kitchen before Morning prayer, nor from twelve at Noon till the Dinr is served up, nor from seven in the Evening till supper is intirely carryed into the little Parlour. And during these Seasons of Exclusion the Kitchen Door shall be bolted when ever the cook shall think fit.

## Sect IV.   Of Shutting up the Gate & retiring to Bed

1. The Gate is to be lockd every Night when the Clock strikes Ten & the Key is to be brought to the Tutor or his Assistant & every Pupil who comes in after that Time is to forfeit twopence for every Quarter of an Hour that he hath exceeded Ten.

2. If any one go out of the House without express Permission after the Gate is locked he is to pay a Shilling for such Offence & should any one get into the House irregularly after the Door is Locked he & each person assisting him in such irregular Entry [shall forfeit a shilling for the first Offence & for the second]* must expect that immediate Information will be sent to his Friends.

3. If any Pupil procure a Key for the Gate he shall not only forfeit it as soon as discovered but be Fined Half a Crown.

4. If any one keep a Guest beyond half an Hour past ten he shall forfeit for every Quarter of an Hour which such Guest stays as if he had stayed abroad himself.

5. If any one Stay out all Night & do not the next Day of his own accord take an opportunity of acquainting the Tutor or Assistant with it & giving the Reason for so extraordinary a conduct he must expect that if it afterward come to the Tutor's Knowledge an immediate Complaint will be lodged with his Friends without any previous Notice taken of it to him.

6. An Account is to be brought to the Tutor every Saturday Morning by the person who has kept the Key of the Gate the preceding week of every one who has been let in during the Time after ten a Clock.

## Sect V.   Rules relating to the Chambers & Closets

1. That the Chambers & Closets be chosen by Persons paying the same Price according to the Seniority of Classes & that if any Question concerning them arise between persons of the same Class who are Boarders on the same Terms it be determined by Lot.

2. Every one entering on any Chamber or Closet is to acquaint the Tutor with the Number of it & to continue in it till he give Notice to the Tutor of his purpose to exchange it & have his Approbation as to the Regularity of that Exchange.

* Crossed out by Doddridge in the original MS.

3. That when any Student leaves a Chamber or Closet he [should] desire the Tutor to go with him into it that it may appear it is left in good Repair or that if it be not proper measures may be taken for fitting it up for the Reception of the person who may next succeed; or for locking it up, if the Tutor judge it more convenient that in present Circumstances of the Family it should be kept uninhabited, or converted to any use different from what it has formerly had.

4. That if Windows be broken, Furniture wantonly demolished, or any other Hurt be done to the House by the Fault of any of the Pupils, the repair of such Damage be charged to the Person by whom it is done. NB This extends to the Instruments of the Apparatus & even to any Detriment which may arise to them by the Carelessness of any person by whom any of them may be borrowed or taken out of their places.

5. No workman is to be employed in any Apartment of the House with out express Leave obtained from the Tutor, & settling it with him, at whose Expense such Work is to be done.

6. Empty Closets & Chambers are to be kept lockd up, & the Keys to remain in the Tutor's Keeping.

## Sect VI.   Rules relating to the Library

1. Every Pupil is to pay a Guinea to the Library when he enters on the Second Year of his Course if he propose to go through the whole, but if he purpose to stay only two years he is to pay but half a Guinea & that from the Time that he enters on the Second Half year.

2. Every one that takes a Book out of the Library is to make a distinct Entry of it in the Library Book prepared for that purpose, adding his Name at length & is in consequence of that Entry to be accountable for the Book while it stands under his Name.

3. When he brings in the Book (which he is always to do at three a Clock every Saturday in the Afternoon if not before References excepted) he is to return it into its proper place in the Library blotting out the Entry he had made of it. And in Case either of these Rules are neglected $\frac{1}{2}$d is to be forfeited for each Book.

4. Reference Books belonging to any Class may be laid together on the Shelf over the Writing Desk & enterd by the word (above) substituted for the Name of the Person who had them left in his possession; if that person be not the last in the Class, in which case he is to put them into their proper places & when any one in a Class delivers those Reference Books to another he is to change the Name or remain accountable for the Books.

5. No Dictionaries Lexicons or Commentators not referd to in Lectures are to be taken out of the Library without express Permission of the Tutor on the penalty of forfeiting two pence for each Book.

6. If any Book be found in any Room above or below & the person under whose Care it is be not in the Room, the person under whose Name it stands shall forfeit two pence for every Folio or Quarto & a penny for every smaller Book.

7. The Library shall be lookd over every Saturday at three in the Afternoon by the Monitor of the week assisted by the Person who is to succeed him a Catalogue is then to be taken of all the Books which are wanting to be called over a Quarter before Seven in the Evening & every Student not attending at that Time shall forfeit a penny distinct from any Forfeiture for being afterwards absent from Family prayers if such Absence should happen.

8. When the List has been called over every Student shall be interrogated as to those [books] wanting & if any be found in his Custody of which on such Examination he have not given regular Intelligence he shall forfeit six pence for every such Book.

9. The Forfeits collected at these Times for offences of the Laws of the Library shall go to the Monitor & any forfeit to be paid by the Monitor himself shall go to the person who is to succeed him in his office.

10. If any one take away the Pen or Ink out of the Library, or the Library Book except wanted in Class or the Catalogue of Books out of the Library he is to forfeit sixpence.

## Sect VII.   Rules relating to the Office of the Monitor

1. Every Academical Student in the Family is to be Monitor in his Turn excepting only the Senior Class for the Time being & if any of them shall in his Turn chuse to officiate as Monitor his Assistance shall be thankfully accepted.

2. The Monitor is to call up every Student at six a Clock in the Morning Winter & Summer Vacation Times only excepted & having rung the Bell twice at ten Minutes after six is to call over all the Names distinguishing in his Bill those who are absent & for every Quarter of an Hour which he delays he is to forfeit two pence. He is also to call over his List before Morning & Evening Prayer as above, as also immediately before all Lectures appointed for the whole Academy together & if he fail to do it or to provide some other person to supply his Place he is to forfeit six pence for every such Failure.

3. He is to review the Library on Saturday at three in the Afternoon & to call over the Catalogue of the Books wanting according to Sect VI No 7 under a Forfeiture of a shilling & he is then to see that a Pen & Ink be left in the Library for publick Use.

4. He is to lay up the Bibles & Psalm Books after prayer in the Cupboard in the long prayer & as an Acknowledgement for that trouble is to claim a Farthing for every one who shall neglect to bring his Psalm Book with him at those Times, if he choose generally to keep it in his Closet.

5. The Monitor is to have an Eye on the Door to see whether any one goes out during Divine Service & to inform the Tutor of it, & is to send the Junior Pupil present to call the Tutor if in the House as soon as he begins to call over the Names.

## Sect VIII.   Rules relating to Conduct abroad

1. No Student is to go into a Publick House to drink there on Penalty of a publick Censure for the first Time, & the Forfeiture of a shilling the second; unless

some particular occasion arise which shall in the Judgement of the Tutor be deemed a Sufficient Reason.

2. No one is begin a Bill at any Place in the Town without the knowledge & Approbation of the Tutor.

3. If any one spread Reports abroad to the Dishonour of the Family or any Member of it he must expect a publick Reproof & to hear a Caution given to others to beware of placing any Confidence in him.

## Sect IX.  Miscellaneous Rules

not comprehended under the former Sections
see the Addenda

3. When the small pecuniary Fines here appointed evidently appear to be despised they will be exchanged for some extraordinary Exercises which if they are not performed must occasion Complaint to the Friends of the Students in Question; for the Intent of these Laws is not to enrich the Box at the Expense of those who are determined to continue irregular, but to prevent any from being so.

4. If any Kind of Rudeness & Indency of Behaviour be practised tho' of such sort as cannot be particularly provided for by such Rules & the Tutor admonish the offender for it publickly or privately without Effect, it must be expected that out of Regard to the Credit & Comfort of the Society he will endeavour to engage the Interposition of such other Friends as may be supposed to have a greater Influence over the Student, whose Misbehaviour is apparent to him; & he concludes that this will be esteemed by all equitable Judges an act of Kindness to the Society & the publick.

5. Accounts with the Tutor are to be balanced twice a year, & all Bills from Tradesmen if such there be are to be deliverd in to the Tutor by the Persons from whom they are due at the Seasons at which they respectively know their accounts are to be made up.

6. No Student is to board abroad unless at the Desire & under the Direction of the Tutor. And those who do so board abroad are nevertheless to attend Family Prayer & Lecture at the appointed Times.

7. The News bought for the use of the Family is to be paid for out of the Box.

8. Six Pence is to be allowed from the Box weekly toward the Support of the Charity School & the Remainder of the Cash (excepting only twenty Shillings to be reserved in Bank,) at the End of every year shall be disposed of in Books or Instruments for the apparatus according to the Vote of the Society to be determined by the Majority of Votes, in which every one who is ending his second year shall have two Votes & the rest but one. This Distribution to be made at the Beginning of the next long Vacation.

9. In the Absence of the Principal Tutor the Assistant Tutor is to be regarded as his Deputy & the same Respect to be paid to him by Seniors as well as Juniors, & his Decisions in relation to all Forfeits becoming due upon these Laws is to be lookd upon as final.

10. It is always to be understood as a most important Part of the Trust reposed in the Assistant to inspect the Behaviour of the Pupils with Regard to these Laws & to give faithfull Intelligence to the Tutor of the Violation of them when it comes to his Knowledge, as also of any other Irregularities of Behaviour which may affect the Character, Comfort and Usefulness of any Students belonging to the Society.

NB. If any Gentleman not intended for the Ministry think fit to do us the Honour to take up their abode amongst us whatever their Rank in Life be, it is expected & insisted upon that they govern themselves by these Rules (excepting those which directly relate to exercises preparatory to the Ministry in which Family Prayer on common Evenings is included) which is required for their own sake as well as that of the Family to whom the admission of such might otherwise prove an Inconvenience.

P. Doddridge D.D. Dec. 10th. 1743
T. Brabant

We whose Names are hereunto Subscribed do hereby Declare our Aquiescence in these Constitutions, Orders & Rules as the Terms of our Respective Admission into or Continuance in the Academy at Northampton:

[fifty-one signatures of students follow]

*Addenda*                          [undated, but possibly 1749]
To Sect I.

15. The Neglect of transcribing a Lecture is to be lookd upon & punished as if neglect of preparing an Exercise.

16. As a Security for the Forfeits to be paid on these or other occasions each Student is at the beginning of a session or when he enters the Academy to deposit five Shillings in the Hands of the Assistant Tutor & the same Sum again when that is forfeited but whatever remains unforfeited at the End of a Session is to be returned to him.

17. Forfeitures in Question are to be adjudged & registered at 8 [o'clock] every Saturday Morning & no Excuses are to be heard by those who are not then present to answer to their Names & offer them.

Subscriptions to the Laws continued:
[twelve signatures of students follow]

These regulations have been transcribed from Doddridge's original MS (New College, London MS L 2/4). Minor alterations to punctuation and spelling have been made.

# Bibliographical Sources

## MANUSCRIPT SOURCES

1. Held at Doddridge and Commercial Street United Reformed Church, Castle Hill, Northampton.
   (a) Church Book, commenced 1694.
   (b) Counsels to the Elders (copy).
   (c) 'Dr Doddridge's system of shorthand' by student Thomas Cartwright.
   (d) Sermons and lectures in both long and short hand, in bound volumes.
   (e) Probate copy of Philip Doddridge's will.
   (f) 'A system of logick, Rules on Behaviour and Short hand; drawn up at Northampton.'
   (g) Letters to and from Doddridge, including a bound volume of twenty-one letters, 1737–43.
2. Held in the Northamptonshire Studies Collection, Central Library, Northampton (part of Northamptonshire Libraries).
   The Doddridge manuscripts, comprising one hundred and ninety-two letters written by Philip and Mercy Doddridge, their children, and others.
3. Held in Dr Williams's Library, London.
   'Constitutions Orders and Rules relating to the Academy at Northampton.' New College, London, MS L 2/4.

## PRINTED SOURCES

### BIBLIOGRAPHY OF THE PRINTED WORKS OF PHILIP DODDRIDGE

Bibliographical details relate to first editions unless otherwise stated. Entries are arranged chronologically. The details given are—*title* (place of publication, publisher, date of publication) and pagination or number of volumes; pagination does not include advertisements; un-numbered pages are in brackets. Translations are not included.

*Free thoughts on the Most Probable Means of Reviving the Dissenting Interest* (London, R. Hett, 1730) 39p.

*Sermons on the Religious Education of children* . . . (London, R. Hett, 1732) xvi, 152p.

*The Care of the Soul urged as the One Thing Needful* . . . (London, R. Hett, 1735) 32p.

*Sermons to Young Persons* (Northampton [printed in London], J. Fowler, 1735) [x], 226p.

*Ten sermons on the Power and Grace of Christ* (London, R. Hett, 1736) [xii], 295p.

*The Absurdity and Iniquity of Persecution for Conscience-sake* . . . (London, R. Hett, 1736) [v], 41p.

*The Temper and Conduct of the Primitive Ministers of the Gospel* (London, R. Hett and J. Oswald, 1737) 80p.

*Submission to Divine Providence in the Death of Children* . . . (London, R. Hett, 1737) viii, 36p. Sermon preached upon the death of his daughter Elizabeth.

*Practical Reflections on the Character and Translation of Enoch* . . . (Northampton, W. Dicey, 1738) [i], iv, 36p.

*The Family Expositor* (London, J. Wilson etc., 1739–56) 6 vols.

*A sermon Preached at Wellingborough, in Northamptonshire, Nov 9 [1738] which was observed as a Day of Fasting and Prayer, on Account of the late dreadful Fire there* . . . (London, R. Hett and J. Buckland, 1739) 40p.

*The Necessity of a General Reformation, in order to a well-grounded Hope of Success in War* . . . (London, R. Hett and J. Buckland, 1740) vi, 7–38p. Dedicated to Col. James Gardiner.

*The Scripture-Doctrine of Salvation by Grace through Faith* . . . (London, M. Fenner, 1741) [vi], 58p.

BARKER, JOHN. *Resignation to the Will of God* (London, R. Hett, 1741) [i], 41p. Funeral sermon for Revd John Newman with additions by P. Doddridge.

*The Friendly Instructor, or a Companion for Young Ladies and Gentlemen* (London, J. Waugh, 2nd edition 1741) ix, 66p.

*Practical Discourses on regeneration in Ten sermons* . . . (London, M. Fenner and J. Hodges, 1742) xvi, 344p.

*Christian Preaching, and Ministerial Service* . . . (London, J. Brackstone and M. Fenner, 1742) 77p. Ordination sermon for Revd John Jennings by Revd David Jennings, with charge given by P. Doddridge.

*The Evil and Danger of Neglecting the Souls of Men* . . . (London, M. Fenner, 1742) [iii], xii, 38p.

*Sermons on several subjects preached by the late Reverend Mr Tho. Steffe* . . . *with some extracts from his letters, in an account of his life and character* (London, M. Fenner, 1742) lii, [iii], 156p.

*The Perspicuity and Solidity of* . . . *Evidences of Christianity* . . . (London, M. Fenner and J. Hodges, 1742) 62p. The first of three letters in reply to Henry Dodwell.

*The Principles of the Christian Religion* . . . *for the use of Little Children* (London, M. Fenner, 1743) vi, 36p.

*Compassion to the Sick recommended and urged* (London, M. Fenner; Northampton, W. Dicey; 1743) [i], xii, 46p.

*A second Letter to the Author of a Pamphlet, intitled Christianity not founded on Argument* . . . (London, M. Fenner and J. Hodges, 1743) 60p.

*A third Letter to the Author of Christianity not founded on Argument* (London, M. Fenner and J. Hodges, 1743) 72p.

*The Christian Warrior animated and crowned* . . . (London, J. Waugh, 1745) xii, 35p. Sermon on death of Col. Gardiner, preached at Northampton 13 October 1745.

FROST, RICHARD. *The Importance of the Ministerial Office* (London, J. Waugh, 1745) 76, 31p. Ordination sermon for the Revd Abraham Tozer at Norwich, with charge by P. Doddridge.

*The Rise and Progress of Religion in the Soul* (London, J. Brackstone and J. Waugh, 1745) xviii, 410p.

*Deliverance out of the Hands of our Enemies, urged as a Motive to Obedience* . . . (London, J. Waugh, 1746) 50p.

*Aenspraek aen de Protestantsche Ingezetenen der Vereenigde Nederlanden* (Amsterdam, 1747). An address to Dutch Protestants; translated into French, but not English.

*Some Remarkable Passages in the Life of* . . . *Col. James Gardiner* (London, J. Buckland, 1747) [xv], 260p.

*A Friendly Letter to the Private Soldiers in a Regiment of Foot one of those engaged in the Important and Glorious Battle of Culloden* (1747).

*An Abridgment of Mr David Brainerd's Journal* (London, J. Oswald, 1748) [i], xi, 107, [4]p. Ed. P. Doddridge.

*Christ's Invitation to thirsty Souls* . . . (London, J. Waugh, 1748) xvi, 35p.

SHEPHERD, JAMES. *Sermons* (London, J. Buckland and J. Waugh, 1748) xii, 176p. Ed. P. Doddridge; including sermon preached by Doddridge on Shepherd's death in 1746.

LEIGHTON, ROBERT. *Expository Works* (Edinburgh, D. Wilson, 1748) 2 vols. Revised by P. Doddridge.

*Tweede Aenspraek aen de Protestantsche Ingezetenen der Vereenigde Nederlanden* (Amsterdam, 1748). Second address to Dutch Protestants; did not appear in English.

*Reflections on the Conduct of Divine Providence in the Series and Conclusion of the late War* . . . (London, J. Waugh, 1749) 39p. To celebrate the national day of thanksgiving following the peace between France and Spain.

*Christian Candour and Unanimity stated, illustrated and urged* . . . (London, J. Waugh, 1750) [iii], 36p. Dedicated to the Countess of Huntingdon.

*The Guilt and Doom of Capernaum* . . . (London, J. Waugh, 1750) xi, 13–40p.

SOME, DAVID. *The Case of Receiving the Small-pox by Inoculation, Impartially considered* . . . *by the late Revd Mr David Some* . . . *published from the Original Manuscript, by P. Doddridge* (London, J. Buckland and J. Waugh, 1750) vi, 7–43p.

*A plain and serious address to the Master of a Family on the Important Subject of family-religion* (London, J. Waugh, 1750) 43p.

*Meditations on the Tears of Jesus over the Grave of Lazarus* . . . (London, J. Waugh, 1751) 36p. A funeral sermon preached at St Albans, 16 December 1750, for Dr Samuel Clark.

WATTS, ISAAC. *The Improvement of the Mind* (London) vol. 2 (1751), ed. D. Jennings and P. Doddridge.


A SELECTION OF DODDRIDGE'S POSTHUMOUSLY PUBLISHED WORKS
(excluding editions of the correspondence and diary)

*Hymns founded on Various Texts in the Holy Scriptures* (Shrewsbury, J. Eddowes and J. Cotton, 1755) xxiv, 325, [19]p. Ed. J. Orton.

*The Family Expositor*, sixth and final volume (London, J. Waugh and W. Fenner, etc., 1756) vii, 641, [i]p. Ed. J. Orton.

*Sermons and Religious Tracts of the late Reverend Philip Doddridge D.D.* (London, printed by assignment from the author's widow for C. Hitch and L. Hawes etc., 1761) 3 vols.

*A course of lectures on the Principal Subjects in Pneumatology, Ethics and Divinity* (London, J. Buckland etc., 1763) [xix], 595, [6]p. Ed. S. Clark.

*A new translation of the New Testament . . . extracted from the paraphrase of . . . Philip Doddridge* (London, J. Rivington, 1765) 2 vols.

*The Evidences of Christianity* (London, J. Buckland, 1770) 24p.

*A Brief and easy System of Shorthand: first invented by Mr Jeremiah Rich, and improved by Dr Doddridge* (London, E. Palmer, 1799) 32p.

*The works of the Revd P. Doddridge* (Leeds, E. Baines, 1802–5) 10 vols. Ed. E. Williams and E. Parsons; includes Orton's life of Doddridge.

*Lectures on Preaching and the several Branches of the Ministerial Office* (London, R. Edwards, 1807) iv, 122p.

*The Leading Heads of Twenty-seven Sermons, preached at Northampton by Philip Doddridge D.D. in the year 1749* (Northampton, F. Cordeux, 1816), ii, 168p.

*Sermons on Various Subjects* (London, J. Hatchard and Son, 1826) 4 vols. Ed. J. D. Humphreys.

*The Miscellaneous Works of Philip Doddridge D.D., with an introductory essay by the Revd T. Morell* (London, J. O. Robinson, 1830) [iv], xiv, ii, iv, 1216p. Printed in double column.

## GENERAL BIBLIOGRAPHY

The details given are—AUTHOR, *title* (publisher, date of publication). Place of publication is given only when in Northamptonshire.

ARNOLD, T. AND COOPER, J. J. *The history of the Church of Doddridge.* (Kettering and Wellingborough, Northamptonshire Printing and Publishing Co., 1895).

BULL, T. P. *A Brief Narrative of the Rise and Progress of the Independent Church at Newport Pagnell* (Wilson, 1811).

BULLOCK, F. W. B. *Voluntary religious societies 1520-1799* (Budd and Gillatt, 1963).

CATER, F. I. *Northamptonshire Nonconformity 250 years ago* (Northampton, Archer and Goodman, 1912).

CHADWICK, O. *The Reformation* (Pelican History of the Church, vol. 3, 1964).

CLARK, P. AND SLACK, P. *English towns in transition, 1500-1700* (O.U.P., 1976).

COLEMAN, T. *Memorials of the Independent Churches in Northamptonshire* (Snow, 1853).

COLLINSON, P. *The Elizabethan Puritan movement* (Jonathan Cape, 1967).

COSTIN, A. C. AND WATSON, J. S. *The Law and Working of the Constitution: documents 1660-1914* (A. & C. Black, 1952) 2 vols.

COUNTRY MINISTER, A. *The State of Northampton from the beginning of the Fire, Sept. 20th 1675 to Nov. 5th . . .* (J. Robinson and W. Cockeraine, 1675).

COX, J. C. AND SERJEANTSON, R. M. *A history of the Church of the Holy Sepulchre, Northampton* (Northampton, W. Mark, 1897).

CREASEY, J. 'Philip Doddridge on Sir John Doddridge' in *Congregational Historical Society Transactions* (1968) vol. 20, pp. 234–5.

DALLIMORE, A. *George Whitefield: the life and times of the great evangelist of the eighteenth century revival* (Banner of Truth Trust, 1970) vol. 1.

DAVIS, A. P. *Isaac Watts: his life and works* (Independent Press, 1948).

DODDERIDGE, S. E. AND SHADDICK, H. G. H. *The Dodderidges of Devon* (William Pollard, 1909).

DOUGLAS, J. D. *The New International Dictionary of the Christian Church* (Paternoster Press, 1974).

EVERITT, A. *The pattern of Rural Dissent: the nineteenth century* (Leicester U.P., 1972).

EVERITT, A. *Perspectives in English Urban History* (Macmillan, 1973).

FERGUSSON, J. *John Fergusson, 1727–50* (Jonathan Cape, 1948).

FLETCHER, J. *The history of the revival and progress of Independency in England, since the period of the Reformation* (Snow, 1847–9) 4 vols.

GARLAND, H. J. *The life and hymns of Dr Philip Doddridge* (Stirling Tract Enterprise, 1951).

GIBSON, J. W. 'Dr Doddridge's Nonconformist academy and education by shorthand' in *Phonetic Journal* (3 April 1886, et. seq.).

GODFREY, B. S. *Castle Hill Meeting* (Northampton, Swan Press, 1947).

GORDON, A. 'Philip Doddridge and the Catholicity of the Old Dissent' in *Addresses, Biographical and Historical* (Lindsey Press, 1922; reprinted separately 1951).

GORDON, A. 'Philip Doddridge' in *Dictionary of National Biography*. Includes a useful bibliography.

HANS, N. *New trends in education in the eighteenth century* (Routledge and Kegan Paul, 1951).

HARRIES, S. G. 'The status of Doddridge's academy' in *Congregational Historical Society Transactions* (1952) vol. 17, no. 1, pp. 19–25.

HARRIS, F. W. P. *The life and work of Philip Doddridge* (1950). Unpublished Oxford University B.Litt. thesis.

HARRIS, F. W. P. 'New light on Philip Doddridge' in *Congregational Historical Society Transactions* (1952) vol. 17, no. 1, pp. 8–18.

HARRIS, F. W. P. 'Philip Doddridge on the method of ordination' in *Congregational Historical Society Transactions* (1963) vol. 19, no. 4, pp. 182–4.

HARRIS, F. W. P. 'Philip Doddridge and charges of Arianism' in *Congregational Historical Society Transactions* (1969) vol. 20, no. 9, pp. 267–72.

HARSHA, D. A. *Life of Philip Doddridge D.D., with notices of some of his contemporaries, and specimens of his style* (Albany, 1864).

HOPE, E. P. 'Philip Doddridge' in *Congregational Quarterly* (1951) no. 29, pp. 342–7.

HUMPHREYS, J. D. (ed.) *Correspondence and diary of Philip Doddridge D.D.* . . . (Colburn and Bentley, 1829–31) 5 vols.

JAMES, A. T. S. 'Philip Doddridge: his influence on personal religion' in NUTTALL, G. F. (ed.) *Philip Doddridge* (1951) pp. 32–45.

JONES, M. G. *The charity school movement: a study of eighteenth century Puritanism in action* (C.U.P., 1938).

KELYNACK, W. S. 'Philip Doddridge' in *London Quarterly* (1951) no. 176, pp. 327–33.

KIPPIS, A. (ed.) *Biographia Britannica* (1778–95 edition) includes entry on Doddridge, which was printed as 'Life of the author' in *The Family Expositor* (F. C. and J. Rivington, 1811) vol. 1.

KISSACK, R. 'Doddridge makes a sermon' in *London Quarterly* (1951) no. 23, pp. 142–5.

KOENIGSBERGER, H. G. AND MOSSE, G. L. *Europe in the sixteenth century* (Longmans, 1968).

LONGDEN, H. I. (ed.) *Northamptonshire and Rutland clergy from 1500* (Northampton, Archer and Goodman, 1938–52) 16 vols.

MACAULAY, T. B. *History of England* (Longman, 1863–4) 4 vols.

McLACHLAN, H. *English education under the Test Acts, being the history of the Nonconformist academies, 1662–1820* (University of Manchester, Historical Series no. 59, 1931).

MARLOW, N. (tr.) *The diary of Thomas Isham of Lamport, 1658–81* (Gregg, 1971).

MURRAY, A. V. 'Doddridge and education' in NUTTALL, G. F. (ed.) *Philip Doddridge* (1951) pp. 102–21.

MURRAY, I. (ed.) *George Whitefield's journals* (Banner of Truth Trust, 1960).

MUSSON, A. E. AND ROBINSON, E. *Science and technology in the Industrial Revolution* (Manchester U.P., 1969).

NUTTALL, G. F. 'Assembly and Association in Dissent 1689–1831' in *Councils and Assemblies* (C.U.P., Studies in Church History no. 7, 1971) pp. 289–309.

NUTTALL, G. F. (ed.) *Calendar of the correspondence of Philip Doddridge, D.D. 1702–51* (Northamptonshire Record Society and the Royal Commission on Historical Manuscripts, 1979).

NUTTALL, G. F. 'Calvinism in Free Church history' in *Baptist Quarterly* (1967–8) vol. 22, pp. 418–28.

NUTTALL, G. F. 'Chandler, Doddridge and the Archbishop: a study in eighteenth century ecumenism' in *United Reformed Church History Society Journal* (1973) vol. 1, no. 2, pp. 42–56.

NUTTALL, G. F. 'Doddridge's life and times' in NUTTALL, G. F. (ed.) *Philip Doddridge* (1951) pp. 11–31.

NUTTALL, G. F. *New College, London and its library: two lectures* (Dr Williams's Trust, 1977).

NUTTALL, G. F. 'Northamptonshire and "The Modern Question": a turning-point in eighteenth-century dissent' in *Journal of Theological Studies* (1965) New Series, vol. 16, pp. 101-23.

NUTTALL, G. F. (ed.) *Philip Doddridge 1702–51: his contribution to English Religion* (Independent Press, 1951) Contents:
    Nuttall, G. F. 'Doddridge's life and times'
    James, A. T. S. 'Philip Doddridge: his influence on personal religion'
    Routley, E. 'The hymns of Philip Doddridge'
    Payne, E. A. 'Doddridge and the missionary enterprise'
    Murray, A. V. 'Doddridge and education'
    Thomas, R. 'Philip Doddridge and liberalism in religion'
    Nuttall, G. F. 'Philip Doddridge—a personal appreciation.'

NUTTALL, G. F. 'Philip Doddridge and the Care of all the churches: a study in oversight' in *Congregational Historical Society Transactions* (1966) vol. 20, pp. 126–38.

NUTTALL, G. F. 'Philip Doddridge—a personal appreciation' in NUTTALL, G. F. (ed.) *Philip Doddridge* (1951) pp. 154–63.

NUTTALL, G. F. 'Philip Doddridge's letters to Samuel Clark' in *Congregational Historical Society Transactions* (1950) vol. 16, no. 2, pp. 78–81.

NUTTALL, G. F. 'Philip Doddridge's library' in *Congregational Historical Society Transactions* (1952) vol. 17, no. 1, pp. 29–31.

NUTTALL, G. F. *The Puritan spirit: essays and addresses* (Epworth Press, 1967).

NUTTALL, G. F. *Richard Baxter and Philip Doddridge: a study in a tradition* (O.U.P., 1951).

ORTON, J. *The Christian's Triumph over Death. A sermon occasioned by the much lamented death of the Reverend Philip Doddridge, D.D.* (J. Waugh etc., 1752).

ORTON, J. *Letters to Dissenting Ministers, and to students for the Ministry . . . with notes, explanatory and biographical* (1806) 2 vols.

ORTON, J. 'Life of Dr Doddridge', preface to Doddridge's *Works*, ed. E. Williams and E. Parsons (E. Baines, 1802–5) 10 vols. Reprint of following work.

ORTON, J. *Memoirs of the life, character and writings of . . . Philip Doddridge . . .* (Cotton and Eddowes, 1766).

PARKER, I. *Dissenting academies in England: their rise and progress, and their place among the educational systems of the country* (C.U.P., 1914).

PAYNE, E. A. 'Doddridge and the missionary enterprise' in NUTTALL, G. F. (ed.) *Philip Doddridge* (1951) pp. 79–101.

PIERCE, W. *An historical introduction to the Marprelate Tracts* (Constable, 1909).

PRICE, E. J. 'The Dissenting academies' in *Congregational Historical Society Transactions* (1930–2) vol. 11, pp. 38–51.

RAZZELL, P. *The conquest of smallpox* (Caliban Books, 1977).

ROUTLEY, E. 'The hymns of Philip Doddridge' in NUTTALL, G. F. (ed.) *Philip Doddridge* (1951) pp. 46–78.

SECRETT, A. G. 'Philip Doddridge and the Evangelical revival of the eighteenth century' in *Evangelical Quarterly* (1951) no. 156, pp. 242–59.

SERJEANTSON, R. M. *A history of the Church of All Saints, Northampton* (Northampton, W. Mark, 1901).

SERJEANTSON, R. M. *A history of the Church of St Peter, Northampton, together with the chapels of Kingsthorpe and Upton* (Northampton, W. Mark, 1904).

SEYMOUR, A. C. H. (ed.) *The life and times of Selina, Countess of Huntingdon* (Simpkin Marshall; Snow; 1839–40) 2 vols.

SHEILS, W. J. *The Puritans in the Diocese of Peterborough, 1558–1610* (Northamptonshire Record Society, vol. 30, 1979).

SKEATS, H. S. and MIALL, C. S. *History of the Free Churches of England* (Alexander and Shepheard, 1894).

STANFORD, C. *Philip Doddridge, D.D.* (Hodder and Stoughton, 1880).

STEDMAN, T. (ed.) *Letters from . . . Job Orton and . . . Sir J. Stonhouse . . . to . . . T. Stedman* (2nd edition, 1805) 2 vols.

STEDMAN, T. (ed.) *Letters to and from the Revd Philip Doddridge* (J. and W. Eddowes, 1790).

STOUGHTON, H. *Philip Doddridge: his life and labours* (Jackson and Walford, 1851).

TAYLOR, J. (ed.) 'Bicentenary volume'. *A history of Northampton Castle Hill Church, now Doddridge . . . (etc.)* (Dryden Press and Congregational Union of England and Wales, 1896). Revised versions of articles which appeared in the *Northampton Daily Reporter;* bound in with *History of College Street Church* (Dryden Press, 1897).

TAYLOR, J. Philip Doddridge, 1702-1751 (Independent Press, N.D.). Pamphlet.

THOMAS, R. 'Philip Doddridge and liberalism in religion' in NUTTALL, G. F. (ed.) *Philip Doddridge* (1951) pp. 122–53.

THORNTON, J. H. 'Dr Philip Doddridge' in *Anglo-Portuguese News* (November 1968) no. 936, pp. 1, 4.

URWICK, W. 'Dr Samuel Clark's charity school' in URWICK, W. *Bible truths & church errors* (T. F. Unwin, 1888).

WADDINGTON, J. *Congregational history 1200–1880* (Snow, 1869–80) 5 vols.

WADDY, F. F. *A history of Northampton General Hospital, 1743 to 1948* (Northampton, Northampton and District Hospital Management Committee, 1974).

WATTS, M. R. *The Dissenters: from the Reformation to the French Revolution* (O.U.P., 1978).

WESLEY, J. *Journal*, abridged by N. Curnock (Epworth Press, 1949).

WOODWARD, J. *To do the sick no harm—a study of the British Voluntary Hospital system to 1875* (Routledge and Kegan Paul, 1978).

# Index

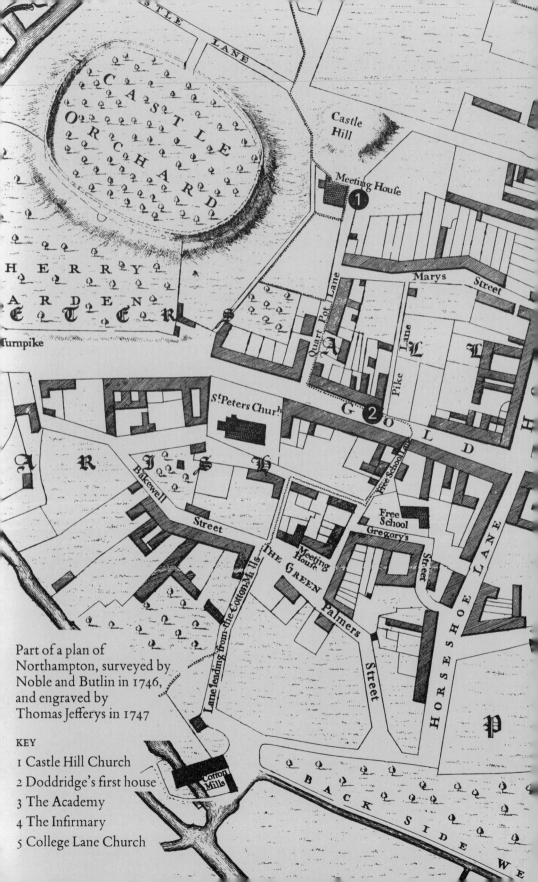

CASTLE ORCHARD

CASTLE LANE

Castle Hill

Meeting House ①

Marys Street

Quart Pot Lane

Pike Lane

GOLD ②

H E R R Y
A R D E N
E T E R

Turnpike

St Peters Church

AR R I S H

Bakewell Street

Free School Lane

Free School

Gregory's Street

HORSESHOE LANE

Lane leading from the Cotton Mills

THE GREEN

Meeting House

Palmers Street

Cotton Mills

P

B A C K   S I D E   W E

Part of a plan of
Northampton, surveyed by
Noble and Butlin in 1746,
and engraved by
Thomas Jefferys in 1747

KEY

1 Castle Hill Church

2 Doddridge's first house

3 The Academy

4 The Infirmary

5 College Lane Church